D1750566

The 5th International Employee Assistance Compendium

Edited by
Dr. Dale Masi,
Professor Emeritus, University of Maryland and
President/CEO of Masi Research Consultants, Inc.

SPONSORED BY LYRA HEALTH

The 5th International Employee Assistance Compendium
Published by Masi Research Consultants, Inc.
Boston, MA

Copyright ©2024 by Dr. Dale Masi. All rights reserved.

No part of this book may be reproduced in any form or by any mechanical means, including information storage and retrieval systems without permission in writing from the publisher/author, except by a reviewer who may quote passages in a review.

All images, logos, quotes, and trademarks included in this book are subject to use according to trademark and copyright laws of the United States of America.

ISBN: 978-0-9770602-2-1

BUSINESS & ECONOMICS / Human Resources & Personnel Management

Cover and Interior design by Victoria Wolf, wolfdesignandmarketing.com. Copyright owned by Dr. Dale Masi.

All rights reserved by Dr. Dale Masi and Masi Research Consultants, Inc.
Printed in the United States of America.

CONTENTS

Introduction and Acknowledgments 1
Dale A. Masi

Sponsor's Perspective 3
Andrew Davies

Editor's Perspective 5
Dale A. Masi

Argentina 9
Eduardo Lambardi, Pilar Lorenzo, and Romina Herrera

Australia 15
Ian Shakespeare

Austria 21
Conny Martens

Bangladesh 31
Ashique Selim

Bosnia and Herzegovina, Croatia, Serbia, and Slovenia 37
Katja Novak

Botswana 43
Onalethata Johnson

Bulgaria 51
Boyan Strahilov

Canada 57
Crystal Smalldon

Chile 63
Maria Elena Subercaseaux

China 69
Hanxiao Mao

Colombia 75
Carlos Felipe Villar

France 81
Emmanuel Charlot

Germany 85
  Juliane Barth and Martin Klein

Greece 93
  Konstantinos Giannakopoulos

Hong Kong 103
  Natalie Cheung

India 109
  Ummul Ranalvi

Ireland 115
  Lucy Dennehy

Italy 121
  Laura Sinatra

Japan 129
  Koji Mori and Kaoru Ichikawa

Kenya 135
  Selina Kemama Njeri

Korea 143
  Jimmy S. Kim

Latvia 147
  Diana Fridrihsone and Ayrat Khabibov

Lebanon and Jordan 151
  Alexandru Manescu and Mohamed Lamaa

Luxembourg 157
  Eliane Bucher

Malaysia 161
  Wilson Tee

Mexico 173
  Deborah Loffler

Mongolia 181
  Khongorzul Amarsanaa and Enkhchimeg Purvee

Netherlands 187
  Francien Resius

New Zealand 191
   Peter Finlayson

Nigeria 197
   Olatunji Odebiyi

Nordic Countries: Norway, Denmark, Finland, and Sweden, plus Poland..........211
   Johannes Edberg

Philippines...217
   Jean Lim

Portugal..225
   Manuel Sommer

Puerto Rico 229
   Marion A. Wennerholm

Romania...235
   Alexandru Manescu

Russia...241
   Daria Fedorova

Scotland...245
   Tony Buon

Singapore 253
   Elizabeth Nair

Slovakia..259
   Zuzana Podkonická

South Africa...265
   Navlika Ratangee

Spain...273
   Miguel Cristobal

Switzerland 277
   Eliane Bucher

Taiwan..285
   Jyh-Hong Lee

Thailand 295
   Athalie de Koning

Trinidad and Tobago 299
    Patricia Elder and Brent Pereira

Turkey 305
    Banu Mercan Öztürk

Uganda 311
    John Mary Ssekate

Ukraine..323
    Natalia Nalyvaiko

United Arab Emirates (UAE): Umm Al-Quwain, Abu Dhabi, Dubai, Sharjah, Ajman, Ras Al-Khaimah, and Fujairah..327
    Hazel Kurian

The United Kingdom..337
    Eugene Farrell

The United States..343
    Jodi J. Frey

INTRODUCTION AND ACKNOWLEDGMENTS

Dale A. Masi

In his essay on Portugal, author Manuel Sommer stated, "The COVID-19 pandemic brought down the barrier of the stigma around seeking psychological help."

As I read the many essays submitted by our authors, it became clear that this statement is very true. I was amazed at how authors around the world talked about the heightened incidence of anxiety and depression in their countries due to the pandemic. Suddenly EAPs were flooded with requests for help, and caseloads for mental health workers doubled and tripled across the globe. India's author, Ummul Ranalvi, stated that the pandemic became a "game changer," exposing the need for mental health services.

Virtual counseling became the norm in most places. Kenya's author, Selina Kamana, stated that "online therapy was a lighthouse during the dark time of the pandemic." Banu Mercan Öztürk from Turkey wrote, "the role of technology and social media in the EAP field has been 'transformative.'" Nigeria's Olatunji Odebiyi pointed out that offshore drillers on oil rigs were now able to access virtual counseling. For the first time Selina Kemama Njeri pointed out that sign language communication was possible with virtual counseling as well.

There were unique differences, however, that give the reader the individual insights for each country. Ukraine's author, Natalia Nalyvaiko, described psychologists providing various levels of support and counseling in bomb shelters, railway stations, and hospitals. China's author, Hanxiao

Mao, pointed out that COVID-19 forced people to think about "life's meaning." Russia's Daria Fedorova stated a tenfold increase in case numbers due to the Russian-Ukrainian war. Legal assistance became a significant area of client inquiry, including requests of how to avoid the military as well as helping those whose family members have been mobilized. Jodi J. Frey, author for the United States, pointed out the EAP Digital Archive at the University of Maryland as a valuable resource for all and available at no cost. Thailand's Athalie de Koning stated the interesting innovation of transparent masks used in order for the counselors to see the client's facial expressions and vice versa. The authors from several countries, including Kenya, Nigeria, Scotland, and the US, saw an increase in substance abuse. An influx of refugees in Poland, Lebanon, and Uganda was mentioned as additional strains on providing services. Two of our authors mentioned artificial intelligence. Laura Sinatra from Italy said that Eapitalia was looking at ways to "integrate with curiosity and a tentative approach." An EAP-specific AI chatbot and Jingjing China provide videos, articles, and recommended counselors.

The above comments were written in the hope of encouraging the readers to take this journey throughout the world by reading each chapter and gaining a vast impression of the urgent need for universal mental health workplace services that only an EAP can provide.

Our authors gave their time willingly, and for that I am eternally grateful. We have only lightly edited the authors' submissions so the reader can experience their original voices, cultural communication styles, and regional spelling.

This *Compendium* is the largest in number of countries and authors. It could not have been done without my fellow professionals who came to my assistance in locating both authors and countries. I am grateful for their immediate response and continued support throughout the project.

In addition to being our sponsor, Andrew Davies provided many contacts from his ICAS World network. His continual support through the project is one for which I am most grateful.

The following peer professionals deserve special thanks: Kenny Maderios, David Levine, Paul Maiden, Katou Ishikawa, Nancy Board, and Denise Johnson.

Any editor does not work alone, and the following staff were ever patient and most supportive: Fred Davis, Peter Tolchinsky, and Ben Kuettel.

My Associate Editor, Dr. Robin Masi Carlson, has been with me for the last three *Compendiums*. As an artist, she designed the cover and advised on the website. Most importantly, she was my trusted advisor, and as my daughter, she kept my spirits up throughout the project.

To all our authors, I am grateful for your responsiveness and patience. Your brilliance gave me insights I will always treasure.

SPONSOR'S PERSPECTIVE

Andrew Davies

I am deeply honoured to present my perspective on *The 5th International EAP Compendium*, edited by the esteemed Professor Dale Masi. Professor Masi has consistently been at the forefront of EAP research and practice, and this publication is a testament to her profound knowledge and unwavering commitment to the field of Employee Assistance Programs. Her reputation has been honed over decades of dedicated work and research, and her contributions have not only shaped the field but also paved the way for future advancements. *The 5th International EAP Compendium* is yet another feather in her cap, reflecting her commitment to fostering understanding and promoting best practices in EAPs across the world.

The 2024 publication presents a comprehensive exploration of the changing global landscape of EAPs, meticulously mapping their evolution and documenting how they are adapting to an array of new issues and challenges. It is a scholarly dialogue that transcends geographical boundaries, enriched by contributions from leading EAP professionals from more than 60 countries. This underscores Professor Masi's global influence and reach and highlights the widespread significance of EAPs in addressing employee mental health and social challenges across the world. Every author's contribution to the *Compendium* stands as a pertinent reminder that a person's mental health and search for and use of care and support are embedded in and shaped by the interactions of a diverse array of social, political, cultural, and environmental factors.

The breadth and depth of topics covered are truly impressive. Key themes and insights include the growing recognition of diversity and inclusivity in EAP program efficacy, the increased reliance on technology as an enabler of EAP services, and the dynamic adaptation of EAPs to a spectrum of mental health needs precipitated by global crises such as climate change, geopolitical conflicts, pandemics, and mass displacement. The depth of her understanding is reflected in the comprehensive exploration of these critical issues in EAPs, and her astute recognition of the COVID-19 pandemic's impact on EAP service delivery provides an enlightening perspective on the changing landscape of the field. Professor Masi wisely navigates this shift, demonstrating her forward-thinking approach and invaluable insights into the most prominent factors driving the evolution of the EAP profession. The critical, and often ignored, influence of socioeconomic, cultural, and political factors on the onset, maintenance, and perpetuation of mental health problems is a consistent theme throughout the *Compendium* and serves as an important reminder of the extent to which contextual factors warrant consideration in shaping our understanding and effective management of mental ill-health. This understanding is crucial in a field that must constantly adapt to rapidly evolving global developments and challenges.

The *Compendium* is a quintessential educational resource for EAP professionals, policymakers, and employers seeking to navigate the complex labyrinth of corporate mental health in an increasingly challenging world. It is not only a collection of academic essays but a beacon illuminating the current state of EAPs and heralding their potential future trajectories. It enables the reader to navigate multiple considerations and details the many issues that those working in the field need to be aware of to provide effective help for those in need. Professor Masi's emphasis on education reflects her commitment to ensuring that EAPs continue to provide essential support in these changing times. Her leadership in the field and relentless commitment to fostering understanding and promoting best practices in EAPs is evident throughout the *Compendium*, making it an essential resource for both seasoned professionals and those new to the field.

Sponsoring this publication is more than just a formal agreement; it is an honour and privilege. Together with all the contributing authors, I stand tall in endorsing Professor Masi's illustrious work that transcends geographical, sectoral, and intellectual boundaries. *The 5th International EAP Compendium* is not just a publication; it is a milestone in the field of EAPs and a testament to Professor Masi's enduring commitment to Employee Assistance Programs and their role in corporate mental health. It underlines the ubiquity and pertinence of EAPs in addressing the mental health exigencies of the modern workforce. My heartfelt congratulations to Professor Masi for this outstanding achievement.

EDITOR'S PERSPECTIVE

Dale A. Masi

As this *Compendium* is the fifth edition, I thought it appropriate to look back on the previous four editions (since 1996) and view the critical points of history in the growth of Employee Assistance Programs and highlight the major touch points of importance.

COMPENDIUM NO. 1 — 1996
Sponsor: EAP Digest

From the 1970s on, there were two parallel tracks of providing services to employees. Prior to this time, occupational social work (OSW) in a few countries, such as India, Ireland, France, Germany, and the US, was the predominant delivery system. With the onset of Employee Assistance Programs in the early 1970s, the dichotomy of the two approaches emerged. The former, more traditional, provided by social workers with a non-directive clinical methodology. The EAP emphasized addiction (especially alcoholism) and included recovering addiction and union personnel staffing programs. The unique element in the occupational alcoholism approach was the involvement of managers and supervisors. There was a major emphasis on training managers and supervisors to be alert to problems with employees that may warrant a referral to the programs. Being aware of signs and symptoms of lost productivity was emphasized. With the strong support of the United States government through the National Institute of Alcohol and Alcoholism, the EAP movement in the US received a tremendous financial and professional level of support. During this period, I was fortunate to consult with many countries and assist them as they became interested in developing EAP programs. I wanted to inspire my students to also develop a love and interest of other countries, and I conceived, upon the suggestion of Carl Tisone, founder of a large US EAP company, the first Compendium. The *EAP Digest* Editor George Watkins was instrumental in supporting the final publication and came to the university to hand-deliver a copy to each student in the program.

COMPENDIUM NO. 2 – 2000
Sponsor: Magellan Behavioral Health

The next five years showed remarkable growth and development in the EAP field.

Internationally, we saw two developments: 1. The growth of local country-based programs and 2. The development of major multinational companies opening EAPs in their overseas destinations and utilizing US EAP companies to deliver services. The former often had to struggle against the financial resources of the US companies. Various models developed. CARIAD (Caribbean Institute of Alcohol and Drug Abuse), under the incredible leadership of Dr. Michael Beaubrun, held an annual School of Addiction Studies for the British Caribbean countries where I was privileged to lecture on EAPs for many years. As a result, programs across the Caribbean developed without outside US interference. South Africa was a standout with local country-based programs starting with the mining industries. On the other hand, the number of US companies marketing EAPs worldwide grew. Our sponsor Magellan was one, along with Human Affairs (HAI) and Personal Performance (PPC). Most importantly, two professional organizations grew: The Employee Assistance Program Association (EAPA) and The Employee Assistance Society of North America (EASNA). The latter emphasized the need for accreditation of programs. The former, because of the presence of a large union membership, fought the professionalism of the field and instead looked at individual certification, without educational requirements.

COMPENDIUM NO. 3 – 2005
Sponsor: ICAS International

As the large US EAP vendors invaded the international market, the local country-based EAPs fought back. The European Forum was organized, and membership included the major countries with EAPs. This was an independent organization from EAPA. It continues to flourish today and holds a comprehensive annual meeting. An occurrence happened in Japan that influenced the growth of EAPs. A law was passed requiring companies to have mental health programs for employees. This was the result of a significant lawsuit won by an employee's wife. The husband committed suicide, and she claimed work stress for the incredible hours he had to work. To the population's amazement, she won the case, and the resulting law was passed as concerned employers considered if they would be vulnerable due to working employees so hard. I was privileged to train human resource personnel in Japan to assist them in establishing employee stress management programs. To this day, Japan continues to have a robust EAP presence.

In the US, the 9/11 attack on the Twin Towers in New York City introduced the importance of EAPs to employees in times of tragedy and crisis. The service of critical incidence response was introduced into EAP services. Previously, worklife programs such as childcare, eldercare, and legal assistance had been added. EAPs continue to offer various services that stretch beyond counseling. Michael Reddy, the founder of ICAS and our sponsor, alerted readers to the implications of the internet for the EAP field.

COMPENDIUM NO. 4 — 2010
Sponsor: Personal Performance Consultants (PPC)

Unfortunately, as EAPs grew across the globe and programs in the US multiplied exponentially, there emerged competition among the EAP providers. Cost-cutting came about and quality was greatly reduced. Instead of imposing accreditation standards and professional standards, the EAP organizations supported the business model and did nothing to rein in the price gouging and exaggerated claims by EAP providers. Benefit consultants in the US jumped in, and the large EAP providers moved dramatically into the international market and often hired indigenous program staff. Professional organizations grew and Asian programs formed the Asia Pacific Employee Assistance roundtable. A few universities tried to enter this arena and train graduates with a specialty in the workplace. Columbia University emphasized mental health, and the University of Maryland, University of Southern California, and Loyola University in Chicago were examples with majors in employee assistance. At Maryland, I developed the Annual EAP Residential School with international students in attendance. These efforts were dwarfed by the proliferation of EAP vendors. EAPs became a big business, and the substance abuse emphasis was diminished. I was invited many times to consult internationally and trained numerous staff in Hong Kong and Japan and became an AMPART (American Participant Expert) when foreign countries requested a speaker on EAPs from the United States. It was a privilege I will always cherish as I met so many wonderful international colleagues and we all struggled to define and refine our emerging profession.

COMPENDIUM NO. 5 — 2024
Sponsor: Lyra Health

Since the previous *Compendium*, there has been an explosion of EAPs worldwide, which has been thrilling and energizing. Our challenge now is to refine our practices and put in some hard work to have a true profession. This will take investments by governments, regulatory bodies, universities, and EAP organizations to cooperate and see the importance of this work. There is no doubt that a healthy mental health workplace is seen as essential by employers. Employees as well as employers recognize the importance of mental wellness and look to EAPs as the solution. The recent pandemic brought this to light and resulted in my seeing the urgent need for this *Compendium*. I had wondered how the pandemic had affected the way services were delivered. I also was aware (how could one not be?) of the growth of technology and its effect on delivery services. Most importantly, I wanted to know how EAPs around the world are adapting to mental health needs as we have new and greatly impactful wars, climate catastrophes, the ever-present COVID-19 virus, the influx of refugees in many countries, and ongoing threats of terrorism. Fortunately, Lyra Health agreed and became our sponsor.

I had the assistance of many colleagues who I have cited in the Acknowledgments, as well as the support of our sponsor, Andrew Davies, to identify the authors to contribute to this *Compendium*. I was not prepared for the tremendous response I received. EAPs in countries from every continent (except Antarctica) responded. This has truly been a labor of love as I read the expert contributions from each author. I can summarize by saying that there is no doubt that EAPs are known worldwide and relied upon as the major source of alleviating the mental health of employees. Unfortunately, the scourge of alcoholism and drug addiction are not as recognized as they should be in many EAP programs. This is unfortunate, and the employer and employee must become much more tuned in to address this pervasive and complex issue. Because of advances in remote technology, virtual counseling has proliferated. I am unclear if this is due to being the best solution or, frankly, because of the demands of counselors who prefer to now work from home.

What is also lost, and I regret this very much, is the lack of contact with supervisors and the workplace itself. EAPs are becoming an outpatient mental health service, and I do not applaud this model because we are missing all the elements of the original EAP Core Technology (see Masi, 2020). I find it greatly ironic that the present EAP delivery model is now more like the original occupational social work model described in my comments on the first *Compendium*.

Regardless of the limitations I may cite regarding the use of technology-based counseling, there is much to applaud. The delivery of EAP services has grown at a tremendous rate and provided support to millions of employees. I have no doubt that with the growth of our EAP organizations and growing interest by governments, we will see a concerted effort to constantly improve. We have grown past adolescence and now must face maturity as an adult service with all the responsibilities that entails.

ARGENTINA

Eduardo Lambardi, Pilar Lorenzo, and Romina Herrera

INTRODUCTION: LAND OF PSYCHOLOGISTS

If there is a country where psychologists have proliferated and where people enjoy therapy, that country is undoubtedly Argentina. It is the country with the highest number of psychologists per capita in the world (222.5 psychologists per 100,000 inhabitants), and its capital, Buenos Aires, is the most psychoanalyzed city on planet Earth. We have no obstacles to go to a psychologist. Therapy is normal, and talking about what one shares with the therapist is also common. The stigma exists, but it is much weaker than in other cultures. However, statistics show that our level of mental health is equal to or worse than the standard. What is happening? How is it possible that in a country where there is an abundance of mental health professionals and where people have no qualms about going to a psychologist, the levels of mental illness are increasing, and the trend cannot be reversed?

We believe that Argentina is a country that generates mental illness due to the conditions of immense socio-political-economic instability in which it is immersed. How is it possible that a country geographically rich in natural resources has 42% of people living below the poverty line? How does a country with free and excellent education have such corrupt and incompetent politicians? How can people live in peace when inflation reaches 140% annually and 28% of workers are poor even with salaried jobs?

LAW AND REALITY

In 2010, Argentina enacted its Mental Health Law, Law 26.657. This law established that, within a period of no more than three years from its enactment, the Executive Power had to allocate 10% of the total health expenditure to mental health. As the reader can imagine, none of this has happened. Until 2022, no annual budget dedicated to mental health could exceed 3%, with only 1.48% in 2022. This simple fact shows the reality of Argentina, where intentions may seem positive, but actions follow a different course than good intentions. We say A but do B. Thus, there is no possibility of success.

As always in life, major crises reveal what people, institutions, countries, and cultures are made of. When catastrophe strikes, nations either succumb or become stronger. During the COVID-19 pandemic in Latin America, the mental health of the population has worsened due to factors such as social isolation, economic uncertainty, and health concerns. Argentina entered the pandemic with drastic decisions of absolute lockdown. It was the country with the strictest lockdown in Occident. Its decisions (which seemed correct at the beginning) turned out to be wrong in retrospect. Despite the drastic lockdown, it could not avoid having a mortality rate higher than the average and, furthermore, its social net was damaged to the point of increasing poverty by 2.5 million people, doubling its inflation rate, significantly increasing low-quality employment, and other negative outcomes that increased the population's stress level. As expected, the health care system collapsed during the pandemic, and especially the mental health systems demonstrated not being prepared to combat the significant increase in needs and demands to address the emotional and mental damages inherent in the pandemic. At the same time that the pandemic was very damaging to people, it is also necessary to recognize that it significantly contributed to the development of Employee Assistance Programs (EAPs), facilitating their growth, visibility, and generating a much more competitive market than before.

THE EFFECTS OF THE PANDEMIC ON EAPS

The pandemic has significantly impacted the development of EAPs in Argentina, and the Latin America region in general. Among the consequences of the pandemic, we observe:

1. Increase in EAP service hiring.

For EAPs, the pandemic has been a phenomenal development opportunity. During the years before the pandemic, EAP LATINA was growing at an annual rate of 9%. In 2020 and 2021, it grew by 63%. These are growth rates in a company that is already in a mature stage because it was the first EAP company in South America. Likewise, during the pandemic, the EAP market expanded. Before the pandemic, most companies that contracted these services were multinationals, or multilatina companies that competed with multinationals. COVID-19 made local and national companies also demand EAP services.

2. Emergence of new competencies for EAPs.

The growing demand for EAP services brought about the emergence of new players. Especially, non-traditional competitors began to appear. These competitors are basically platforms that offer virtual psychological counseling. Several platforms began to offer virtual psychological assistance services, and some even dared to add legal, financial, and medical counseling. Virtual medical service platforms joined the competition with EAPs by incorporating psychological assistance services into their offerings. In Argentina, there are no official statistics to demonstrate the growth of all these "competencies." However, a quick look at the market today shows that several of these offers survive and develop. Since the platforms, so far, are not offering typical EAP services such as 24/7 assistance, critical incident, legal and financial counseling, training for managers and supervisors, fitness for duty evaluations, etc., it is not unusual to see some companies having a traditional EAP and a mental health platform contracted together.

3. Lower customer loyalty with EAP providers.

The industry's growth and the proliferation of new providers caused customers to behave with less loyalty. Before the pandemic, the EAP business in Latin America (including Argentina) had an annual churn rate of approximately 3%. During the pandemic and in 2022, it grew to approximately 12 or 14%, and in 2023, it is stabilizing around 5 to 7%. Although this may seem like a negative index for EAP providers, the truth is that it is very positive because it speaks to the market's adaptation to growing competition. There are more customers joining to buy EAP services, more providers offering different alternatives, and consequently, greater customer mobility.

4. Changes in the modality of traditional service provision.

Prior to the pandemic, 82% of EAP users in Latin America, including Argentina, accessed the service through 0800 or telephone modality, and 18% did so through digital means such as email or chat in a wellness app or portal. After the pandemic, only 43% of users access it by phone, and 57% through digital access. This trend continues to increase after the pandemic, and everything indicates that the phone as a mode of access is becoming extinct. Likewise, before the pandemic, 73% of psychological cases were attended face-to-face, 24% by phone, and 3% virtually. After the pandemic, only 32% are attended face-to-face, 25% by phone, and 43% are attended virtually. These drastic changes in the ways of offering traditional EAP services forced providers to invest in technology, develop better and more secure platforms, and train their professionals in different attention dynamics than before the pandemic. The virtuality in professional counseling processes brought three marked benefits:

- *Improved accessibility:* It allowed improved access to mental health services for people who might otherwise have geographic barriers, limited mobility, or difficulties accessing in-person care.
- *Flexibility in schedules:* It facilitated people to schedule counseling sessions according to their needs and daily commitments.
- *Greater access to specialists:* People were able to access mental health specialists who may be located in other cities or regions, thus expanding the availability and diversity of professionals with specific expertise.

5. Changes in the style of mental health professionals' care.

Although we do not have clear statistics on this, we do observe that just as workers value remote work and many are not willing to return to the pre-pandemic in-person mode, mental health professionals are also undergoing the same process. After the pandemic, many mental health professionals decided not to provide in-person care anymore, only doing so virtually. This brought about two new challenges. The first is selecting professionals in those areas where the former professionals decided not to provide in-person care anymore. The second challenge is the increase in fees for professionals who still provide in-person care. In Latin America, we have seen that, on average, mental health professionals ask for 20% more than their traditional fees (pre-pandemic) for in-person care.

6. Greater demand for basic services.

In Argentina, as in many other countries, the average utilization has experienced an increase of approximately 20% compared to pre-pandemic levels. However, while in other countries the increase has been in psychological cases, in Argentina, the increase has been in financial consultations. This shows that the EAP is a tool sensitive to people's real problems. In Argentina, the poor management of the pandemic has generated an inflation of more than 100% annually, a new social class of "poor salaried workers," a 6% drop in the purchasing power of salaried workers, and a deep fear of "falling into poverty" for normal workers.

FINAL WORDS

EAPs in Argentina, like in the rest of the countries in Latin America, have proliferated alongside the COVID-19 pandemic. This proliferation seems very positive from a business perspective and the need for expansion of assistance services. At the same time, there is a human, almost existential concern, which is the worsening of the general population's mental health levels. It seems contradictory that we can increase access to assistance services but cannot reverse the growing trend of major mental health problems. We, the authors of this article, believe in human beings and their transformation faculties. We imagine that what we are capable of building with our clients will have a positive impact on the world. The pandemic put mental health on the employers' agenda. Why couldn't we all together put mental health on the politicians' agenda and their budgets? Why couldn't we build healthy conversations with the people who make decisions about the fate of humanity? Let's continue working for a better world. We are proud to be health agents.

ABOUT THE AUTHORS

Eduardo Lambardi, Clinical Psychologist, Master's Degree.
Pilar Lorenzo, Clinical Psychologist, Master's Degree.
Romina Herrera, Communication and Journalist, Master's Degree in HR.

We are three employee assistance professionals. Pilar is the Professional Services Manager, Romina the Operations Director, and Eduardo the General Director and Founder of EAP LATINA. Our company was born 25 years ago and delivers EAP and wellness services in the 18 Spanish-speaking countries in LatAm. We serve nearly 3 million people, and we are infinitely grateful to the EAP industry and community for having given meaning to our professional careers.

AUSTRALIA

Ian Shakespeare

Even prior to the COVID-19 pandemic, mental disorders were a leading contributor to the global health burden due to, inter alia, cost, diminished productivity, relationship dysfunction, workplace conflict, and absenteeism. However, since the pandemic, we have experienced increases across the globe (replicated in Australia) in the two most prevalent and disabling mental disorders of anxiety and depression, with an up to 36% increase in recorded anxiety disorders globally; Australia is between 9.7% to 14% (The Lancet, 2021).)

Importantly, the impact was high across the entire population lifespan and was not gender specific, and critically (suggesting a new approach is required), there has been no reduction in prevalence for either depression or anxiety since 1990, despite evidence of interventions aimed at reducing their impact (The Lancet Psychiatry, 2021). These escalating mental health issues prior to the pandemic, plus the immediate and ongoing impact of the pandemic across all aspects of our lives—shutdowns, significant social restrictions such as mask wearing and social distancing, and school and work closures—has changed and continues to change the way we live, work, socialize, and think. Researchers from the Australian National University (ANU) used data from the three waves of COVID-19 that measured Australians' mental health every few weeks during the acute lockdown phases. In surveying 704 Australian participants, what they found was that people who reported higher levels of anxiety and depression early in the pandemic were more likely to hide their emotions later, leading to a self-perpetuating cycle of higher levels of anxiety and depression. Clearly it was time for a new approach.

While many in our society have been struggling to come to terms with the constant developments in technology changing the way we work (demands and expectations), as well as the impact of globalization (enabled by technology) and social media on our lives, the pandemic appears to have created a "perfect storm" of uncertainty. This has led to a rapid increase in demand for support services such as psychological counselling at the very time (2020–22) when face-to-face services were restricted due to shutdowns and when demand far outstripped the supply of professionals to provide the services. There were periods in Australia when an employee may need to wait over two weeks for an online counselling session and over two months (if it all possible) for a face-to-face session. Therefore, it became incumbent on EAP companies to quickly adjust their service provision infrastructure and also develop communication strategies for all stakeholders, given that the history (and therefore expectations) of EAPs in Australia has been predicated largely on face-to-face (over 90%) counselling sessions with an experienced and accredited psychologist.

The impact initially on the demand for EAP services was a small decrease in demand due to the lockdowns and the lack of available face-to-face service, coupled with a view that "this will be over in two to three months," and we can cope with our situation until the pandemic passes. As this was not the reality, the initial decline in service demand ramped up over that three-month initial period (March to May 2020) to the point where service KPIs were not and could not be contractually met. This led to a rapid segue from not only face-to-face counselling to virtual video counselling, but innovation in what other services could be provided online as well as being beneficial to both the organisation and the employee. This led to the creation of a range of "COVID-19 impact" workshops, online questionnaires, information sessions, and HR support sessions that discussed a broad and constantly moving range of topics associated with working remotely. These included, inter alia, coping strategies at home, communicating remotely with colleagues, managing workloads, work-life balance, performance management, habit formation and adjustment, and the benefits of online services.

Given that adjustment was a requirement for everyone, we created an online "Adjustment Wheel" at SMG Health, where employees could self-assess where they needed to make adjustments in their lives, then link to a range of online, interactive services to support those adjustments. All these options assisted in gaining greater acceptance for online services and contributed to increased demand. Significantly, it also contributed to a greater demographic diversity of employees accessing services as the workshop/information sessions provided useful information as to what EAP could provide that many employees were unaware of, and therefore were not likely to have used the service in the past. While most EAP services in Australia have always (well, at least over the past decade) provided these ancillary services, they have only ever made up a small proportion of the total service delivery, with counselling (particularly face to face) making up the vast majority of service delivery. The focus on face-to-face counselling has also been reinforced by human resource departments that have seen the EAP as synonymous with psychological counselling and therefore internally promoted them as such, unwittingly reducing utilization and also the potential effectiveness as preventative services. This has also been seen in the dollar value placed on "traditional EAP" (counselling at $150 to $180 per hour) compared with coaching and consulting services ($200 to $300 per hour).

However, with most major dilemmas (such as a pandemic), there is often a silver lining, albeit one that needs to be sought out, analysed, and developed for present and future benefit. While the COVID-19 pandemic placed significant and totally unexpected challenges on the EAP industry in Australia, as it did all other industries, it also provided the opportunity for all stakeholders (boards, management teams, employees, human resource departments, and occupational health and safety personnel) to reassess not only the potentiality of EAPs as being a core preventative service in the mitigation of ever-increasing mental health issues but also acceptance of the flexibility of those services in using multi-format platforms and technological innovation in service delivery. For example, the significant but fluctuating demand for services through the pandemic required strategies to maximise attendance at counselling sessions. As such, the introduction of both text and email appointment confirmations led to a significant decrease in the incidence of non-attendance at booked sessions. Also, the greater acceptance of online services provided the opportunity for an improved employee-counsellor alignment. For example, with employees seeking support for issues with their children, or those seeking specific relationship counselling, online capability meant we were able to connect the specific need with the specific expertise, no matter where in Australia either resided. Other technological developments, though not instigated by the pandemic, were certainly hastened by its impact. These include online chat for those seeking specific advise or guidance but not wanting to initially enter a counselling program; an increase in coaching services, particularly in relation to issues such as diet, exercise, medical issues, and work life balance; real-time reporting with companies increasingly concerned about the mental health status of their workforce; a reduction in hard copy promotions as "touch free" was seen not only as a healthier option but a more efficient and economical method of promoting EAP. We must ensure that the opportunities afforded by the pandemic, our nimbleness in responding to those opportunities, and the technology now available are not stalled.

While COVID-19 is no longer a pandemic (according to the World Health Organization) and demand for EAP services has trended back to pre-pandemic utilization but with a greater acceptance of the value of online service delivery, its impact remains far-reaching. The implications for the development of more innovative organisational adaptation and service delivery to satisfactorily respond to future changes and challenges are significant. If we as mental health service providers continue to rely on traditional EAPs that don't address the fundamental underlying issues that contribute to poor mental health, then I posit that we will continue to see low utilization and further escalation of employee stress, anxiety, and depression-related illnesses.

The advent of COVID-19 gives us the opportunity, a once-in-a-lifetime opportunity, to reappraise how we respond to the human impact of rapid and major change that was already happening as a result of the continual technological advancements over the past 20 years. We now live and work in a world where change is the only constant and therefore require strategies that acknowledge this and understand the implications for all employees and organisations if we don't develop new and innovative strategies for the times. We must seriously consider taking a more integrated and holistic approach to employees and organisational well-being and productivity. This means acknowledging the criticality of each of the core pillars of health—physical, emotional, social, and existential (spiritual)—and engaging with our client organisations as to how each of these (in terms of ongoing programs) becomes accepted as business as usual throughout the organisation. That is, employee wellness policies become on an equal footing with all company policies and procedures and are reviewed and adjusted annually as required. Without that level of commitment and innovation from EAP providers and client organisations, it is likely that in the future, as the "change constant" rolls on, our responses to those changes will again become out of date, and human suffering and lost opportunities will result.

ABOUT THE AUTHOR

Ian Shakespeare has worked in the field of employee well-being globally and in Australia for over 30 years. He is currently the Director of Shakespeare Consulting Pty Ltd, and prior to that was CEO of SMG Health Pty Ltd, Senior Vice President Asia Pacific at Optum, CEO of PPC Worldwide Australia/APAC, and CEO of OSA, all of which were Employee Assistance Program companies. He is a former President of Asia Pacific Employee Assistance Roundtable (APEAR) and former Director of the International Council of Stress Management Professionals (IPSMP). He has a Bachelor of Behavioural Science, Graduate Diploma in Education, Graduate Diploma in Counselling Psychology, and a Master's in Business Administration (MBA). He has written a number of papers and presented at many forums both within Australia and globally on employee well-being topics and has provided advice to businesses on mental health issues for many years. During his 30-plus years in the EAP sphere, he has experienced many impactful issues (global financial crises, tsunamis, major fires and floods, globalization) that have required organisations to adjust. However, none of these has been more impactful or more challenging than the COVID-19 pandemic. Consequently, it required a certain nimbleness in how we as EAP professionals responded.

AUSTRIA

Conny Martens

AUSTRIA: THE CRADLE OF PSYCHOTHERAPY

Austria is a small country in the heart of Europe with almost 9 million inhabitants and about 83,900 square kilometers, but it is important in many areas of life. Not only because famous musicians such as Wolfgang Amadeus Mozart were born here but also because psychotherapy has its roots in Austria. Over the centuries, various approaches and schools have developed to treat mental illness and promote people's well-being.

The roots of modern psychotherapy go back to the 19th century. It was at this time that Sigmund Freud, considered one of the founders of psychoanalysis, began to develop his revolutionary ideas. He contributed significantly to the emergence of psychotherapy as an independent discipline. His groundbreaking concepts about the unconscious and the interpretation of dreams had a profound impact on psychological practice and laid the foundation for later therapeutic approaches. Alongside Freud as the founder of the so-called First Viennese School, and Alfred Adler who was considered the founder of the Second Viennese School, Viktor Frankl, also an Austrian neurologist and psychiatrist, developed logotherapy as the third school, an existential form of therapy that focuses on the meaning and significance of life. His best-known work, *Man's Search for Meaning* describes his experiences in a concentration camp. It inspired many people and had a lasting influence on the development of psychotherapy.

LEGAL FOUNDATIONS

In the 1950s, the Austrian Society for Psychology (ÖGP) was founded, which functioned as an organisation for psychotherapeutic training. The psychotherapeutic profession has been regulated by law in Austria since January 1991. On this date, the Federal Act on the Practice of Psychotherapy (Psychotherapy Act) came into force. Since then, psychotherapy has been an indispensable part of the Austrian health care system. A special feature in Austria is that currently, there are a total of 24 (sic!) recognised psychotherapeutic directions in this country, which are divided into four clusters: Psychoanalytic/psychodynamic (PPT), behavioural (VT), humanistic (HPT), and systemic (SPT).

It was not until the 1990s that society in Austria came to the realisation that "Work must not make you ill!" This led to the adoption of the Workers' Protection Act in 1994. In the run-up to the law, the business community feared that it would incur immense costs and that the administrative effort would be disproportionate to its success. But the law became a success story. With the changes in the world of work, the factors that cause illness at work have also changed. It is now recognised that mental illness is on the rise as a result of work stress.

LEGAL "DUTY OF CARE" OF THE ENTREPRENEUR

In Austria, according to the ABGB (Allgemeines Bürgerliches Gesetzbuch – General Civil Code), the employer has a duty of care toward the employee, which is also detailed in the Employee Protection Act. In addition to the classic areas such as noise protection and health protection regulations, there is an exciting decision by the Supreme Court (OGH) that drastically expands employers' duty of care. This decision has motivated some companies in Austria to offer an EAP in order to meet this very broad understanding of the duty of care.

WORKERS' PROTECTION ACT 2013
Evaluation of mental stress

Politics has taken the changed situation into account: Since the 2013 amendment to the Employee Protection Act, companies have been obliged to evaluate mental stress for the first time.

From an occupational science perspective, the term "mental stress" is first defined neutrally: Mental stress is "the totality of all detectable influences" that come from outside and have a psychological effect on a person. Mental stress, on the other hand, is a person's reaction to mental strain. We speak of mental stress when there are working conditions that experience has shown can lead to disturbances in physical and mental well-being. Employers are obliged to ensure the safety and health of workers in all aspects related to work. This also includes measures to prevent work-related hazards through appropriate work organisation. The latest knowledge in the field of work organisation must be taken into account. Employers shall identify and assess the causes of work-related mental stress and take measures to improve the psychosocial working environment. The results of the identification and assessment, as well as the measures taken, shall be documented in a suitable and comprehensible manner.

In the 10 years since the introduction of the law, a lot of positive things have happened in Austria, which finally paved the way for EAP. When the EAP Institut was founded in Vienna in 2012, there was a great need to explain what was meant by employee assistance, as this offer was almost completely unknown. Only a few innovative companies or large corporations that knew about EAP from their home countries knew what was behind the three letters.

Since COVID-19 and multiple crises, not only have the working conditions changed permanently and led to higher psychomental and psychosocial stress, but the search for adequate and helpful offers to support employees has also increased. Even more performance, social competence, and emotional stability were demanded of managers and staff.

The situation deteriorated noticeably, especially in the area of mental illnesses, so the Austrian health insurance companies soon sounded the alarm: The proportion of insured persons with sick leave due to mental impairments has risen dramatically in recent years. The costs of mental illnesses in Austria amount to 3–4% of GDP. That is the equivalent of about 12 billion euros per year. Thus, it is fair to say that since the pandemic and the associated challenges for companies to keep their employees mentally healthy, the willingness to introduce an EAP has increased exponentially. There are now a number of occupational health providers who also offer EAP. However, there are only two companies that have specialised exclusively in EAP and have been on the market for more than 10 years.

Who is allowed to provide psychological counselling in Austria?

EAP is not legally regulated in Austria. Therefore, the question arises as to which professions should generally provide counselling for employees in the sense of an EAP and what the legal situation is for these professions in Austria. Since counselling of employees is a very sensitive area, and often, employees seek counselling who may also have underlying mental illnesses, it is extremely important that counsellors are sufficiently well trained so that they can also recognise possible underlying mental illnesses and, if necessary, make a referral to a competent specialist.

The following professional groups are allowed to provide psychological counselling in Austria: 1. psychotherapists, 2. psychologists, 3. psychiatrists, 4. life and social counsellors, and 5. mediators.

All the occupational fields mentioned deal with psychological problems, disorders, and psychological issues. The following presentation is intended to help distinguish between the occupational groups, primarily on the basis of training, and also to assign them, at least typical, areas of activity. In practice, there are numerous overlaps. Depending on the qualifications acquired and additional training completed, members of all the professional groups listed sometimes also offer counselling, coaching, supervision, and mediation.

Life and social counselling represent the so-called "fourth pillar of health policy" in Austria, which is a "special feature" within the European health system. LSBs are very well suited for EAP counselling due to their training and the topics they are allowed to cover in counselling.

As a restricted trade requiring a licence, this professional group is affiliated with the Austrian Chamber of Commerce. The focus of counselling is on preventive health care and supports individuals, couples, families, and groups in improving their quality of life. LSBs are not allowed to conduct psychotherapy or treat people with "pathological disorders" (anxiety, panic disorders, etc., according to ICD 10).

The following subject areas are explicitly listed by the legislator. They are activities of the profession of life and social counselling and may therefore only be carried out on the basis of a licence corresponding to this profession, whereby a precise division is made according to counselling topics of personality development, self-discovery, problem-solving, improvement of relationship skills, and psychosocial counselling with the exception of psychotherapy.

In the private-personal sphere
- Life situation analysis and location determination, i.e., support in self-awareness and reflection of one's own work on personal goals and planning for the future.
- Development of a mission statement, self-strengthening and value analysis.
- Decision-making and action competence, i.e., preparation of decisions and analysis of decision-making behaviour, development of action, and solution strategies.
- Leisure-time activities to strengthen personal resources, personal educational concepts, and their emotional handling of money, i.e., support in coping with financial-problem situations and responsibility in handling financial resources.
- Topics related to single life, i.e., dealing with psychosocial consequences of single life, reflection on relationship patterns.
- Topics related to coping with crises, i.e., support in psychosocial/personal crises, accompanying affected persons, relatives, and helpers during crises and disasters.

In the professional field
- Career choice and career development according to personal resources, i.e., professional position determination and career planning.
- Development of application strategies, personal success concepts and strategies, time management, and dealing with stress.
- Strengthening of personal resources to increase motivation, job satisfaction, and performance.
- Dealing with personal consequences of unemployment, pension, and support with specific issues of professional activity such as burnout.
- Support in achieving a balance between work and private life (work-life balance).
- Development of a healthy psychosocial environment (e.g., health counselling, dealing with fears, issues of demarcation).
- Addiction counselling, addiction prevention.

Life stage themes
- Dealing with illness and death, i.e., mourning work, assisting the dying, coping with loss.
- Validation, i.e., personality development of the elderly, counselling of relatives and nursing staff with regard to communication and coping with stress.
- Counselling, coaching, and care in the relationship-oriented field and in connection with personal relationship issues.
- Partnership and marriage issues, i.e., analysis and processing of conflicts, crises, and changes in the couple's relationship.
- Family issues, i.e., analysis and processing of family climate, family dynamics, and divorce and separation issues.
- Educational issues, such as general pedagogical issues, special educational problems and behaviours, and issues in the areas of school and teachers.
- Sexual issues and social relationship issues.
- Conflict issues and conflict management, such as analysis and processing of conflicts of needs and values, developmental conflicts, avoidant behaviour, and conflict management strategies.
- Mediation and group and team topics, such as analysis and processing of group dynamics and interaction processes.
- Supervision, such as field-related and task-oriented topics for people in professional or voluntary work.

Communication topics
- Conversation and metacommunication, i.e., analysis and training of verbal and nonverbal communication possibilities, recognition of different levels of communication, and development of metacommunicative skills.
- Social communication and learning; logic, emotion, and intuition in social communication.
- Conversation and leadership behaviour, how to reflect on different conversation behaviours, development of partnership communication behaviour, and conversation techniques.

COMPANY SIZES IN AUSTRIA AND THE CHALLENGE OF SPECIAL EAP CONCEPTS

In 2021, around 358,600 companies in the market-oriented economy were small- to medium-sized enterprises (SMEs), i.e., 99.6% of all Austrian companies in the market-oriented economy.

Around 87% of SMEs were micro-enterprises with fewer than 10 employees. This size category also includes one-person enterprises (those with a single employee), which accounted for about 41% of all enterprises in 2021. About 11% of SMEs were classified as small enterprises (10 to 49 employees), and 2% as medium-sized enterprises (50 to 249 employees).

These figures show that in order to be successful in Austria, EAP concepts have to be individually tailored to the size of the customer. In addition to the few large companies and companies with a corporate structure, there are mainly micro-enterprises in Austria. They have an enormous need to keep their employees in the company, to motivate them positively, and to support them mentally, but they hardly have the resources to offer occupational health services. Therefore, in addition to classic EAP services, digital online platforms offering psychological counselling are also developing in the Austrian market. The EAP Institut, which is based in Vienna, offers counselling in German as well as in 10 other languages. The counsellors are mainly psychotherapists who live in Vienna.

ADDENDUM

1. How has the pandemic affected delivery of EAP and mental health and substance abuse services?

When the pandemic started, Austria had its first lockdown in March 2020. We noticed a state of shock as people were faced with a lot of uncertainty and anxiety as well as fear of death. Therefore, for the first two to three weeks during our first lockdown, we could see a decrease in the calls that we received as people were occupied with ensuring that their basic needs were covered for an uncertain period of time. Once people got out of this state, we noticed an increase in the need for coaching as well as crisis intervention. At the beginning, we received a lot of requests for private issues such as family matters or relationship matters. Our clients wanted to switch to online counselling sessions and felt safer in doing so in the comfort of their own homes. During this time, our EAP delivery services and mental health services were completely digitalized. We offered chat consultations via telephone and video-based sessions frequently, and made sure to make them accessible for all our clients. We adapted our services to our clients' needs and found individualized solutions for each client to ensure the highest quality of service in regards of sticking to our GDPR. One of the most significant discoveries that we made was that more children and teenagers were in need of mental health services, and we even had our highest number of referrals to psychiatrists as well as psychotherapists during this time. Within our company and the EAP service that we deliver, we did not notice an increase in substance abuse-related topics.

2. How has technology been utilized in delivering services?

Even before the pandemic hit, we had been developing and growing our technology services as well as digitalization to ensure that we reach each and every client and cover their needs. We have developed a well-being platform for our clients, where they can access podcasts and videos as well as meditations and exercises for both body and mind on different mental health topics to prevent mental health issues and keep them mentally well. Also, we have expanded our video-based services on different platforms to ensure that everyone can gain access and use our services at their convenience. Furthermore, our already-existing EAP app includes chat consultations. The number of our chat consultations has increased since the start of the pandemic.

3. How have you incorporated diversity and inclusion?

Diversity and inclusion has been one of our focus areas for the past two to three years or so. We have created different workshops as well as trainings on diversity and inclusion, where we discussed the following topics:

- How do you form dynamic and efficient work teams with your colleagues? Colleagues not only have individual potential but also exhibit different characteristics, such as age, gender, social and geographical backgrounds, internationality, as well as any disabilities, and they are shaped by different life situations, experiences, worldviews, and competencies.
- How does this diversity enrich both the team or the company and individual colleagues?
- How do you treat each other with mutual respect, even in the face of differences?
- And how do you avoid any behaviour that contradicts this principle?

Furthermore, in terms of our internal diversity, we make sure to live a culture where each and every one feels welcome and included. We do take the time each week to give our employees and colleagues time to voice their thoughts, feelings, and anything they want to share. It is highly important to us to have a wide diversity within our team in terms of gender, cultural background, age, religion, etc., to ensure that every individual client finds a right fit with one of our counsellors.

ABOUT THE AUTHOR

Dr. Conny Martens (Founder and Managing Director)
EAP-Institut management consultancy GmbH
Hegelgasse 19/10
1010 Wien
Vienna Austria

c.martens@eap-institut.at
www.eap-institut.at

ABOUT THE EAP-INSTITUT

- Type of company: GmbH
- Family business (5 children as co-partners, 1 of whom is an active partner)
- Data protection certified
- Memberships: EAEF, first Austrian member
- Viktor Frankl Centre Vienna
- Respact (CSR)
- Trade licences: Management consultancy and psychological counselling
- Founded in 2012, around 200 EAP counsellors, 10 languages
- Headquarters: Vienna, 2nd office in Baden

RESOURCES

EAP Providers of Employee Assistance Programmes that have been in existence for more than 10 years:

EAP Institut management consultancy GmbH
Hegelgasse 19/10
1010 Vienna
Emperor Franz Joseph Ring 5/3
2500 Baden near Vienna
info@eap-institut.at
http://eap.world

Mavie Work GmbH
Landstraßer Hauptstraße 95/1/4a
1030 Vienna
kontakt@maviework.care

Workplace health promotion facilities and associations:

Netzwerk Betriebliche Gesundheitsförderung
4020 Linz, Gruberstraße 77
05 0766 - 14103526
oenbgf@oegk.at

Österreichische Gesundheitskasse
Wienerbergstraße 15-19
1100 Wien
Telefon: +43 5 0766-0

Ministery of health
Stubenring 1
1010 Wien
iii2@bmaw.gv.at

Occupational health institutes (and EAP):

IBG Innovatives Betriebliches Gesundheitsmanagement GmbH Mariahilfer Straße 50/14
A-1070 Wien www.ibg.at

Health Consult

Gesellschaft für Vorsorgemedizin Ges. m. b. H

1010 Vienna, Freyung 6

info@health-consult.at

BANGLADESH

Ashique Selim

BACKGROUND

The first Employee Assistance Program (EAP)[1] in Bangladesh[2] went live in September 2019 when Psychological Health and Wellness Clinic (PHWC)[3] opened its 24-hour phone line to HSBC staff in 2019. I started my company PHWC in 2018 with the goal of setting up the first of its kind clinical mental health service, providing the highest quality of individual care in the private sector along with an organisational well-being program, including EAP. PHWC is a social enterprise of SAJIDA Foundation,[4] which is a value-driven, non-government organisation that embodies the principle of corporate philanthropy, with 51% shareholding of Renata Ltd, one of the fastest-growing pharmaceutical and animal health product companies in Bangladesh.

Currently, PHWC has a clinical unit with five psychiatrists, 14 full-time psychosocial counsellors and six associates who have provided care to over 4,500 individual clients since inception. We have an organisational well-being service providing EAP to 14 organisations through ICAS,[5] with almost 3,000 lives and a further 8,500 lives of local employees across 16 organisations.

---

1   EAP: https://eapassn.org/page/definitionandcoretechnology
2   Bangladesh country profile: http://bdembjp.mofa.gov.bd/public/storage/pdf/Country_Profile.pdf
3   PHWC: https://www.phwcbd.org
4   Sajida Foundation: https://www.sajida.org
5   ICAS: www.icasworld.com

PRE-COVID-19

Around the time of PWHC's formation, ICAS International won the global bid for providing EAP to HSBC. I understand that ICAS commits to providing a local phone service to companies to ensure language and cultural compatibility. As there was no EAP in Bangladesh, I was approached by ICAS and, with their support, we were able to go live in about a year.

The enthusiasm for local EAP contracts in the private sector was not as high as I thought it would be. The lack of awareness of mental health in general, not to mention the novelty of the "new and innovative" EAP, did not get much interest. Most multinational companies already had a global EAP contract and so were not interested. Local banks and financial institutions were not sensitized and so were not interested. ICAS themselves only had a few contracts in Bangladesh, and the numbers of lives were low.

Bangladesh had an influx of refugees from Myanmar in 2017, which resulted in almost a million Rohingya moving into refugee camps in the Cox's Bazar region of Bangladesh.[6] This resulted in a large-scale humanitarian response led by the Government of Bangladesh, UN organisations and various international and national NGOs and civic society. The scale of the response and the importance of the mental health needs of the refugees resulted in several organisations looking for mental health support for their own staff members. This provided an opportunity, and we provided EAP to primarily non-government organisations (NGO) in the initial period.

Almost as soon as we launched our service, DIY EAP companies started to appear in the market. The lack of awareness of what the services entail and the lack of commitment to quality (e.g., hiring unqualified staff) meant that these services were able to undercut our prices significantly, and they started to gain traction in the market. Predictably, once organisations received a poor quality of care, organisations were then further closed to the idea of exploring EAP.

COVID-19

Bangladesh went into full lockdown in March 2020. At that time, our 24-hour phone service was live and contracted tele-counselling was part of the service. Since prior to COVID-19, most of our clients were based in a different city, we were accustomed to providing remote counselling over the telephone or video calling. This experience allowed us to quickly move into a purely online service for both clinical and organisational services. We were able to reduce overheads by letting go of physical premises and hiring more staff, as we did not have the need for office space. The initial lockdown had an overall net positive impact on our business. People in general were more

---

6 Rohingya Crisis: https://www.unicef.org/emergencies/rohingya-crisis

interested in the topic of mental health, and the conversation was becoming more widespread. We had more enquiries into EAP and contract numbers increased.

Social media played an important role in the spread of awareness of mental health and the need for well-being. Webinars were being broadcast, and the previously limited audience was now significantly higher. There was a negative side to this too. Bangladesh has no statutory regulatory body when it comes to counselling or psychotherapy. This has allowed unqualified people to make false claims about their credentials and to reach an audience in need of professional help.

In January 2019, we had our second lockdown, and in April/May, the third and final lockdown. In the initial period of the COVID-19 crisis, I found that employees were keen to engage in online counselling and webinars, but soon this enthusiasm waned, and there was far less engagement.

POST-COVID-19

As the direct impact of COVID-19 was receding, I found that many of the organisations we were providing services to were taking mental health more seriously and hiring their own resources, which meant that EAP was no longer needed. The Ukraine invasion by Russia also meant that there was a global shift in refugee funding from the Rohingya crisis to the Ukraine crisis. This resulted in a significant reduction in our contracts. Hence, we found that there was a reduction in the demand from the NGO sector. At the same time, private businesses were recovering from the impact of the lockdowns and we had developed a reputation in the market for being a quality provider. This resulted in an increase in interest from private businesses, and our contracts started to increase.

EAP IN BANGLADESH

My experience of setting up an EAP service and trying to sell this in a new market was an interesting journey. I have realized that taking the approach of having an Organisational Wellbeing Program with a supporting EAP is an easier sell. Human resource departments are quite rudimentary with a focus on hiring, salaries, and logistics. There is little use of data for staff engagement, satisfaction, or well-being. There is a market for workshops and seminars on topics such as stress management or empathic listening. Using this as a gateway to building a trusting relationship with companies and then trying to upsell seems to be the way forward.

Bangladesh has a young economy, having only just celebrated our 50 years of independence. Coming out of very high poverty levels has meant that the government is investing heavily in infrastructure and basic necessities of the citizens. Most of our workforce is engaged in agriculture, and there is a trend where this is shifting into manufacturing. Financial services are limited, and insurance is quite rudimentary. We are a major ready-made garments manufacturer with an estimated 3 million people working in the sector.[7] The high use of contractual staff with little education means that EAP, in its existing form, is not cost-effective or appropriate for the manufacturing industry.

In general, Bangladesh is quite a homogenous society with the majority of people belonging to the same ethnicity and religion. As a result, ethnic and religious minorities are often not part of the mainstream conversation. Bangladesh has had the longest-sitting democratically elected female head of state. This, along with significant national initiatives in education, legislation and employment, has meant that female empowerment has come a long way since our independence. Bangladesh also officially recognizes transgender individuals as part of a "third gender." While this term remains controversial, I think that it is a step in the right direction. Our psychology and counselling curriculum has a big emphasis on being nonjudgmental with clients, irrespective of their differences. In our organization, this conversation continues in ongoing training and case discussion. Recently, ICAS has provided two rounds of diversity training, which was available to their preferred partners.

There exists a significant opportunity to develop an innovative, tech-supported well-being service for manufacturing, considering most employees have limited education and limited access to technology. The model consists of a tiered approach with training of peer support staff on the factory floor, with further training and support for supervisors, EAP services for mid to low management, and a premium service for executives. This, backed with robust research, may help to develop a package that can help tap into an untapped market.

---

7   Bangladesh economic status: https://www.worldbank.org/en/country/bangladesh/overview

ABOUT THE AUTHOR

I am a psychiatrist by training, and over the past seven years have been working in Dhaka, Bangladesh, as a clinician and an entrepreneur. Having spent the earlier half of my career in the UK, I returned to Bangladesh in 2016 with the hope that I could contribute to the overall lack of mental health care in the country[8,9]. Bangladesh is currently a least-developing country on the verge of becoming a developing country by 2026.[10]

RESOURCES

Md. Salim Hussain – Associate Professor – Department of Industrial and Organisational Psychology, Dhaka University, salim087@du.ac.bd.

Dr. Ashique Selim, MRCPsych (UK), MB BS (Bangladesh), Consultant Psychiatrist and Managing Director of PHWC, Advisor to Mental Health Program Sajida Foundation.

---

[8] MH services in Bangladesh: https://www.who.int/docs/default-source/mental-health/special-initiative/who-special-initiative-country-report---bangladesh---2020.pdf?sfvrsn=c2122a0e_2

[9] Mental health challenges in Bangladesh and the way forward.

[10] Hasan, K., Jannat, Z., Shoaib, S., *Ann Med Surg* (Lond). 2022 Aug; 80: 104342.

BOSNIA AND HERZEGOVINA, CROATIA, SERBIA, AND SLOVENIA

Katja Novak

BACKGROUND

The concept of an Employee Assistance Program (EAP) does not have an extensive history in Slovenia, Croatia, Bosnia and Herzegovina, and Serbia. Progress in this field was made by the Educational and Research Institute Ljubljana, headquartered in Slovenia, which ventured into the realm of EAP nearly 15 years ago. Collaborating with an international EAP provider, our institute pioneered the introduction of EAP services in Slovenia and other former Yugoslavian countries, including Croatia, Serbia, and Bosnia and Herzegovina.

Initially, our focus was primarily on offering EAP services to subsidiaries of big multinational companies. In the local companies, there was still a limited awareness regarding the significance of employees' mental health and overall well-being, and this resulted in hesitancy among employers to invest in EAP services. However, this dynamic has gradually evolved, albeit at varying speeds across the different countries. To understand better why EAP is gaining recognition as an important element of strategies aimed at enhancing and sustaining employee health and well-being, it is essential to delve into the historical context of these nations.

Slovenia, Croatia, Bosnia and Herzegovina, and Serbia, along with Montenegro and Northern Macedonia, were constituents of the Socialist Federal Republic of Yugoslavia (SFRY), commonly referred to as Yugoslavia. Under Josip Broz Tito's leadership, Yugoslavia adopted a unique form of socialism that emphasized self-management, non-alignment in international affairs and a system of brotherhood and unity among the ethnically and culturally diverse groups within the country. During Tito's rule, Yugoslavia experienced relative stability and economic development, but after his death in 1980, ethnic tensions and economic challenges resurfaced. In the early 1990s, the breakup of Yugoslavia occurred amid a series of violent conflicts and wars. The Ten-Day War, which occurred in 1991 in Slovenia, marked the first armed confrontation during the breakup of Yugoslavia. After this short-lasting war, Slovenia transitioned into an independent state.

The wars that followed the breakup of Yugoslavia (Croatian War of Independence, Bosnian War, and Kosovo War) resulted in a significant loss of life, population displacement and widespread destruction. The Croatian War with Serb forces lasted from 1991 until 1995. The Bosnian War with Serb forces took place from 1992 to 1995. Wars had a profound impact on the political, social and economic landscape of Croatia, Serbia, and Bosnia and Herzegovina. All countries transitioned from a socialist economy to a market economy. Slovenia joined the European Union in 2004, followed by Croatia in 2013. Both Serbia and Bosnia and Herzegovina aspire to join the European Union and have taken steps toward integration. In all these countries, there are some nuances between the health care systems, but all in all, health insurance is mandatory for all citizens and it plays a crucial role in financing the health care system. The system is designed to offer accessible and affordable health care services to all individuals, regardless of their income or social status. Alongside the public health care system, there are also private clinics that provide additional options for health care services, often with out-of-pocket payments.

As the socio-political and economic landscapes continue to evolve in these countries, the growing recognition of EAP's role in nurturing employee well-being stands as a testament to the gradual shift in attitudes and priorities. In all these four countries, we are, for now, the only EAP provider—offering 24/7 support for employees and their immediate family members.

THE IMPACT OF SERVICES DURING THE PANDEMIC

During the COVID-19 pandemic, our services were governed by the strict safety regulations. For some period of time, we could not deliver face-to-face counselling. This presented quite a problem for us due to the prevailing reliance on in-person counselling, which clients favoured over telephone sessions. In response, we introduced an online (video) counselling option as an alternative, which was very positively embraced by our clients.

Amid the pandemic's early stages, we noticed that certain client companies refrained from promoting our EAP services despite our proactive efforts and carefully curated promotional materials. This reluctance signalled a need for heightened awareness among client companies about the potential value EAP services could offer during times of crisis. Thus, we undertook vigorous initiatives to engage human resources (HR) departments, outlining the many ways in which employees could benefit from EAP services during the pandemic and assisting them in the consistent promotion of the services.

At the beginning of the pandemic, we observed the decline in the number of EAP users. This could be attributed, in part, to the lack of promotional activities in the client companies and the overwhelming demands individuals faced in managing various aspects of the pandemic (childcare, adjusting to working from home, health concerns, etc.). However, as the population acclimatized to the new reality over the subsequent two to three months, the utilization of the EAP started gradually increasing because people were facing a wide array of mental distress. During the pandemic, there was extensive coverage in the media emphasizing the critical importance of prioritizing one's mental well-being and actively seeking assistance when grappling with challenges. This increased media attention played a significant role in gradually dismantling the social stigma previously associated with addressing mental health concerns. This may also contribute to the higher utilization rates of EAP in all four countries.

The pandemic also coincided with a growing acknowledgment among both employees and employers regarding the profound impact of the pandemic on psychological welfare. Thus, more and more companies were interested in offering the EAP services to their employees, prompting a more proactive stance toward employee support.

THE EFFECTS OF ONLINE/VIRTUAL COUNSELLING

Prior to the pandemic, the concept of online or virtual counselling was a relatively uncommon approach. Slovenia, Serbia, Croatia and Bosnia and Herzegovina are quite small countries; therefore, it is not very time-consuming to visit the counsellor for a face-to-face session, and people in these countries have a preference for direct personal interactions. The pandemic changed that a lot. Most of the people had to work from home, and technology became an indispensable lifeline for communication. This paradigm shift undeniably impacted the traditional preferences, prompting both our counsellors and clients to embrace the realm of virtual counselling. Post-pandemic revelations prompted us to recalibrate our approach. While face-to-face counselling remains prevalent and continues to be the method of choice for many, a significant transformation has taken root. An evident shift is underway, with an increasing number of clients opting for virtual counselling sessions. In our experience, virtual counselling is as effective as face-to-face counselling. The virtual realm, once considered distant and detached, has proven itself as a realm where genuine connections can be fostered and meaningful support can be extended. The convergence of technology and therapeutic expertise has brought about an unforeseen dimension of access and convenience for those seeking assistance, regardless of geographical limitations.

THE ROLE OF TECHNOLOGY AND SOCIAL MEDIA

Technology has rapidly evolved into a pivotal cornerstone within the EAP field. The contemporary norm of seeking information on the internet has spurred us to harness technology's potential, especially in response to the challenges posed by the pandemic. In a bid to offer comprehensive support, we inaugurated a dedicated web page for client companies. This digital hub serves as a repository of vital information about our EAP services, further enriched by an extensive array of resources encompassing articles, videos, infographics, and interactive questionnaires spanning a diverse spectrum of health and well-being topics.

A distinctive feature of our digital platform is the integration of a user-friendly contact form through which employees can initiate correspondence with our counsellors. Upon submitting their queries or concerns, a prompt and personalized response from the counsellor is sent to their specified email address. Real-time chat counselling isn't presently offered due to the relatively modest demand via the described contact form, but we remain attuned to emerging communication trends. As we acknowledge the propensity of younger generations to favour such instantaneous modes of interaction, we anticipate the introduction of chat counselling somewhere in the near future.

Regarding social media, we are prominently using Facebook and LinkedIn to raise awareness of the importance of employees' mental health and overall well-being and to promote the pivotal role EAP plays in nurturing a thriving workforce. We believe that being present on social media is bolstering the efficacy and accessibility of our EAP offerings.

In conclusion, technology has revolutionized the landscape of Employee Assistance Programs, making it more accessible, efficient, and adaptable to the diverse needs of today's workforce.

EFFORTS TOWARD DIVERSITY AND INCLUSION WITHIN THE FIELD

In recent years, the discourse surrounding diversity and inclusion has gradually gained traction within our societal dialogue, although it might not yet hold the same level of prominence as in some highly developed countries. Our strategic approach extends beyond mere acknowledgment. We are proactively building a network of counsellors to cater to the diverse needs and expectations of our clients. Whether it's addressing cultural nuances, language preferences, or understanding unique life experiences, our diverse network of counsellors stands as a testament to our commitment to providing empathetic, personalized support.

Inclusivity is a core principle that guides our interactions and decision-making processes. Through this intentional approach, we are trying to create an environment where every client feels seen, heard, and understood. By fostering a culture of diversity and inclusion, we are not only enriching the experiences of our clients but also contributing to the broader narrative of societal progression.

ABOUT THE AUTHOR

Katja Novak, BA in Psychology
Educational and Research Institute Ljubljana
E-mail: katja.novak@iri-lj.si
Phone: 00386 41 519 773
LinkedIn: https://www.linkedin.com/in/katja-novak-08050b71/

RESOURCES

Employee Assistance Program Adria
https://eap-adria.com

Slovenia
Ministry of Health
(Ministrstvo za zdravje)
Štefanova ulica 5
1000 Ljubljana
https://www.gov.si/drzavni-organi/ministrstva/ministrstvo-za-zdravje/

The National Institute of Public Health
(Nacionalni inštitut za javno zdravje)
Trubarjeva cesta 2
1000 Ljubljana
https://www.nijz.si

Croatia
Ministry of Health
(Ministarstvo zdravstva Republike Hrvatske)
Ksaver 200a
10000 Zagreb
https://zdravlje.gov.hr/

Croatian Institute of Public Health
(Hrvatski zavod za javno zdravstvo)
Rockefellerova 7
10000 Zagreb
https://www.hzjz.hr/

Serbia
Ministry of Health
(Ministarstvo zdravlja Republike Srbije)
Nemanjina 22-26
11000 Beograd
https://www.zdravlje.gov.rs/

The Institute of Public Health of Serbia
(Institut za javno zdravlje Srbije)
Dr Subotića Starijeg 5
11000 Beograd
https://www.batut.org.rs/

Bosnia and Herzegovina
Ministry of Health
(Federalno ministarstvo zdravstva)
Maršala Tita 9
71000 Sarajevo
https://www.fmoh.gov.ba

BOTSWANA

Onalethata Johnson

INTRODUCTION

I am a clinical pharmacist by training, holding a PharmD (Doctor of Pharmacy), working as the managing director at ICAS Botswana (ICASBW), a licensee of ICAS World established in 2009, formerly as GO Corporate Wellness Solutions. ICASBW, like many providers in the country, provides employee wellness/health and well-being programmes, which are inclusive of EAPs. ICASBW recognises that employee well-being, addressed holistically, is a critical enabler of individual and organisational productivity and performance. We are the country's foremost specialist in the provision of comprehensive employee health and well-being programmes (EHWP). Over the years, I have amassed extensive experience in the field (in its various names), with my initial contact with the "wellness" concept having been in a hospital employee wellness area during my clerkship/clinical rotations in Columbus, Ohio. Further to that, I was government seconded to the consultancy charged with setting up the National Antiretroviral Therapy (ARV) Programme, Masa, back in 2000–2002. I subsequently led the Debswana HIV/AIDS Impact Management Programme (2004–2012), which I was instrumental in eventually evolving into an employee wellness programme.

Botswana is a small country of just over 2.3 million people, located at the center of Southern Africa, between South Africa, Namibia, Zambia, and Zimbabwe. With its economy built on a foundation of diamond mining, Botswana spends around US$466 per capita on health, making health care generally accessible to an average citizen. There's no EAP-specific legislation in Botswana, but rather, occupational health and safety is regulated by various pieces of legislation, including the Factories, Agrochemicals, Mines, Quarries Works and Machinery, Radiation Protection, and the Workers' Compensation Acts.

Due to limited research on workplace health in Botswana, related literature is very scanty, hence the unclear origin of EAPs. What is available, however, implies that employee assistance was preceded by occupational health and safety-focused interventions, providing mostly preventative services, including workplace health promotion initiatives offered through welfare, wellness, or occupational health units. These "informal" initiatives became more formalised in the late '80s as a result of the HIV/AIDS pandemic, which had severely hit Botswana. In an effort to mitigate associated challenges, the Government established structures to address issues of HIV stigma and discrimination, as well as, critically, to ensure that health care workers were well-equipped to cope with the physical and emotional demands of their jobs. The private sector also set up workplace HIV/AIDS programmes to abate its negative impact and secure continued productivity.

We must consider wellness as rooted in "medical sciences" and more associated with physical health, emphasising the adoption of positive health practices and lifestyle choices. This is more or less at the exclusion of or with minimal mental/psychological aspects, which traditionally form the focus of EAPs. Along with all that, workplace programmes seem to have been founded from HIV/AIDS prevention and care, and we can understand why the shape of these "EAPs" became skewed toward employee wellness programmes (EWPs)—the perspective they have taken from the onset and have grown from.

EWPs in Botswana, which are inclusive of EAPs, have evolved further, with today's programmes changing form and scope to adopt a more holistic, integrated well-being perspective, now seen as a business imperative rather than as employee benefits or welfare issues, also aimed at enhancing business objectives through people. In addition to personal issues and challenges, the focus is now on addressing any issue faced by today's employee that can negatively affect their health and well-being and therefore productivity.

THE IMPACT OF SERVICES DURING THE PANDEMIC

Botswana, just like the rest of the world, was not spared from the global crisis and the unparalleled disruption of COVID-19. In response, the government of Botswana, too, developed strategic response plans through which measures such as physical distancing, isolating and quarantining, and restricting movement, among others, were imposed to contain the spread of COVID-19 and mitigate its effects on the population. Inopportunely, the requisite changes in normal life necessitated by these measures led to "unintended" outcomes. In addition to the unrelenting rise in COVID-19 prevalence and the related suffering and deaths, the business closures and the financial strain due to the loss of livelihoods posed a perfect recipe for mental distress.

We experienced a sharp rise in the demand for psycho-social support services due to the prevalent mental health challenges such as isolation and the related breakdown of the social connections we all thrive on as humans, the high levels of stress associated with job insecurity or even the loss of income for some, the uncertainty and fear, and a sense of despondency pertaining to the health and life of loved ones as COVID-19 mortality increased by the day. This rise in the demand for services undeniably heightened the attention on mental health and EAPs more than ever before. We did indeed (at ICASBW) see a parallel increase in the EAP uptake through our special COVID-19 intervention programmes.

Further, the pandemic led to a number of observations about the EAPs:

- A proliferation of new mental health service providers that set up clinics all over the country to contribute to the management of the crisis.
- New COVID-19-specific interventions were developed to augment existing EAPs, some of which included COVID-19 check-ins (at ICAS), group COVID-19 debriefing for teams following a positive COVID-19 test result of a team member or COVID-19 death, and more social good in the form of a wider, more inclusive extension of services to family members and relatives who may have not been originally included as beneficiaries.
- Emergence of "new" services such as workplace-based temperature checks, in compliance with the Ministry of Health and Wellness guidelines on coronavirus transmission, prevention and early detection, and engaging health care auxiliaries possessing a certificate in health care assistance.
- Leveraging technology and setting up counselling helplines to keep basic counselling services available where conventional (in-person) provision of mental health services could not hold due to restrictions and interventions.

The effects of online/virtual counseling
The increasing availability of the internet, coupled with the current digital technology advances such as smartphones, have given EAP/EWP service delivery a facelift in the form of online counselling. While face-to-face counselling still has a place and cannot be substituted, particularly in respect of more severe emotional and psychological challenges, online/virtual counselling has many positive effects, including:

- Convenience for people who may have challenges with accessing conventional delivery modes of therapy, such as in-person, face-to-face services. In today's world of open-plan offices where confidentiality is often difficult to maintain, this means users can, through online counselling, receive therapy in the comfort of their private spaces and at convenient times.
- Enhanced ability to remain anonymous through live chat counselling, etc., thereby lessening the stigma associated with mental health and counselling and providing the comfort necessary to those who may still be uncomfortable with openly accessing counselling support.
- Increased reach and an alternative mode of counselling delivery, which seems to be the preference for Gen-Zs and other tech-savvy employees.
- Equitable service access for employees who work outside the main metropolitan areas of Botswana, where there is a dearth of counselling and mental health professionals.

The benefits of online counselling do not only accrue to the individual user of the services but also to the employer organisation. Programme uptake and utilization are inputs of programme impact outcome. Increased reach and diversified accessibility bring an improved programme uptake and thereby an amplified potential of the programme's impact on the organisation.

While the overall effect of online counselling has been positive, there are still observations of resistance to adopting this mode of service delivery resulting from the perception that face-to-face is the best. As a result, we see an almost-equal split between those who prefer digital counselling and those who prefer the conventional way.

THE ROLE OF TECHNOLOGY AND SOCIAL MEDIA

Because of the great advances in technology and the significant increase in the use of social media such as WhatsApp, Zoom, Microsoft Teams and others, many organisations have adopted the use of technology and social media as part and parcel of doing business. Furthermore, the need for massive change in all aspects of life brought about by the COVID-19 pandemic "forced" organisations to rapidly shift from face-to-face to online products and services as a means of survival and ensuring continued operations.

With the demand for employee psycho-social support clearly heightened, this shift toward digital solutions could not have come at a better time when access to the required support services using the usual means was challenged. EAPs and wellness programmes leveraged these ready resources to address the service disruptions created by the pandemic. At the height of the pandemic, face-to-face contact was a luxury, and the need to social distance badly impacted the ability to maintain consistent EAP service delivery. Digital technology enabled employees to remotely access the services and support they needed with relative ease.

From the face of it, there appears to be appreciation and acceptance by the industry in Botswana of the need to approach wellness from a technology-leveraged perspective. Whereas previously, only a handful of service providers, like ICAS Botswana, were already powering technology to widen the reach of their services, telephonic counselling and online therapy are steadily becoming the norm of doing business to complement the traditional, in-person, face-to-face interventions. Some therapists are believed to have resorted to online/telephonic counselling to bridge the gap created by travel restrictions, quarantine, and isolation in light of the toll that COVID-19 had on people's mental state. In addition to facilitating ease of access to EAPs, social media such as Facebook and LinkedIn are used quite widely to position wellness as a business imperative, promote employee well-being, and offer related tips.

ICASBW now offers, as a basic option, virtual/video counselling through Microsoft Teams and Zoom, based on established protocols to ensure that professional standards and confidentiality are maintained. Using bespoke business intelligence systems and programme utilisation and engagement data (AI), ICAS generates informative reports from which client organisations can be proactively advised for more targeted interventions to prevent psychosocial issues and behavioural risks. In a further effort to leverage technology and the Fourth Industrial Revolution (4IR) and to expand reach, wellness digital platforms, which employees can download on their mobile devices, are offered for employees to safely and confidentially access comprehensive health and well-being information, tools, and assessment, including on mental well-being. Most recently introduced was an ICAS (on the go) app that gives employees a chat functionality for quick access to counselling through the touch of a button, and it is available 24 hours a day.

While there's good, the use of social media can also be a drain on well-being, leading to tremendous stress, anxiety, loneliness and poor self-esteem, all of which pose a high risk for depression, self-harm and suicidal ideation. There has, in fact, been an observed upsurge of youth suicides in the recent past, plus increased referrals of youth by their parents for psycho-social support.

DIVERSITY AND INCLUSION EFFORTS

Employee wellness endeavours to look at a person holistically from all dimensions. As a result, a multidisciplinary intervention approach is critical to the success of the interventions offered. Certainly, a modern employee has to contend with a wide spectrum of challenges, thereby requiring different skill sets to address them. As the industry grows, there has been a proliferation of professions other than counselling getting involved in the EAP space. For example, in addition to the clinical/counselling psychologists and social workers, financial advisors, legal professionals, nurses, behavioral scientists, and others have joined "EAP professionals" in providing the synergy required for optimal intervention outcomes. There is still a long way to go for optimal integration, but that certainly is the ultimate goal if EAPs are to have a "visible" impact. We've seen an increase in the training of key health responders in basic psychosocial skills to offer, as a minimum, psychological first aid before referring clients on for substantive interventions. The hope for the future is to have a local EAPA chapter and see formal training of EAP professionals.

ABOUT THE AUTHOR

Onalethata Johnson, PharmD, is the managing director at ICAS Botswana (ICASBW).

RESOURCES

EAPASA: www.eapasa.co.za/about-eapa-sa/what-is-an-employee-assistance-program.

Minimum Package: Botswana Workplace Wellness Program for Health Workers. Table - PMC (nih.gov).

Service Providers:

ICAS Botswana. Onalethata Johnson, PharmD. Managing Director. Email: onalethata@icasbotswana.co.bw Phone: +267 3190019 Fax: +267 3190018. Website: https://www.icasbotswana.co.bw

Well@Work Corporate Wellness Programme – BOMAid. Ntukunu Makubate, Wellness Coordinator. Email: bomaid@bomaid.co.bw Phone: +267 3633100 Fax: +267 3184230 Website: https://www.bomaid.co.bw/wellwork-corporate-wellness-program/

DaisyR Solutions. Daisy Lejowa, Managing Director. Phone: +267 3133109 Fax: +267 3133119 Website: http://www.daisyrs.com

Key Wealth. Email: info@keywealth.co.bw Phone: +267 3114034 Website: https://www.keywealth.co.bw

Storkforth Health. Dr. Mogwera Mogalakwe, MD. CEO Email: hq@storkfort.com Phone: +267 3974578 Website: https://www.storkfort.com

Botswana Substance Abuse Support Network (BOSASNet). (NGO) Prisca Mokgadi, Executive Director. Email: director@bosasnet.org.bw Phone: +267 3959119 Fax: +267 3951333 Website: http://www.bosasnet.com

BULGARIA

Boyan Strahilov

AT THE BEGINNING

I suppose as in many other companies, the professional development of PIK Center was quite difficult at the beginning. Mental health care was limited to offering psychological counselling to private clients in our office. In 2010, we began providing EAP services as a partner to one of the global EAP providers. But in most of the cases, the client organisations in Bulgaria had no information that this kind of service existed at all. At that time, we put really great efforts into reaching out to the HR departments to make them aware of the services available for their employees. Only three years later, we managed to get our first client. At that time, we were only two professionals at PIK Center, and we did absolutely everything—from promoting the idea of EAP to providing counselling to employees. These first steps weren't easy, and this continued for several years.

Gradually, other global EAP providers began to seek contact with us. Their interest was aroused by the need to serve their global clients with divisions in Bulgaria and the opportunity to sign new contracts, since they also cover Bulgaria. At that time, we were in demand for one main reason: We were the only one offering EAP in Bulgaria. Moreover, we were the only one applying Solution-Focused Brief Therapy in our practice and offering a 24/7 EAP line. Nevertheless, the Bulgarian companies to which we offered EAP perceived the idea as an unnecessary luxury rather than an important asset for their organizations.

PANDEMIC CHALLENGES

The situation changed a lot in the early 2020s with the onset of the pandemic. COVID-19 has brought about drastic changes in work patterns, shaken up the workforce, and caused HR professionals to focus on employee mental health. The abundance of negative news that the mass media produced and the uncertainty about the future in the longer term took shape as elements of a "hidden advertising campaign" for EAP in Bulgaria. Many companies have realized the necessity to take care of the mental health of their employees and the need to procure EA programs or at least provide the opportunity to access psychological counselling.

In all kinds of organisations, the focus on the pandemic acted as a catalyst and put the emotional well-being of employees in the top priorities. A search for EAP began, which bifurcated in two directions. The first line of interest was from brokers and agencies that wanted to market and sell the service—they had hardly heard of EAP before. The second was from companies and organizations that needed help for their employees due to the rising anxiety and stress in the pandemic situation. Most of those organizations seeking EAP tended to state the need for a psychologist, without a clear idea of how the counselling relationship should be structured or how such a service could be provided. This led to a series of additional trainings and clarifications on how EAP works and what the meaning and benefits of implementing such a program are.

Despite the huge interest, potential client-organisations were rather cautious; they wanted to try it out, preferring to sign contracts for a few months or a year at most. During this period, according to our statistics, utilization of EAP services in Bulgaria reached levels of 15% to 20% on an annual basis. But that still seemed to be not enough for employers. Some HR managers' perceptions of EAP utilization were as high as 60% to 80%, as unrealistic as that was.

PSYCHOLOGICAL COUNSELLING: ENRICHING THE TYPES

An important component of the EAP service that developed rapidly with the onset of the pandemic and has remained stable over time is online counselling. Due to the specifics of the situation, employees and their families were willing to use any online platforms to access counselling, regardless of their security and complexity. Online counselling has found its stable place among the types of psychological work. For the past three years, clients who state their preference for online counselling have formed a stable group of about 20% to 22% of all psychological counselling requests. Some of the organisations that wanted to implement EAP as a service deliberately sought online counselling in combination with other types of psychological services. Others even set conditions stating that they prefer only online and remote forms of psychological counselling. This was prompted by the fact that many employees continue to work from home offices or use the hybrid work option. Also, the offices of some organisations are located far from the centre of Sofia, where the counselling premises are.

At present, the largest share of psychological counselling in Bulgaria is occupied by telephone counselling, with about 45%. This can be explained with easy accessibility and the possibility of timely service provision by the consultants. Face-to-face counselling is preferred from about 33% of the individual clients. Lastly is the demand for advice via chat. This is partly due to the lack of offering this type of service in Bulgarian. In general, it can be concluded that chat counselling is a very unpopular service in Bulgaria.

CULTURAL FEATURES

The observed penetration of global providers in Bulgaria is accompanied by an interesting phenomenon introducing a contradiction in the understanding of how an EAP service could be successfully implemented and developed locally. It can be said that in the actions of some of the global providers, on the one hand, there is a clear opposition between the declared readiness to provide freedom to local experts in the implementation of EAP services in Bulgaria, and on the other hand, the hidden desire for total control and imposition of unified (sometimes in contradiction with local regulations and laws in Bulgaria) EAP processes and procedures. It seems that more trust in the local expertise is needed to get a working EAP formula worldwide.

We (from PIK Center) have witnessed and suffered from the unilateral imposition of work requirements (especially in the area of personal data collection) in the last few years under the slogan "We want the EAP service to be the same worldwide." We strongly disagree—there is no way to unify the approach to the psychological work in the US, China, and Bulgaria, for example. Cultures are different, and customer reactions to a certain service approach (and mandatory collection of personal data) are also different. Our practice shows that the uniformity of the approach in dealing with clients in Bulgaria results in building resistance in them to use the services, which leads to a reduction in the EAP utilisation. So, we are wondering: Is this really the idea of EAP? And where does that leave the genuine understanding of mental health care? Because the emotional support of the employees needs to be tailored to the specific culture in which it is applied. Otherwise, it could be even considered as an act of violence. A good example of this is the politics of some of the global providers to the LGBTQ community. We also take good care of the mental health of this specific group, but Bulgaria still lacks a stronger focus in this direction, unlike many other countries. Looking into their specifics too deeply starts to annoy the LGBTQ clients themselves. They have problems, just like anyone else, and we are careful not to shift the focus of the consultation from the client's real problem by focusing too much on their identity. LGBTQ people are treated and supported in the same way that we support the rest of the EAP clients.

MORE LOCAL EXPERIENCE

We mainly apply SFBT, CoLeC and Single Session Therapy in counselling. In our psychological work, we have found out that it is better to teach clients to ask useful questions themselves rather than counsellors questioning them about their problems and guiding them to ideas about how to deal with the difficulties they face. Clients learn to ask good questions about their own needs, and on that basis, they build strategies and find solutions. We have called this approach CoLeC (Conversations Led by Clients). The approach works well for clients in Bulgaria who seek help on the EAP line. They find their way out of difficulties and achieve their goals much more quickly than with other therapeutic approaches or psychological techniques. Moreover, they are happy to discover that it is better to be the active party in such a process of interaction.

NEXT EAP STEPS

Mental health care is increasingly coming into focus as an employer's responsibility and long-term commitment. But much still needs to be done in Bulgaria in terms of making EAP a more popular and workable service. There should be real social commitment from the leadership of companies, not just a show of it as an excuse or a tick in the checklist. This includes:

- Managers of organisations to be sensitised and educated as to gain insight into the advantages of constant mental health care for their employees.
- Employers to be given more information about the importance of mental health and possible prevention activities in the field of emotional health (including the use of EAP services).
- HR teams to be educated about their role in implementing EA programmes. And we need to keep working to change the attitude of management toward such programmes to help them see EAP as an investment in employees rather than as a cost that needs to be contained over time.
- And last but not least, to train more professionals in the field of helping professions who can adequately respond to the needs of the clients.

My colleagues and I know that this is not an easy task, but we believe that the efforts in this direction are worthwhile. Technology has its place in our work, but it cannot replace the human factor in achieving good mental health. Therefore, we will continue working hard to develop the human potential.

ABOUT THE AUTHOR

Boyan Strahilov is the Managing Director of PIK Centre Ltd., Sofia – the first company delivering EAP Services to different client-organizations in Bulgaria. As professionals he and his colleagues offer different type of psychological services focused on mental health since 1999.

Boyan Strahilov
Managing Director at PIK Center Ltd.
boyan@pikcenter.eu
+359 877 951555

CANADA

Crystal Smalldon

INTRODUCTION

The COVID-19 pandemic has brought about profound challenges across the globe, affecting people's physical and mental well-being. In Canada, like in many other countries, the pandemic's impact on mental health has been significant. In this essay, we will delve into the multifaceted implications of the pandemic on counseling services in Canada. We will explore how the pandemic accelerated the adoption of telehealth and virtual counseling, the critical role of technology and social media, and the commendable efforts made toward diversity and inclusion within the counseling field. Additionally, we will provide a resource list with recommendations for professionals keen on networking within the counseling sector in Canada.

THE IMPACT OF SERVICES DURING THE PANDEMIC

The COVID-19 pandemic disrupted the traditional delivery of counseling services in Canada, prompting a swift and transformative response from mental health professionals and organizations across the country. At the onset of the pandemic, face-to-face counseling sessions faced severe restrictions due to safety concerns and social distancing protocols. This forced counselors and therapists to adapt quickly to ensure continuity of care for individuals in need of mental health support.

TELEHEALTH AND VIRTUAL COUNSELING

Telehealth and virtual counseling emerged as one of the most significant adaptations to the challenges posed by the pandemic. Therapists and counselors turned to telehealth platforms and videoconferencing tools to connect with their clients. This transition allowed individuals to access counseling from the safety and comfort of their own homes.

The impact of virtual counseling during the pandemic was twofold. On the positive side, it ensured the uninterrupted provision of care to many Canadians who required mental health support. Moreover, it demolished geographical barriers, making counseling services accessible to remote and underserved communities, where in-person counseling had previously been a challenge due to distances and limited resources. However, on the flip side, virtual counseling presented challenges to some individuals, including those with limited access to technology or unstable internet connections.

The effectiveness of virtual counseling became evident as therapists adapted to the medium. While in-person interactions have unique advantages, therapists found innovative ways to maintain the quality of therapeutic relationships. They focused on building rapport and ensuring clients felt heard and supported during virtual sessions.

INCREASED DEMAND FOR SERVICES

The COVID-19 pandemic also led to an increased demand for counseling services in Canada. The prolonged period of uncertainty, social isolation, and economic instability contributed to heightened stress, anxiety, and depression levels among the population. As individuals grappled with the uncertainty of the pandemic's trajectory and its associated challenges, many sought solace and support in the form of counseling.

This surge in demand underscored the necessity for greater investment in mental health infrastructure and services. Mental health providers and government agencies alike recognized the urgency of addressing the mental health crisis in tandem with the pandemic. The pandemic highlighted the need for sustained efforts to expand access to mental health services and reduce the stigma associated with seeking help for mental health concerns.

THE EFFECTS OF ONLINE/VIRTUAL COUNSELING

Online/virtual counseling became a crucial lifeline for many Canadians during the pandemic. The advantages of this mode of counseling became evident as it offered greater accessibility, convenience, and the ability to maintain therapeutic relationships while adhering to public health guidelines.

ACCESSIBILITY AND CONVENIENCE

One of the primary benefits of online/virtual counseling was its enhanced accessibility and convenience. Individuals no longer needed to travel to counseling centers, making mental health support more attainable for those living in remote areas or facing transportation challenges. Moreover, it provided a solution for clients with mobility issues, busy schedules, or caregiving responsibilities who might otherwise have struggled to access in-person therapy.

MAINTAINING THERAPEUTIC RELATIONSHIPS

Therapists successfully adapted to the virtual format, finding innovative ways to maintain the quality of therapeutic relationships. While in-person sessions offer direct physical presence and nonverbal cues, virtual counseling demonstrates its effectiveness in preserving and, in some cases, even deepening therapeutic connections. Counselors employed strategies such as active listening, empathy, and creative interventions to bridge the gap between the digital screen and the client's emotional world.

THE ROLE OF TECHNOLOGY AND SOCIAL MEDIA

Technology and social media played pivotal roles in connecting individuals with mental health resources and support during the pandemic.

ONLINE SUPPORT COMMUNITIES

Social media platforms witnessed a surge in mental health-related content and support communities. Many Canadians turned to platforms like Facebook and Reddit to share their experiences, seek advice from peers, and find solace in knowing they were not alone in their struggles. These online communities provided a sense of belonging and understanding during a time of social isolation, acting as informal support networks.

MENTAL HEALTH APPS AND RESOURCES

In addition to social media, several mental health apps and online resources gained popularity during the pandemic. These digital tools offered self-help strategies, guided meditation exercises, and resources for managing anxiety and depression. They provided individuals with actionable steps to bolster their mental well-being, often complementing formal counseling services. These apps empowered individuals to take an active role in managing their mental health and cultivating resilience.

EFFORTS TOWARD DIVERSITY AND INCLUSION WITHIN THE FIELD
The field of counseling in Canada has been actively working to ensure greater diversity and inclusion, both among counselors and clients.

CULTURAL COMPETENCY TRAINING
Counselors and mental health professionals recognized the paramount importance of cultural competency. Training programs and initiatives focused on understanding diverse cultural backgrounds and providing culturally sensitive care have gained prominence. This proactive approach ensures that counselors are equipped to address the unique needs and perspectives of clients from various cultural, ethnic, and linguistic backgrounds.

REPRESENTATION AND ACCESSIBILITY
Efforts to increase representation of diverse voices within the counseling field have been ongoing. This includes recruiting counselors from various cultural backgrounds and ensuring that counseling services are accessible and culturally relevant to all Canadians. Recognizing that diverse populations may face distinct mental health challenges, such efforts aim to bridge existing gaps in access and care.

CONCLUSION
The COVID-19 pandemic has indelibly reshaped the landscape of counseling services in Canada, ushering in a new era of innovation, adaptability, and inclusivity. As we reflect on the impact of the pandemic, it becomes evident that the counseling field in Canada has demonstrated remarkable resilience and resourcefulness in the face of adversity. The acceleration of telehealth and virtual counseling, driven by necessity, has not only ensured the continuity of mental health care but has also transcended geographical boundaries, making support more accessible than ever before. While some challenges remain, particularly concerning equitable access to technology, this shift toward virtual services has undoubtedly widened the horizons of mental health care in the country.

Simultaneously, the pandemic's role in bolstering technology and social media's significance in mental health support cannot be overstated. Online support communities have become havens for individuals seeking solace and understanding, underscoring the importance of peer support networks in times of isolation. Furthermore, the proliferation of mental health apps and resources empowers individuals to take an active role in their well-being, complementing the professional guidance provided by counselors. These technological advancements will likely continue to shape the future of mental health care in Canada, emphasizing the importance of maintaining a balance between digital and human interactions within the field.

In tandem with technological advancements, the counseling field in Canada has made commendable strides toward diversity and inclusion. Culturally competent care is increasingly emphasized, ensuring that mental health services resonate with the diverse tapestry of Canadian society. The active promotion of representation among counselors from various backgrounds and the commitment to accessible and culturally relevant care have collectively strengthened the sector's ability to cater to the unique needs and perspectives of all Canadians. As the field continues to evolve, these efforts will be instrumental in addressing the mental health disparities that persist within the country. In conclusion, while the pandemic presented unprecedented challenges, it also prompted a transformation within the counseling field, promising a more inclusive, accessible, and tech-savvy future for mental health support in Canada.

ABOUT THE AUTHOR

Crystal Smalldon is a current Registered Social Service Worker, Psychotherapist, Canadian Certified Addiction Counsellor, Canadian Indigenous Addiction Counsellor, Canadian Certified Telemedicine Addiction Professional, Internationally Certified Drug and Alcohol Counsellor, Alcohol and Drug Counsellor Level 2, Medication Assisted Treatment Specialist, and an associate member of the Canadian Society of Addiction Medicine.

Crystal is also the Executive Director of the Canadian Addiction Counsellors Certification Federation as well as the Executive Director for multiple other not-for-profit organizations that certify addiction counsellors and services across the globe.

RESOURCES

For professionals interested in networking within the counseling field in Canada, several valuable resources and organizations offer opportunities for connection, growth, and collaboration.

The Canadian Addiction Counsellors Certification Federation (CACCF) is a not-for-profit Ontario registered organization that has been in operation for 39 years. The CACCF promotes, certifies, and monitors the competency of addiction-specific counselors in Canada using current and effective practices, which are internationally recognized. They certify thousands of Addiction Counselors across Canada. The CACCF is internationally recognized as the gold-standard provider in addiction credentialing both in Canada and on the international stage. They follow best practices related to the issuance of addiction credentialing as clinically researched and confirmed by the International Certification and Reciprocity Consortium. Their mandate is to protect the public. The certifications CACCF issues along with their professional conduct review process provide public protection for counselors, employers, regulatory agencies, clients, and their families.

ONLINE COUNSELING PLATFORMS

Get-aHead offers a comprehensive Software as a Service (SaaS) platform tailored for mental health practitioners, aimed at enhancing the quality of care they provide. This innovative platform is designed to train, assess, and continually improve the effectiveness of mental health professionals in delivering care across various domains. Presently, Get-aHead's services extend to several critical areas of mental health, including psychology, psychiatry, social work, addiction counseling, and health coaching. By leveraging cutting-edge technology and evidence-based methodologies, Get-aHead supports practitioners in honing their skills, staying up-to-date with industry best practices, and ultimately delivering more impactful and tailored mental health care to their clients across diverse disciplines.

MENTAL HEALTH CONFERENCES

Participating in mental health conferences in Canada, such as the Canadian Mental Health Association's Annual Conference, can be a transformative networking opportunity. These conferences bring together professionals, thought leaders, and experts in the field, offering a platform to establish meaningful connections, share insights, and stay updated on the latest developments in mental health.

CHILE

Maria Elena Subercaseaux

EAPS IN CHILE: NEW CHALLENGES

EAS was the first provider in Chile of Employee Assistance Programs (EAP) and has been operating since 2004. As well, EAS is part of EAP LatinA Corporation, a Latin American company that has been in the market for more than 26 years. EAS and EAP LatinA work together to provide Employee Assistance Programs to prestigious companies throughout Latin America.

In all these years of history and with more than 200 client companies in Chile, EAS works to deliver a service that responds to the needs of both the client company and its workforce.

EAS has a network of more than 100 specialized professionals: psychologists, lawyers, accountants, nutritionists and medical professionals (doctors and nurses) trained to offer this service 24/7/365, always working to prevent and solve personal difficulties that affect work performance and well-being.

The mental health of employees is an issue that cannot be ignored in the business world. Organizations should focus on ensuring a healthy work environment and adopting policies and practices that encourage the prevention and treatment of mental health problems. This will not only benefit workers but will also contribute to improving the productivity and performance of the company in general.

It is important to mention that Employee Assistance Programs (EAPs) are not as widespread in Chilean organizations compared to some other countries, especially those in North America and Europe. However, the concept of EAPs has been gradually gaining recognition in Chilean workplaces, particularly in larger, multinational companies that adopted international HR practices.

Unfortunately, in recent years, Chile has suffered several natural, social and political events that have seriously affected the mental health of the Chilean population, such as the 2010 earthquake, the social outbreak of 2019, political instability and crime, uncontrolled immigration and, finally, the great crisis generated by the COVID-19 pandemic and the consequences of a long confinement during 2020 and 2021.

MENTAL HEALTH IN CHILE: SOME FIGURES

- According to figures from the Superintendency of Social Security (Suseso), two out of every three workers (67%) who presented a recognized occupational disease of work origin during 2022 correspond to mental health diagnoses. The figure represents an increase compared to 2021, the year in which it reached 52% of the total.
- The Mental Health Thermometer in Chile, carried out by the Catholic University and the Chilean Security Association in April 2021, showed worrying results:
  - Almost half of Chileans (46.7%) reported symptoms of depression.
  - More than 20% had eating, energy and sleeping problems.
  - 15.2% lost interest in things and 12.1% felt hopeless.
  - The proportion of people with suicidal ideas quadrupled from November to April 2020.
- Furthermore, according to the study "Health Problems in Chile" by the Global Health Monitor (Ipsos, 2022), mental health is the main health problem that people currently face in Chile since three out of five interviewees (62%) point it out.
- With this result, Chile far exceeds the world average (36%) and occupies the second position on the international list, being surpassed only by Sweden (63%). Concern about mental health rose from 50% in 2020 to 62% in 2022, which reveals a significant growth in this concern in the last three years. In addition, obesity is in the third position of the main health concerns in Chile, with 38% of mentions. However, like mental health, Chile occupies the second place among the countries most concerned about obesity, only behind Mexico (55%), which demonstrates citizens' special concern about this issue.
- Finally, according to the Sodexo Quality of Life Index 2022, the pandemic caused an increase in levels of stress, violence, depression, uncertainty and anxiety, and it left repercussions that are reflected in both the economy and people's health.

After all this, we can conclude that taking care of the mental health of employees is not only important for their overall well-being, but it can also have a significant impact on the productivity and success of the company as well as the general well-being of our country.

THE GROWTH OF EAPS

As a consequence of these events, and especially the COVID-19 pandemic, EAP services began to be increasingly required. They have played a key role in supporting employees, families and organizations, helping them to cope with these issues. Stress management techniques, helping people adapt to remote work and manage work-life balance, counselling to cope with caregiving responsibilities due to school closures, and education for employees in order to understand emotional and psychological aspects of these issues are some examples.

These situations obliged us to customize our EAP services and adapt them to our clients' new needs, creating reduced and short-term services with our PEACE (Extraordinary Emotional Support and Contention Program), which was required in our country during this period. In addition, we implemented a strong platform to deliver daily online training in different topics as well as mindfulness practice, all of which has been appreciated by client companies, workers and families.

NEW WAYS TO DELIVER COUNSELLING

Although teletherapy was becoming popular around the world some years ago, in Chile, it was scarcely used until the COVID-19 pandemic in 2020, when it became popular due to mandatory confinement. Since then, virtual counselling has continued to be used because of its advantages, such as accessibility for people who live in rural areas (Chile is a long, long country but with fairly good access to the internet and mobile phones) or who have transportation issues or parking costs, etc. Also, people can access a wider range of hours for individual sessions and receive counselling in any place they are. Even more important, clients can access professionals of their choice who work far away or even abroad. For most people, privacy is very important, and online sessions reassure this condition. Clients need to carefully check the best platforms in terms of security and data protection. Finally, as costs for clients can be reduced, so can the costs for therapists and other EAP professionals because they can reduce office costs.

Even though online or virtual sessions have been a very good alternative, we can point out several disadvantages, such as the loss of nonverbal language, less engagement, distraction during the sessions, and problems managing technology.

TECHNOLOGY AND SOCIAL MEDIA IN RELATION TO EAP SERVICES

We can point out advantages and disadvantages. In the first group, we have websites, apps, chats and other elements that make it easier to access EAP services, allowing people to obtain instant information and support in real time. As an EAP provider, we have been forced to update our offerings and develop new apps and websites to address a younger workforce composed mainly of millennials, a multi-screen and hyper-connected generation that prefers to access the service through apps such as WhatsApp and other media.

In terms of marketing, technology and social media make it easier to disseminate the service, allowing us, as providers, to spread information among employees of the organizations. As for the disadvantages, we can mention the information overload that people constantly receive, both from their internal and external networks. This situation may be a source of stress and distraction for employees. Overall, we consider these technological advances a great support for the EAP services.

CHILE: FROM ISOLATION TO INCLUSION

In relation to diversity and inclusion within the EAP services, it is important to mention that in Chile, this has been changing rapidly. As some of you may know, our country is a very long, narrow and isolated territory, with a magnificent and diverse nature: Atacama Desert to the north, Andes Mountains to the east, the Pacific Ocean to the west, and lakes, islands, channels, millenary forests and magnificent glaciers to the south, reaching the Antarctic.

Historically, it was not customary to have many foreigners in the workforce, but in the last decade, we have been receiving a great number of immigrants from other Latin American countries. In addition, laws for inclusion and protection of minorities have been enacted, so our EAP services have had to meet the needs of a diverse workforce. Organizations were obliged by a law of inclusion to hire a certain percentage of disabled workers, and we were asked to coach leaders and their teams in this aspect. About four years ago, EAS recognized the need to integrate with the EAP LatinA structure, which, as I mentioned earlier, delivers services to all Latin American countries. It happened that many of our clients in Chile began operations in other countries, and many of EAP LatinA's clients had operations in Chile, so unifying our structure and processes was an imperative. The need arose to recruit professionals of different ethnicities, genders, sexual orientations and cultural backgrounds, which involved understanding and respecting the cultural values, norms and traditions of their clients.

Another important issue is the possibility of offering counselling in languages other than Spanish, such as English, Portuguese, and others as needed. This service is especially needed by expats. Finally, it is worth mentioning that we implemented a strong front line with a wide range of hours for easy access to the EAP services by a diverse workforce of employees and families, with a call center receiving calls 24 hours a day, 365 days a year.

SECURITY AND DATA PROTECTION

Finally, I would like to refer to a very important topic: the security of information and protection of personal data, a condition required by our client companies. We are proud to report that EAP LatinA Corporation, the company to which EAS belongs, is the only EAP provider in South America that has ISO-27001 certification for information security management.

ABOUT THE AUTHOR

Maria Elena Subercaseaux is a Psychologist and Executive Director of EAS Chile.

CHINA

Hanxiao Mao

HOW THE PANDEMIC DROVE MENTAL HEALTH DEVELOPMENT IN CHINA

The COVID-19 pandemic that began at the end of 2019 has profoundly changed people's social and working environment. Social changes, lockdown measures, isolation, work restrictions, declining income, and the fear toward physical health and the future have collectively affected the mental health of employees. Employers should play and have played a crucial role in maintaining employees' mental health by providing them with necessary resources and tools during critical and special periods.

As a leading provider of mental health services in China, CIIC EAP has provided various types of mental health services to nearly a thousand organizations during the three difficult years.

CIIC EAP collected 25,677 samples of desensitization data and did mathematical statistical analysis. The results indicate the following five points.

1. The epidemic has had a huge impact on employees' mental health. We found that 49.04% of users were affected by the emotional impact of the epidemic, with the most common negative emotions including anxiety (57.35%), depression (25.46%), anger (10.38%), and fear (6.81%). Employees showed poorer performance in the dimensions of anxiety and depression, confidence level, social function, and physical health. There were also differences in emotional arousal among employees of different genders, ages, and industries. Women experienced more depression and anger, while men experienced more anxiety and fear. For young employees aged 26 to 30, they were more likely to experience negative emotions than older people. In addition, service industry employees had higher levels of anxiety compared to industrial industry employees.

2. Under the impact of the COVID-19 pandemic, employees had more difficulties in work than in life. Among all counseling issues related to COVID-19, work stress was the most popular issue and reached its peak in May 2022 (when Shanghai was totally locked down) and December 2022 (when the Chinese government adjusted control measures and the majority of the population got the infection at that time). Work pressure mainly came from two aspects: work itself and work adaptation. The issues of "work itself" included increased workloads, a challenged marketing environment, and the incapability to meet targets. The issues of "work adaptation" included a home environment that was not suitable for work, poor communication among colleagues, decreased attention, and unclear boundaries between work and life. During the three-year epidemic period, the proportion of "work itself" in all employee issues significantly increased.

3. The COVID-19 epidemic urged people to reconsider meaning. The experience of "impermanence in life" made people start to think about the value and significance of life. More employees discussed their understandings of the world, life, values, and other aspects in counseling sessions. They considered exercising and improving their abilities in various aspects to better cope with their future life. This kind of thinking and awareness would help them better cope with the pandemic and enhance their resilience.

4. The COVID-19 epidemic brought dual pressure on managers' emotions and managerial work as well. During the epidemic, "how to be aware of and identify employees' emotions" has become the top concern for managers, and they usually weren't equipped with the basic knowledge and skills.

5. More flagged cases were identified during the pandemic. The proportion of flagged cases increased 5.26% compared to the average proportion from 2009–2019. Among all industries, the manufacturing industry showed the largest proportion of flagged cases.

As the pandemic got worse, more and more demands emerged from organizations and employees that required EAP providers to be able to offer services in a swift manner and via a virtual modality. In 2018, CIIC EAP had already launched an online portal based on H5 webpage technology with four functions, including counseling booking, trending articles, psycho-educational video clips, and self-help screening tools. In 2020, CIIC EAP decided to invest more and updated this portal to contain other features, i.e., enabling an embedded video function to conduct video counseling, online pre-evaluation surveys allowing counselors to collect information before the first session, online post-satisfaction surveys making providing feedback easier, a mindfulness module providing systematic practice to users, and AI interaction.

The most important upgrade is that users are able to browse 100+ counselors and review their background, feedback, and availabilities for the next two weeks and select their preferred counselor, date, time, and modality. Usually, users are able to book a session within 48 hours, and if they need more timely service, a 24/7 hotline is always available. From 2020 to 2022, 65% of counseling sessions were booked from the online portal, and 35% of sessions were through the 24/7 hotline. For internet and technology companies, the percentage of online bookings reached 88%. Obviously, people favor the autonomy, convenience, and promptness brought by technology.

Other than online booking, the other three popular modules are AI interaction, mindfulness, and self-screening tools. Under the impact of the pandemic, people were keen to figure out what happened to them, wondering, "Am I normal for feeling scared and anxious?" and "What is the next step I should take?" CIIC EAP invented the first EAP AI called "Jingjing" (which means "I need a break") and embedded it into the online portal. Through education and the evaluation of negative emotions such as anxiety, depression, and anger, users better understand those negative emotions and their own mental health status. Jingjing also provides solutions such as emotional comfort, self-help resource tools, self-screening tools, and counselor recommendations to guide users to explore appropriate resources.

THE IMPACT OF TECHNOLOGY

In terms of counseling modalities, telephonic counseling is always the most popular way to conduct counseling in China due to convenience, shyness, stigma, and the distribution of professionals. However, with the development of technology, more and more people prefer to adopt virtual sessions instead of in-person and telephonic. CIIC EAP found that there is no significant difference in effectiveness and satisfaction among telephonic, in-person, virtual, and on-site counseling.

Besides counseling services and self-help resources demonstrating online trends, virtual training and workshops also showed a dominant modality. In 2022, 83% of trainings in CIIC EAP were conducted through online conference systems, i.e., Zoom, Microsoft Teams, and Tencent. Compared to 2019, only 12% of trainings were through the web. Even since the pandemic ended, online training still holds advantages, such as lower costs to organize, more available options, larger attendee capacity, and replay options. In 2023, 57% of trainings were online from January to May in CIIC EAP.

To meet an organization's temporary and critical needs due to the negative impact of COVID-19, CIIC EAP modified annual services to one-month and three-month short-term services. At the beginning of 2020, the City of Wuhan was locked down. From April to June in 2022, the City of Shanghai was locked down. These two major events caused panic and confusion for employees and organizations in Wuhan and Shanghai. Those organizations that hadn't had an EAP program were required to select a qualified provider within a limited time and budget. CIIC EAP decided to offer a standard set of timely, comprehensive, and short-term services to organizations to meet their critical needs and save the purchasing cost, which received positive feedback from clients. Over 60% of short-term service clients converted into long-term partnerships.

DIVERSITY AND INCLUSION

The concept of "diversity and inclusion (D&I)" comes from the West. For local national companies, D&I is not promoted that much. For multinational companies in China, due to the global influence, local offices are required to promote the D&I concept and conduct a serial of training topics. In China, D&I mainly focuses on gender, multigeneration, and bias. China has as high as a 61% female labor participation rate, which means that gender equity and feminine power are popular topics for the workplace. With the emergence of the younger generation into the labor market, how to understand and better communicate with Gen Z is usually a challenge for managers, especially for those born in the '70s and '80s. Usually, webinars and lunch 'n' learns are the most popular ways to promote D&I. Some organizations conduct D&I Week each year as a routine. Unlike Western countries, LGBTQI is not an open topic that organizations would select to discuss publicly; however, we see a need for more counseling related to LGBTQI. In terms of professionals, counselors with LGBTQI training and clinical experience are essential. However, the number of qualified professionals is very small in China.

ABOUT THE AUTHOR

Hanxiao Mao, MS, CEAP, is the Program Director at CIIC EAP Center.

RESOURCES

CIIC EAP Center: http://www.ciiceap.com/ eap@gunaitong.com
Nanjia Counseling Center: http://www.nanjia.org/
Sino-American Family Therapy Institute, SAFTI: http://saftiaquarespace.com
Tang xinli: https://www.tangxinli.com/
United Family Healthcare: https://ufh.com.cn/
Parkway Healthcare: https://www.parkwaychina.com/
Ningbo Kangning Hospital: http://www.nbknyy.com/
HOPE 24/7 crisis hotline: +86 400-161-9995
Beijing Huilongguan Hospital: https://www.bhlgh.com/

COLOMBIA

Carlos Felipe Villar

In 2022, the World Health Organization (WHO) stated that there was an urgent and indisputable need for acting on mental health.[11] It is undeniable that mental health over the past years has become more and more visible and relevant, and the awareness of its positive and negative impacts on society has increased. A survey carried out by Ipsos in 2022 in 34 countries found that 47% of the respondents stated that COVID-19 was the biggest health problem facing their country, followed by mental health, cancer, and stress.[12] This means that the second-biggest problem perceived by the surveyed adults in their countries in 2022 was mental health, which is not a minor issue. This statistic reflects the increasing awareness of the importance, impact, and role of mental health in the everyday.

However, although the awareness, actions, initiatives, and strategies on mental health have risen, they remain insufficient and inadequate.[13] According to the 2022 Mental Health Report developed by WHO, health systems worldwide tend to prioritize other health conditions over mental health. On average, only 2% of the assigned health care budgets in countries around the world are directed to mental health.[14] This means that mental health, although perceived as an

---

11 World Health Organization (WHO): Mental health (who.int)

12 Ipsos Survey cited in Statista study on Mental Health in Colombia, www.statista.com

13 World Health Organization (WHO): Mental health (who.int)

14 World Health Organization (WHO): Mental health (who.int)

important issue, is not receiving the attention and support it deserves and needs. Therefore, access to mental health services remains a challenge for countries and their health systems, and there are gaps and imbalances, specifically in governances, resources, and services.[15]

Amidst the above-mentioned, the bright side is related to the fact that it has become more common to think about our mental health and well-being and to identify and create initiatives that contribute to mental health and well-being. In 2020, in a survey developed by Wellcome Trust, around 33% of individuals in Latin America reported that at least once in their lifetime, they were so anxious or depressed that they could not continue their regular daily activities as they normally would for two weeks or longer. Compared to other regions, Latin America ranked the highest, above Australia and Central Asia.[16] Beyond the explicit and descriptive outcome of this statistic, it is important to highlight the fact that people are starting to recognize and accept that they have had difficulties related to mental health issues, which configures the first step for looking for help and support. In other words, people are speaking up and the conversation about mental health in Latin America is gaining relevance in a historical moment where health systems recognize the importance of mental health and well-being but can't keep its pace in terms of responding to demands. Over the years, mental health has gained relevance and visibility. In a survey developed by Wellcome Trust in 2020, 46% of individuals worldwide aged 15 years and older stated they thought mental health was more important than physical health, while another 46% felt mental health was just as important as physical health.[17]

Given this increasing awareness, it is a fact that health systems cannot always provide timely and quality support and orientation to the population, and therefore, EAPs within workplace settings have gained even more relevance as an actor among many others that can support health systems in terms of mental health and well-being. The WHO in the 2022 Mental Health Report argues that given the increasing importance of mental health, some people do not look for help or support mainly because of three specific factors: poor quality of services, low levels of health literacy in mental health, and stigma and discrimination.[18] So, to contribute to mental health, there is a need for multisectoral action in order to create strategies that tackle the challenges of an increasingly growing population.[19] And within this scenario, organizations and EAPs have played,

---

15   World Health Organization (WHO): Mental health (who.int)

16   Wellcome Trust cited in Statista study on Mental Health in Colombia: www.statista.com

17   Wellcome Trust cited in Statista study on Mental Health in Colombia: www.statista.com

18   World mental health report: transforming mental health for all. Geneva: World Health Organization; 2022. License: CC BY-NC-SA 3.0 IGO.

19   World mental health report: transforming mental health for all. Geneva: World Health Organization; 2022. License: CC BY-NC-SA 3.0 IGO.

are playing, and will play an important role within the system within its reaches and limitations.

EAP Latina Colombia was created in 2006 in Colombia with the purpose of being one of those initiatives needed to contribute to mental health and well-being, adding to the effort that EAP Latina was already making in Argentina, Chile, and Mexico. The history and evolution of Employee Assistance Programs (EAP) in Colombia have had a different evolution than other countries in the region. Its development has been marked not only by introducing the EAP service but by contributing to the transformation of a work culture that was not used to prioritizing mental health and well-being at the workplace. During many decades, the idea of seeking mental health support was considered neither by organizations nor employees. Unlike other countries in the region where it has been common to discuss mental health in work settings and counseling is normalized, in Colombia, mental health has traditionally been seen as something that should stay in individual and private spheres and does not need to be talked about publicly. As mentioned, stigma and discrimination, together with low levels of mental health literacy and poor quality of services, have historically played a central role in diminishing the access and use of mental health services in Colombia. However, this has been changing, and nowadays, the situation is different.

EAPs in Colombia, together with public and private health systems initiatives, as well as with political, cultural, and social influences, have contributed during the past 20 years to the creation of a culture that is starting to support and validate mental health and well-being in work settings. When EAP Latina Colombia started its operations in Colombia in 2006, there were few organizations interested in hiring the program, mainly because there was a lack of understanding of its impact on business. In fact, the acceptance of the idea that there is a positive correlation between well-being and work performance is relatively new and is associated with the above-mentioned culture that positions mental health as a priority among people in organizations.

Before the COVID-19 pandemic, within the Columbian culture that did not tend to prioritize mental health in work settings, the essence of EAPs was somehow distorted. Different companies started to offer not only counseling, legal, financial, and nutritional services but also many different services like plumbing, locksmithing, holiday and party planning, and even shoe shining. So, EAPs were measured and evaluated by some organizations not only by the professionalism but by the number of services that were offered. That, besides the fact that there was an expectation of a utilization rate above 80%, following the logic that if a benefit is acquired it should be used. Thus, it was understood that if any organization did not reach such a utilization rate, something was not working within the organization. Those were not easy times for reaching organizations and implementing EAPs.

The COVID-19 pandemic was a game-changer in Colombia for EAPs, given its impact on the well-being and mental health of people. The COVID-19 pandemic accelerated the cultural change around the importance of mental health and well-being in workplaces. Quickly, organizations started to look for mental health support for their employees, and it became relevant. EAP Latina was there, ready to help and offer services adapted to organizational needs.

In Colombia, a study conducted by Martínez-Cabezas et al. (to be published) focused on estimating the prevalence of depression and anxiety before and after the COVID-19 pandemic, using the Individual Registry of Health Services Delivery Data from 2016 to 2020, and argued that there was an important increase before and after the COVID-19 pandemic.[20] The article study suggests that although there was a tendency in terms of increment, during March and August 2020, the number of cases decreased, which might be explained by the lockdown and the difficulties in accessing services. Specifically, during this time, EAPs in Colombia were trying to figure out how to best support organizations, employees, and their families by finding alternatives that strengthened the use of technology in the realm of well-being and mental health. These results align with the statistics presented by the Colombian Ministry of Health, which, in response to the coronavirus pandemic, launched a hotline aimed at providing mental health counseling and assistance to the population. Between April 2020 and April 2021, mental health problems accounted for approximately 34.26% of all interventions within this initiative.[21] Specifically, anxiety symptoms were ranked first on the list of reasons for contacting the service, followed by stress.[22]

The COVID-19 pandemic shaped EAPs in Colombia, not only by increasing the awareness and need for mental health support in work settings but by fostering its reach through the use of technology in the delivery of its services and emphasizing the focus on prevention by preparing organizations and employees to cope with everyday challenges. At the beginning, there was some resistance to accessing virtual counselling, but with a dose of resignation and self-reflection, it started to become more popular. Perhaps because it was the only option or because the need was so great, the number of employees and their families using the virtual services of EAP Latina increased significantly. In this sense, whilst the COVID-19 pandemic and the new technologies contributed to give access, it also contributed to the normalization of the importance of talking about ourselves, our issues, and our worries in organizational settings. As of 2022 in Colombia, 46% of adults stated that mental health was the biggest health problem facing people and 36% stated that stress was the biggest health problem facing people in 2022.[23]

---

20 Martínez-Cabezas, S., Pinilla-Roncancio, M., Carrasquilla, G., Casas, G., & González-Uribe, C. (2023). Prevalence Of Depression And Anxiety In Colombia: What Happened During Covid-19 Pandemic? *Medrxiv*, 2023-02.

21 Ministerio de Salud y Protección Social (Colombia), cited in www.statista.com

22 Ministerio de Salud y Protección Social (Colombia), cited in www.statista.com

23 Ipsos Survey cited in Statista study on Mental Health in Colombia: www.statista.com

A few months after the official ending of the COVID-19 pandemic, the tendency for considering mental health and well-being as important is still present and its effects are here to stay. However, it is not easy to foresee the future, since a dose of uncertainty remains about the effects of the COVID-19 pandemic on mental health and well-being in general terms, and specifically in workplace settings. Although virtual counseling gained popularity, given its benefits in terms of accessibility, there is a lack of research that can support its effectiveness compared with face-to-face counseling in the long term. EAPs should invest in research to support these new ways of delivering counseling.

There is an increasing need to keep shaping and adapting EAPs to the current trends in political, social, and cultural environments looking for ways to adapt the services and continue contributing to society. In a survey conducted by Gallup between 2020 and 2021 in Latina America and the Caribbean, the adults considered that the approach most frequently considered helpful in alleviating anxiety or depression was spending time outdoors, followed by improved lifestyle behaviors and talking to a mental health professional.[24] For EAPs in Colombia, it is important to read the context and shape its approach and services accordingly to the needs of organizations, their employees, and their families.

ABOUT THE AUTHOR

Carlos Felipe Villar is the Project Leader of EAP Latina Colombia.

---

24 Gallup Survey cited in Statista study on Mental Health in Colombia: www.statista.com

FRANCE

Emmanuel Charlot

A FEW WORDS ABOUT STIMULUS

Founded in 1989 by Patrick Légeron, a psychiatrist, Stimulus is specialized in the management of mental health, emotions and behaviors in the workplace. To achieve this, it draws on a number of areas of expertise that enable it to carry out audits, consultancy and training services, and psychological and social support (both remotely and on-site), as part of EAP or not.

Since 2016, Stimulus has been part of the "Human & Work" group, whose aim, through its four subsidiaries in France, is to support companies on the topics of mental health (Stimulus), inclusion and diversity (Equilibres), leadership and coaching (Talentis) and career transitions (Nexmove). In 2023, each company in the Human & Work group became a "mission-driven company" sharing a common purpose: "Building together an inclusive, responsible and serene workplace."

IN THE LAND OF ASTERIX,* EAPS ARE STILL RESISTING ...

Despite the hot news that should be encouraging French companies to take an interest in so-called "full EAP," French companies are still rather poorly equipped, unlike American, Canadian or British companies. It has to be said that for over 20 years, French companies have been equipping themselves with basic psychological support lines, primarily in response to their legal obligation to protect the physical and mental health of their employees.

... but with the COVID-19 crisis and the growing awareness of the importance of mental health, things could change very quickly.

Today, we're talking less about preventing psychosocial risks and more about improving mental health. In France, we're accustomed to saying that words have meaning: While it was still impossible to use the words "mental health" in France three years ago, we spoke rather of emotional health, or even psychological health, so as not to refer to psychic health from the psychiatric angle. Today, these words are in everyone's mouth, from mental health professionals to employees, and HR departments.

The COVID-19 pandemic we experienced in 2020–2021, the return of war to Europe with Russia's attack on the Ukraine, and one natural disaster after another around the world have all contributed to the increase in mental health problems and the need to address them.

The COVID-19 crisis has considerably changed attitudes and practices. What we have seen is a kind of general "coming out" about mental health: celebrities talking about their depression, the head of a major company revealing his illness and how it affects his psychological health, a sportsman or woman revealing their addiction, etc. In fact, everyone is speaking more willingly and more widely, particularly with the sounding board provided by social networks. Logically, when the crisis hit, many French companies took the plunge and set up punctual psychological hotlines.

Over the same period, the use of these services increased significantly, particularly among younger employees (aged 20 to 30). This age group, which used to be fairly discreet in the statistics, now accounts for one in five calls (compared with one in ten before the COVID-19 crisis).

Because of its worldwide nature, the COVID-19 crisis enabled HR departments of major companies to discover that several local initiatives, such as the setting up of an EAP, had been launched by some of their subsidiaries. This prompted them to take a closer look at all these initiatives and, for some of them, issue RFPs to harmonize the programs more closely.

Also, employees' use of psychological support services has increased significantly. Given the difficulty of finding a mental health professional quickly, employees have tended to make greater use of company resources, both internal and external (EAP and on-site presence).

As for Stimulus Care Services, the Stimulus brand dedicated to psychological support services and EAP, business simply doubled between 2019 and 2020 and continued to be very strong in 2021. The crisis has clearly marked a turning point in awareness of the importance of French people's mental health.

There has also been a significant change in the way people contact EAP professionals. Whereas before 2020, EAPs provided psychological support to employees mainly by telephone, employees have discovered and are making more massive use of all the channels made available to them by EAP providers, in line with changes in the way products and services are consumed in everyday life (following the example of the explosion in the number of medical appointments booked on the platform of French unicorn Doctolib and the boom in medical teleconsultations). Today, access to the EAP service is largely by online appointment booking and chat (30%), and follow-up sessions are increasingly taking the form of video conferences (22% versus less than 5% before COVID-19) ... although, of course, the appeal of an EAP still lies in its primary feature of offering immediate access to a qualified psychologist 24/7, particularly for dealing with crisis situations.

Similarly, the debate surrounding the legitimacy of employers taking care of employees' personal problems has all but disappeared. With the spread of remote working, it is now very difficult to draw a line between one's professional and private life, and everyone agrees that it is obviously preferable to take the individual as a whole, without distinguishing between the professional and personal life. In fact, more than 60% of the requests received by Stimulus Care Services today concern situations in the personal sphere.

The changing job market and working patterns radically reinforced the interest and usefulness of EAPs in France.

In 2020, the employment rate among 15–64-year-olds in France was at its highest level since 1980. This means that employers are facing a scarcity of candidates and that the balance of power has shifted; in other words, it's now up to the company to seduce the candidate! This job market is now much more conducive to employer branding policies, with companies competing with each other to come up with ideas to promote work-life balance (hybrid work, autonomy, four-day week) and retention and commitment (trainings, services to support parenting, meaning at work, company's contribution CSR aspects, office layouts conducive to teamwork, etc.). In this context, EAPs obviously have an important role to play, enabling companies to support employees in their well-being and quality of life at work (seven out of ten employees consider it very important for their company to act in favor of their well-being, according to an Institut Elabe survey for Unedic, April 2023).

Purely digital players entered a market dominated by traditional players until today.

The COVID-19 crisis has not only raised awareness of the importance of mental health, but it has also inspired entrepreneurs to launch their own companies. Since 2020, about 60 start-ups have been launched in this field, half a dozen of which have raised several million euros. A number of other start-ups are trying to raise funds of their own but without much success, as the financial markets have put a stop to all-out investments. Finally, some others have had to throw in the towel. These start-ups emphasize the usefulness of their content and focus on the preventive aspect, whereas the traditional players in the psychological helpline and EAP sector—the oldest of which have been present in France for over 30 years—have focused on both individual and collective management of mental health in the workplace.

Several of these start-ups have joined forces to form an association called Mental Tech (mentaltech.fr), while the established players regularly exchange ideas within the association they set up in 2011 and called FIRPS (firps.org). Nevertheless, there has been a significant slowdown in fundraising for those still trying to raise funds, as the context of the financial markets has generated a more demanding selection process. Finally, some others have had to throw in the towel.

AND WHAT ABOUT THE FUTURE?

French companies were quick to mobilize in favor of psychosocial risk prevention and were forced to do so mainly because of dramatic events in 2008 (a wave of suicides in major French companies).

In a world of work that is changing even faster than in the past, and where all the pre-COVID-19 certainties are being shattered, these same companies are beginning to understand that dealing with mental health in the workplace is no longer a constraint but a necessity if they are to continue to develop, and to do so, they must rely on their main asset: people.

EAPs and, more generally, all initiatives designed to support employees in their mental health, as well as those aimed at improving work-life balance, have a bright future ahead of them.

ABOUT THE AUTHOR

Emmanuel Charlot is the Managing Director of Stimulus in France.

*Astérix is a 29-album French comic strip series created in October 1959, featuring a small Gallic village that fights alone against the Roman invaders thanks to a magic potion prepared by a druid.

GERMANY

Juliane Barth and Martin Klein

Twenty years after the introduction of the EAP concept in Germany, the service is well known and accepted in the larger companies and public service. Occupational Social Work (OSW), which already had a more than 100-year tradition when EAP appeared on the market, also flourished. Starting with factory inspection and factory care, OSW has continued in organizations until today and since the 1980s has focused on addiction counseling, systemic counseling and case management for troubled employees. While the larger countrywide EAPs are associated in the EAEF (www.eaef.org), the occupational social workers (in-company or ex-company) are clustered in the Bundesfachverband Betriebliche Soziale Arbeit e.V. (BBS e.V.), the National Association for OSW, which has comprehensively repositioned and modernized itself over the past five years. A milestone was a series of interviews with important protagonists such as federal constitutional judges, presidents of the Bundestag, minister presidents, ministers, writers, directors and journalists on their views on the importance of social coexistence and OSW, which received nationwide attention (https://www.bbs-ev.de/i2.html).

Numerous crises, including the pandemic, technical acceleration, global networking and digital communication possibilities have greatly changed the world of work. Characteristic is an increasing consumption of mental energy for problem-solving, emotional regulation and successful cooperation. Together with an increasing workload, this can lead to psychosocial stress among employees and their families, health impairments and performance loss.

Therefore, many organizations offer counseling services to their employees and their families voluntarily and without legal obligation. EAP is mostly provided by independent EAP companies staffed with psychologists and social workers.

The OSW is provided by internal and/or external professionals, who usually have a degree in social work, further qualifications and many years of counseling experience. It is important that counselors should be professional secrets, according to § 203 of the German Criminal Code.

The support in everyday life and the variety and complexity of personal and social problems in and outside the organization can be roughly divided into three areas of services:

1. **Individual support:** Social and legal counseling, family care, psychological counseling, addiction counseling, crisis intervention, resource procurement, case management and coaching of managers.
2. **Group-related services:** Mediation, critical incident interventions and prevention services.
3. **Organization-related activities:** Coordination and planning of support within and outside the organization—occupational integration management, mental risk assessment and care management.

IMPACT OF THE PANDEMIC ON CUSTOMERS AND PROVIDERS

The pandemic affected the organizations differently. In the case of the so-called "system-relevant" organizations such as hospitals, police, supermarkets or public administrations, which were often not so well funded, the hope arose that public applause and expressed appreciation could lead to improved framework conditions. However, this seems to have been truly realized in only a few areas.

The pandemic caused, in all organizations, as is probably the case worldwide, a digitalization push. Home offices, video conferencing and digital tools for collaboration were introduced, learned and taken for granted at a speed that was hardly imaginable before. At the same time, a new distinction was introduced in organizations that ran across the blue- and white-collar workers distinction. The new distinction runs on the basis of which job was transferable to the home office and which was not. The new distinction is related to who belongs to the near-risk workers and who belongs to the far-risk workers through all levels of the hierarchy. This is associated with conflicts, solidarity effects, and fairness issues, which also became OSW issues.

Another finding emerged in how much organizations had been trimmed for efficiency prior to the pandemic and how much buffer they had been left with. The buffer, the "slack" of the organization, was reduced from a rationalization perspective (cf. Kühl, Stefan 2023, p. 136 ff.). In the pandemic, the costs of this rationalization became clear: Just-in-time production could no longer take place, warehouses were lacking, hospital beds were not available in sufficient numbers, and cashiers in supermarkets, administrative staff and personnel to maintain internal order became scarce. Additional resources were activated without a view to costs.

The pandemic confronted companies with employees who had to cope with anxiety, uncertainty, change, digital communication, health issues, elder care, the challenges of home offices (including working at the kitchen table or in children's bedrooms), home schooling and marital conflicts. Some staff members became invisible for colleagues and supervisors, others had stress because they had to come to work while coworkers or family members were allowed or forced to stay at home. Conflicts arose around different views on vaccination and lockdown or resulted from a lack of privacy or the possibility to relax when locked down in a small apartment.

Companies with EAP services turned to their providers to ask for help with promoting the services and facilitating web-based trainings on topics such as "Managing people in home offices," "Managing stress," "Conflict resolution," etc. EAP staff quickly learned to deliver these services online as well as to present their annual reviews in web meetings. Other companies that had hesitated to buy EAP services decided to do that immediately. They did not all stay customers for a longer period, as the EAPs were not always properly implemented and there was a lack of understanding of a realistic expectation of utilization rates and the efforts it takes to attain a reasonable utilization. Some companies had to cut costs because of the impact of the pandemic. Nevertheless, in terms of business and despite all the challenges, 2020 and 2021 were very good years for some, and for some providers, they were the best years ever.

Sales activities of global EAP companies put pressure on their local providers, who struggled with recruitment and onboarding while working from home offices. At the same time, the face-to-face counselors working for EAP companies were mostly well-booked after having made their adjustments to the situation. Highly qualified counselors were utterly needed. There was an increase in utilization of legal issues and mental health, especially depression and anxiety, that needed appropriate treatment. Loneliness and anxiety to go back to the workplace came next.

AUDIO AND VIDEO SERVICES

EAP staff, of course, had to deal with the same challenges as their clients. While most of the EAP companies state that the shift from personal counseling to audio and video went smoothly, there were learnings with regard to the management of video counseling and with data protection.

In Europe, the processing of special personal data is prohibited if it reveals, for example, racial and ethnic origin, political opinions, religious or ideological beliefs or trade union membership. This also applies to the processing of genetic or biometric data for the unambiguous identification of a natural person, and health data or data on a person's sex life or sexual orientation (cf. Art. 9 [1]

GDPR). However, there are defined exceptions. It is allowed if there is an explicit and purpose-related consent of the data subject. This is a consequence of the fundamental right to informational self-determination. In addition, this sensitive data may only be processed by specialist personnel who are subject to a duty of confidentiality in accordance with the German Criminal Code. This must be considered when selecting counselors and case managers.

Many organizations have introduced a videoconferencing system for internal and external digital communication and expected these to be used for counseling sessions. However, the video conferencing system must comply with telemedical security standards (cf. KBV, 2022). These standards include that the transmission of the video consultation should take place via a peer-to-peer connection without the use of a central server, all content must be encrypted during the entire transmission process according to the state of the technology end-to-end encryption, and that not even the video service provider is allowed to see or store the content. Even the metadata/technical linking data must be deleted after three months at the latest and may only be used for the processes necessary for handling the video consultation. The disclosure of data is prohibited.

Video conferencing systems always grant access to the special category of data because the images can reveal racial and ethnic origin, and the processing of biometric data enables unique identification. The organization is responsible for doing everything possible to ensure that particularly sensitive data is processed in a way that protects data privacy. This includes technical and organizational measures, access restrictions to data, encryption, pseudonymization, training and sensitization of organizational members, establishment of suitable procedural channels, etc. (cf. Klein/Schermaier-Stöckl, 2022, p. 74 ff.).

Video counseling has been accepted quite easily by the customers. However, some clients prefer face-to-face counseling due to a lack of privacy at home and, in the meantime, the percentage of face-to-face services is almost as before the pandemic. But clients now expect video counseling to be delivered as a regular service next to audio and face-to-face. This requires secure platforms as well as appropriate working spaces for the counselor and the client. Thus the expectation with regard to the levels of service has gone up while prices are being expected to go down.

The implementation of apps with a chat function was welcome in some companies; in others, it needed to go through a longer and not always successful review process for approval by data protection officers and work councils. While there might be a need for a 24/7 live chat facility, for providers, this can be challenging if the utilization is low and the customers are not willing to pay extra fees for this service.

DIVERSITY

In Germany, many organizations have been talking about diversity for a long time. Individuals or social groups with different characteristics, such as skin color, nationality, gender and religion, for example, should be taken into account when filling positions. In addition, the focus is on equal participation and recognition in order to overcome discrimination. It must not and should not matter whether we are men or women or in between, whether we come from this or that milieu, whether we are black or white, whether we have a local or a distant origin. Even if we have to realize that, unfortunately, it does matter from time to time. For certain groups, therefore, there are very good reasons in society to insist on recognition and participation. Minority rights must be made strong. But there is also a flip side to the emancipatory effort for diversity. When insisting on this, it is evident in the renewed fixation on characteristics such as skin color, nationality or religion. Not the human being is in the foreground, but his characteristics. This should be avoided.

There are expectations in some organizations that, for example, counseling should only be offered by a person who has the same characteristics (see prior list) as the person being counseled. But that would mean that we would now always have to look closely because it does seem to make a difference whether someone has white or black skin color, is of a different gender, and is homosexual or not. When you think like that, you think in terms of particular identities. Organizations that want to live diversity do not reduce people to any of these characteristics. Occupational social work is characterized by the fact that it is normal to be different. It is about the individual being able to be the way he or she wants to be and reflecting together on how best to deal with this. The possibilities of dealing with differences are also very diverse.

Moreover, with regard to the diversity of counselors, the situation in Germany cannot be compared with the US or Canada. As we are not, per definition, an immigration country, we do not have a large number of qualified and certified counselors with diverse cultural backgrounds and language skills. It can already be challenging to find counselors who feel comfortable with counseling in English. EAP companies and OSW usually find individual and creative solutions to meet clients' needs and monitor these with careful case management.

OTHER DEVELOPMENTS

When the lockdown due to the pandemic ended, the war between Russia and Ukraine began. This created shock, pain and uncertainty on the side of the clients as well as the counselors and was an additional challenge for people who already felt overwhelmed or mentally instable.

Companies were keen on providing support for their affected employees. They demanded counseling in Ukrainian and Russian languages and asked for support for families that were hosting refugees or trying to help relatives in Ukraine. Critical Incident experts were asked to be available at Berlin train stations to offer support to refugees. Ukrainian and Russian employees who used to work together closely and easily due to their cultural proximity now suddenly belonged to different conflict parties, which led to a lack of recognition, to isolation and anxiety and feelings of discrimination that were not always easy to cope with.

Regarding market development, prices are still going down. This forces EAP companies to make their processes leaner and keep their wages low, which is a challenge regarding quality as long as there are not enough other services that create the necessary income. At the same time, new, more digitalized companies are entering the market, where eligible users can choose their preferred counselor online and make an appointment without going through an intake and referral process. This is attractive for the younger generation that feels more comfortable using the internet than making contact on the phone. These companies often have investors funding them and can offer competitive prices. However, although these companies are perceived as EAP companies (EAP in Germany is still perceived as a "telephone hotline" or an "external counseling service"), some of them lack an understanding of the basic principles of EAP, such as the two-client-awareness and the EAP core technology. More movements in the market result from the fact that the generation of EAP pioneers in Germany is now retiring and selling their companies. These companies that have been set up and managed by clinicians now become part of a larger organization with a different approach to management and perhaps a different view on the services offered, which will be interesting to follow.

ABOUT THE AUTHORS

Juliane Barth studied psychology, education and sociology at the University of Flensburg and management and policies at the Hogeschool van Amsterdam. She was trained in Gestalt and Transactional Analysis, Family Counseling, Systemic Coaching, Critical Incident Stress Management and is a certified Case Manager (DGCC). She received EAP training by ICAS International, Prof. Dale Masi and Ms. Rensia Melles. She was co-founder, Clinical Director and CEO of Corrente AG, one of the EAP pioneers in Germany and Europe. She was also co-founder of the Employee Assistance European Forum (EAEF) and served as Vice President, Treasurer and member of the EAEF taskforce Standards and Guidelines. Since 2022, she has worked as a freelance counselor and consultant. Having more than 20 years of experience in delivering EAP services, her mission is to continue teaching the concept of EAP to professionals in the field.

Prof. Dr. Martin Klein studied social work and economics. He is a professor for concepts and theories of social work and currently Vice Rector of the Catholic University of Applied Sciences NRW, Cologne. As a co-founder of the German Society for Case Management and Case Management Trainers (DGCC) and Chairman of the National Association of Occupational Social Work in Germany, he is engaged in voluntary work.

RESOURCES

https://www.bbs-ev.de
https://icas-eap.de/
https://www.insite.de
www.otheb.de
https://hanza-resources.com/
www.corrente.de
www.familienservice.de

REFERENCES

KBV – Kassenärztliche Bundesvereinigung (2022): Vereinbarung über die Anforderungen an die technischen Verfahren zur Videosprechstunde gemäß § 365 Abs,1 SGV.

Klein, M/Schermaier-Stöckl, B (2021): Vertrauen in der Betrieblichen Sozialen Arbeit. Schweigepflicht – Datenschutz – Zeugnisverweigerungsrecht. Beltz-Juventa.

Kühl, S. (2023): Der ganz formale Wahnsinn. 111 Einsichten in die Welt der Organisationen. Vahlen.

Our thanks go to Michael Schneider (Senior EAP Corporate Consultant at ICAS Germany), Dr. Matthias Conradt (Managing Director at Insite Interventions), Dr. Amina Özelsel (Founder, CEO and Clinical Director at Hanza Resources), and Sarah Barth-Boshuizen (Occupational Psychologist and Managing Director of Cinnux B.V.) for the time they made to share their experiences and perceptions.

GREECE

Konstantinos Giannakopoulos

Pulso is a spin-off of Leuven University with joint ventures in Lisbon, Paris and Athens. It provides a wide range of psychosocial well-being and HR-related services and products. Since 2018, Pulso has been a member of the German hospital group "Asklepios Kliniken," one of the largest operators of private clinics and health care facilities in Germany. Pulso is globally recognised as a visionary and innovative company of reference in the field of Employee Assistance and innovative evidence-based tools and services for assessing and impacting psychosocial well-being. Today, Pulso is operating via affiliated companies and partners in many European countries, including Benelux, France, Germany, Portugal and Greece.

THE IMPACT OF SERVICES DURING THE PANDEMIC

The COVID-19 pandemic was an unprecedented event that rapidly changed the daily routines of employers and employees. In Greece, the unfolding health crisis was initially managed with strict non-medical measures such as lockdowns, restrictions of travels, teleworking and social distancing. The first lockdown was enforced by the Greek government in March 2020, and a second lockdown was introduced in November 2020. The EAP market in Greece had to face three major challenges, namely 1) to ensure continuity of business by deploying a decomposed time-space modus operandi with the use of digital solutions, 2) to act proactively and respond successfully to the increased needs of the companies and 3) to cultivate a well-being state of mind for employers regardless of the pandemic or other critical mass events.

Although the experience from previous health crises, mostly in China, demonstrated that stressors during the lockdown involved mainly boredom, frustration, anxiety, fears of infection and confusion produced due to inadequate information (Brooks et al., 2020), a research project carried out in Greece during the first lockdown indicated moderate pandemic-related stress levels (peritraumatic stress) in the general population and medium resilience capacities that demonstrated a buffering effect (Nikopoulou et al., 2022). However, specific professions such as health care professionals demonstrated a psychological burden and high risk for burnout.

Notwithstanding the immaturity and underdevelopment of the Greek EAP market compared to North America and Central and Western Europe, many big- and medium-sized Greek companies requested various services related to psychosocial interventions during the pandemic. Such requests included: a) standard EAPs with the main service as the psychosocial support of employees and their direct family members, b) "flash" or short-term EAPs along with the pandemic, c) webinars and trainings on stress management, resilience and remote working and d) psychosocial barometers and surveys.

The impact of the provided services can be viewed on individual, organizational and societal levels. On an individual level, the main benefit of EAPs associated with alleviating symptoms of fear, anxiety and depression for the employees, resulted in an increased sense of control (Parlpani et al., 2020). Especially for employees with mental health disorders or for employees in industries or workplaces with inherent high health risks and stressors, EAPs offered prevention and treatment referral services. Lockdowns and school closures created imbalances in the daily routines of working parents, thus the request for work-life balance was also supported by EAP services, mostly by delivering individual counselling and webinars on remote working and parenting.

On an organizational level, existing EAP clients had the opportunity to reform and properly resource their EAPs as well as to put them on a sound financial footing. Interestingly, some clients decided to upgrade their session model and increase the number of provided services. Remote training on well-being served not only the skills development of the workforce but also the cohesion enhancement within and between teams, notably as pandemic-driven digital nomads were meeting together as a team during training facilitation. Likewise, new EAP clients experienced the value of a needs-driven and company-specific EAP and recognised that operational excellence and business continuity and success are associated with a psychologically healthy working environment, be it physically or digitally mediated. Concluding, the key outcomes of EAPs during the pandemic were the retainment of engagement and loyalty on high levels as well as the decrease of stress and the risk of burnout, especially for teleworkers with children and adolescents.

On the macro level, EAP providers raised awareness about the importance of mental health in the workplace, elucidating that stressors from different environments can disrupt the comfort zone of the employees and lead to limited productivity, absenteeism, presenteeism, shades of undesirable behaviour, unpleasant teamwork, etc. Beyond the organized EAP providers, single mental health experts, counsellors and psychologists entered the EAP market, providing well-being-related services.

Two significant evolutions signalized and validated the assumption that successful business activities require a workplace free of psychosocial risks. The first is the new law on violence and harassment in the workplace (Law 4808/2021), which specified the legal framework regarding all forms of harassment in the workplace, including violence, mobbing and sexual harassment, and strengthened the psychosocial risk assessments. The second important evolution was the implementation of the first Wellbeing Conference in Greece, held on 31 January 2023 in Athens, discussing the importance of mental health on workplace performance in the post-COVID-19 era.

However, evidence indicates that there is more room for the growth of the EAP market in the post-COVID-19 era in Greece. Only four in ten employees in the private sector and one in ten in the public sector believe that their organization takes care of the mental health and well-being of employees.[25]

THE EFFECTS OF ONLINE/VIRTUAL COUNSELLING

Remote counselling within EAPs requires digital competences and flexibility to modify and adjust the counselling/therapeutic setting. To better understand the effects of online counselling, these are accounted in the beginning, during and after the pandemic.

In the beginning of the pandemic, the optimistic view of a short break from the daily routines created a loose perception among counsellors and psychologists for using digital ICT infrastructure to deliver counselling sessions. The very first weeks of the pandemic, neither counsellors nor EAP beneficiaries were allowed to meet face to face. Thus, the long-ended lockdown forced mental health professionals and EAP beneficiaries to excessively use digital infrastructure such as Skype, Zoom, Microsoft Teams, and Viber and to modify the therapeutic setting by developing netiquette.

During the pandemic, the digitally mediated counselling environment demonstrated an unfamiliar experience of togetherness for both counsellors and EAP beneficiaries. Guidelines, recommendations and tips were developed by EAP providers to ensure the unbiased interaction flow, the confidentiality and the protection of personal data. With regards to the scope and content

---

25   The survey on the mental health and well-being of employees in Greece was implemented in 2021 by a consortium comprised of Ernst & Young, Hellas EAP and the University of Athens. The report is available online: https://www.hellaseap.gr/wp-content/uploads/2021/12/mental_health_report_2021.pdf

of counselling, EAP users reported high satisfaction and effectiveness of the interventions. For a specific group of EAP users, the physical distance and the feeling of sitting comfortably in their place enabled a secure emotional expression during the sessions. On the other side, employees living with their families found it difficult to sit in a quiet room and speak openly and honestly to the counsellor. It is worth mentioning that the months following the first lockdown, the government allowed face-to-face sessions for mental health services. Nevertheless, teleworkers preferred the remote EAP services with only a few cases for face-to-face sessions.

This evolution inevitably and forever modified the EAP counselling modus, then in the post-COVID-19 era, as EAPs effortlessly embedded a hybrid model of sessions up to the needs of the EAP user. From this point of view, the internal differentiation in a) face-to-face, b) remote or c) hybrid counselling reflects a major modifying effect of the pandemic on the EAP delivery mode.

THE ROLE OF TECHNOLOGY AND SOCIAL MEDIA

From the perspective of socio-technical systems (Kling & Sawyer, 2005), it is not technology per se that accelerated the EAP services during and after the pandemic in Greece but rather the interaction between technology, EAP providers, companies and EAP experts. Thus, the dynamic ecosystem of EAP in Greece created recently new online platforms for well-being, wearables and applications for physical and mental health self-assessment, digital tools for psychosocial risk assessment, webinars on well-being-related issues, client-specific tools for monitoring the implementation of EAPs, etc. In doing so, big companies in Greece announce requests for proposals (RFPs), which eloquently require accounts for well-being online platforms, tools for assessing risk behaviours at work, digital libraries for well-being, etc.

Remote working, especially teleworking, seems to account for an effective measure to improve work-life balance. However, it also creates stressful conditions for employees with less work autonomy or if teleworking arrangements are applied for a long time. A recent study showed that 31% of employees in Greece proposed the deployment of preventive well-being measures for teleworkers, such as 50-minutes online meetings and one day free of online meetings, while 30% proposed the development of remote working policies.[26]

The role of social media is important for the Greek market in terms of increasing public awareness and understanding the value of psychosocial interventions in the workplace, as well as promoting best practices from countries with long traditions in EAPs and well-established

---

26 The survey on the mental health and well-being of employees in Greece was implemented in 2021 by a consortium comprised of Ernst & Young, Hellas EAP and the University of Athens. The report is available online: https://www.hellaseap.gr/wp-content/uploads/2021/12/mental_health_report_2021.pdf

well-being cultures for the workplace. A key channel for promoting EAP-related content is LinkedIn. Having said that, Facebook, Instagram and X (Twitter) are still valid, but it seems that LinkedIn better suits the needs for promoting EAPs due to its professional and business nature.

A recent ERASMUS+ project called "THRIVE@WORK" reported that HR Managers in Greece deployed various well-being measures over the last five years, including access to digital resources and materials utilizing their intranet or external online well-being platforms.[27]

EFFORTS TOWARD DIVERSITY AND INCLUSION WITHIN THE FIELD

As an EU member, Greece adheres its national legislation to the European Commission directives. In this context, the antidiscrimination Law 4443/2016 complied with the European Directives on Equal Treatment Law[28] and replaced previous legal acts covering discrimination on the grounds of racial and ethnic origin, religious or other beliefs, disability, age, and sexual orientation. Additionally, this law discusses antidiscrimination issues related to chronic illness, descent, family or social status, and gender identity or characteristics.

Recently, Greece ratified Convention 190 of the International Labor Organization for the Elimination of Violence and Harassment in the Workplace, resulting in the launch of a new law on violence and harassment in the workplace (Law 4808/2021). Following that, companies with more than 20 employees are obligated to apply policies and procedures for preventing harassment, assessing psychosocial risks, and promoting inclusion in the workplace. In line with this evolution, EAP providers in Greece have designed and implemented interventions, since 2021, mostly in the form of webinars, trainings and consulting for preventing and tackling harassment in the workplace.

Since 2019, about 150 private enterprises with over 50,000 employees have signed the Greek Diversity Charter, an initiative of the European Commission to promote diversity in business. Founding members are OTE-Hellenic Telecommunications Organization S.A. and Alfa-Beta

---

27 More details about the research findings are available in the "EU Handbook for the development of well-being programmes" which is online accessible: https://thriveatworkproject.eu/resources/ The THRIVE@WORK project is funded by the European Commission and aims to promote stress prevention and well-being at work by encouraging Human Resources professionals, Vocational Education and Training trainers, CEOs and owners of companies to dedicate resources and invest in programmes for the psychosocial well-being of their staff. Partners for this project are GRANTXPERT CONSULTING (Cyprus), JOB-PAIRS (Greece), CESIE (Italy), CATRO (Bulgaria), PULSO GROUP (Belgium) and INSTITUTE OF DEVELOPMENT LTD (Cyprus).

28 More specifically, Law 4443/2016 inserted in the Greek legal framework i) the Directive 2000/43/EC on the application of the principle of equal treatment of persons regardless of racial or ethnic origin, ii) the Directive 2000/78/EC on the formation of a general framework for equal treatment in employment and occupation and iii) the Directive 2014/54/EU on measures to facilitate the exercise of workers' rights in the context of free movement of workers.

Vassilopoulos – Supermarket Chain. By signing the Diversity Charter, the organization commits to promoting diversity and equal opportunities for its working staff.[29] Despite the growing interest and importance of diversity and inclusion policies in the workplace, little research has been implemented in Greece (Kyparissiadis, 2019).

Companies' focus with regards to diversity is more on the aspects of gender and sexual orientation. This trend characterizes more frequently multinational companies, which share a global diversity culture. Additionally, big Greek and multinational companies—with employees with different nationalities, languages, age groups and other special characteristics—respect and announce diversity, even if this just validates their pre-existing diversified work staff. The last two years, big- and medium-sized Greek companies have announced diversity policies in their workplaces, but more in the sense of a compliance with the globally penetrated political correctness rather than a realistic approach for embracing diversity.

In private companies, diversity policies and issues are integrated in the Social Responsibility Department. In some cases, the Hellenic Labour Inspectorate, the Independent Authority of the Greek Ombudsman as well as social partners, can provide information, guidance or consulting to private companies for managing diversity, trainings for recruiting people with disabilities, and mentoring for dealing with diversity conflicts, etc. However, there is still room for establishing diverse and inclusive working environments in Greece, mainly by raising awareness and establishing collaborations between authorities, organizations and companies. EAP providers already contribute to this convergence by offering services for building awareness of the benefits of a diverse and inclusive working environment, cultivating attitudes of antidiscrimination, establishing a culture of respect and acceptance of others as well as supporting leaders and managers in unlocking the hidden potential of their workforce. In this context, well-being services interrelate with other consulting services such as developing recruiting procedures that comply to diversity or ensuring leadership commitment and buy-in.

Only a few clients demand a diverse counsellor's network within the EAP services. More often, companies ask whether the EAP providers' network is diverse, while there are few requests for at least one LGBTQ+ and/or one black counsellor in the available counsellors' network. Such requests come mainly from multinational company clients and less often from big national companies. Paradoxically, during the EAP intake process, their employees don't purposefully ask for a diverse counsellor, signifying that the "flat-rate diversity approach" often encounters country-specific cultural bias. The focus is more on the specialization and the expertise of the appointed counsellor that has to match and effectively respond to the particular issues of the

---

29   More details about the Diversity Charter in Greece: www.diversity-charter.gr

employee. Having said that, requests to EAP providers for a normative re-engineering of their work staff toward diversity conflict with the open-minded, anti-discriminatory, democratic, sensitive and non-dogmatic state of mind of mental health professionals. According to the Code of Conduct of Psychologists in Greece, their main responsibility engages respect for all humans and their rights, objectivity, dignity, conscientiousness and high sense of responsibility. Thus, requests that force diversity within the mental health field don't really add value and rather underline the importance of the established and valid Code of Conduct.

ABOUT THE AUTHOR

Dr. Konstantinos Giannakopoulos is a Clinical Psychologist, Group Analyst and Couple Therapist with a Ph.D. in Social Sciences from the Otto-Friedrich University of Bamberg. He is Vice President of the Hellenic Institute for Group Analytic and Family Psychotherapy and Member of the Employee Assistance European Forum (EAEF). He is working as Regional Manager for Pulso Southeast Europe in Athens, Greece.

RESOURCES

In Greece, well-being-related services include mainly Employee Assistance Programmes with a focus on psychosocial support, trainings and psycho-education, crisis management, psychosocial risks assessments and integrated services for well-being policies and mental health strategy.

Professionals interested in networking in the field of EAPs in Greece should display various skills and competences as well as knowledge of the mental health sector. Although there is no valid framework for EAP professionals in Greece in terms of a strict and pre-defined job profile, EAP providers in Greece comply with specific standards for providing EAPs of high quality and added value.

In this context, mental health professionals who are interested in joining the EAP network as external contractors should be in principle licenced Psychologists, display a Master's Degree in Psychology or a completed training in Psychotherapy or Counselling at an accredited Institute for Psychotherapy, have at least three years of professional experience, have their own private office, possess digital competences and have a good knowledge of the mental health system in Greece, including private and public mental health services and NGOs.

Moreover, professionals who are interested in joining EAP companies for carrying out surveys, psychosocial risk assessments and trainings should, in principle, have a background in Social Sciences, with most preferable Sociology, Organizational Psychology, Human Resources Management or Economics, sufficient statistical knowledge, experience in quantitative and qualitative research methods, communication and presentation skills, teamwork and critical thinking.

REFERENCES

Brooks, S. K., Webster, R. K., Smith, L. E., Woodland, L., Wessely, S., Greenberg, N., &

Rubin, G. J. (2020). The psychological impact of quarantine and how to reduce it: rapid review of the evidence. *The lancet, 395*(10227), 912-920.

Kling, R., Rosenbaum, H., & Sawyer, S. (2005). *Understanding and communicating social informatics: A framework for studying and teaching the human contexts of information and communication technologies.* Information Today, Inc.

Kyparissiadis, G. (2019). A changing country: Diversity management in Greece. In

Diversity within Diversity Management (Vol. 21, pp. 217-238). Emerald Publishing Limited.

Nikopoulou, V. A., Gliatas, I., Blekas, A., Parlapani, E., Holeva, V., Tsipropoulou, V., ... & Diakogiannis, I. (2022). Uncertainty, stress, and resilience during the COVID-19 pandemic in Greece. *The Journal of Nervous and Mental Disease, 210*(4), 249.

Pappa, S., Athanasiou, N., Sakkas, N., Patrinos, S., Sakka, E., Barmparessou, Z., ... & Katsaounou, P. (2021). From recession to depression? Prevalence and correlates of depression, anxiety, traumatic stress and burnout in healthcare workers during the COVID-19 pandemic in Greece: A multi-center, cross-sectional study. *International journal of environmental research and public health, 18*(5), 2390.

Parlapani, E., Holeva, V., Voitsidis, P., Blekas, A., Gliatas, I., Porfyri, G. N., ... & Diakogiannis, I. (2020). Psychological and behavioral responses to the COVID-19 pandemic in Greece. *Frontiers in psychiatry*, 11, 821.

HONG KONG

Natalie Cheung

SURVEY ON THE EFFECTIVENESS OF EAP COUNSELLING SERVICES IN HONG KONG

To understand the effectiveness of EAP in improving employees' workplace outcomes and health conditions, we have been conducting an effectiveness survey using Workplace Outcome Suite (WOS) from 2011. Over the years, we collected 627 responses, about 60% of which were received after 2019 (i.e., during the pandemic era).

The survey found that up to 2022, over half of Hong Kong employees who sought counselling services from our EAP suffered from poor physical and mental health, with 38.8% reporting "very high work stress" and 19.5% considering suicide or self-harm. This alarming data has raised calls for government support for mental health initiatives in the workplace.

The survey also revealed that local employees are faring worse than international peers, with 49% and 48.4% unable to engage at work or dissatisfied with life, respectively. These rates are about 20% and 10% higher than international averages. The survey also reported 34.8% of employees are too afraid to go to work and took leaves due to personal concerns, resulting in an average of 6.1 sick days in the month preceding the month when the respondents received counselling services.

These findings highlighted the effectiveness of EAP in addressing these issues. After joining the EAP, nearly 60% of those who had initially reported their physical and mental well-being as "poor" or "very poor" rated their well-being as "good" or "very good," indicating significant improvement. Further, 93.1% of those who had considered suicide or self-harm no longer had such thoughts after receiving the intervention.

Nowadays, it is estimated that less than 30% of the working employees in Hong Kong are covered by the protection of EAP. While EAP services are mainly engaged by large corporations or multinational corporations (MNCs), over 98% of the companies in Hong Kong are small- and medium-sized enterprises (SMEs), accounting for over 45% of the workforce. As the leading EAP provider in Hong Kong, we have a mission to promote the values of EAP service and engage more employers in the endeavours of caring for their employees. The survey's results prompted the FDC to recommend that the government should subsidise SMEs to implement EAPs for facilitating the development of a healthy and productive workforce and for retaining talent.

However, employers are encouraged to promote mental well-being in the workplace through various policies and initiatives. It is highly suggested that employers organise Mental Health First Aid training for their staff members and set the ratio of Mental Health First Aiders based on job types, company size, and employee characteristics. This allows early identification and support for employees experiencing mental distress. Employees are advised to develop healthy living habits by building a positive mindset, making use of their strengths in handling work/life challenges and by expanding their stress-coping strategies to improve their physical and mental well-being.

THE EFFECTS OF ONLINE/VIRTUAL COUNSELLING

In recent years, Hong Kong has faced many difficulties, COVID-19 brought unprecedented challenges, and employees of all companies and institutions have been affected. In fact, the mode of EAP's service delivery was hugely impacted under the influence of the pandemic. Before this global crisis, over 60% of the services were provided in-person, and around 30% of counselling clients received the services via phone. During that era, online counselling was not yet popular in the Hong Kong community.

However, since 2020 when social distancing was advised, our service has explored and implemented online counselling, considering the case nature and readiness of the clients. Up until 2023, over 52% of our counselling services were offered virtually (online counselling: 27%; phone counselling: 26%).

As we are equally committed to providing online clinical services of the highest professional standards, clinical protocols and consent forms guiding online counselling were set out for the clients and counsellors. For the clients, the documents explained and gathered their consent about the data security standards and confidentiality limitations in using online counselling. It also served to educate them about the choices of suitable spaces for the counselling itself, technical preparation, and contingency plans when undergoing a virtual session.

Also, the protocol prepared our counsellors for the clinical application and suitability assessment of their online clients. A few exclusion criteria included the level of suicidality, psychiatric conditions, and the conflict level of couple clients. These criteria determined if online work could be delivered. Recurrent supervision and review of the use of online counselling was given as well. To ensure that the level of data security was in compliance with the local standards, online platforms such as Zoom, Google Meet, and Microsoft Teams were reviewed and selected in collaboration with our IT Office and our global partners.

THE ROLE OF TECHNOLOGY AND SOCIAL MEDIA

To further advance the quality of our 24/7/365 hotline service, we collaborated with a vendor that was an expert in telecommunication, and we revamped our current call centre system since 2020. A new system and equipment powered by web-based call centre features were implemented to ensure seamless support to our corporate clients through the hotline service. During the pandemic when office access was interrupted, the new system enabled our team to offer uninterrupted and quality hotline services remotely with a secure platform that meets high standards of data security. The system also allows for a comprehensive understanding of call-answering performance, the enhancement of quality assurance by collecting post-call satisfaction surveys via a computerized system, easy management in allocating call answering agents in supporting the phone lines around the clock, as well as taking advantage of voicemail systems when calls are occupied. It greatly raised our capacity to support today's clients who have diverse needs and live in different horizons.

In addition to the revamping of our 24/7/365 hotline service, we adopted a web-based system and conducted the counselling sessions via an online system. The demand for conducting the staff training or wellness promotion sessions via webinars and online platforms was huge too. Currently, over 50% of the training programs and wellness promotion programs are conducted via online platforms. Furthermore, we are developing the EAP APP to make the service more accessible to the clients we serve. However, we are not using social media in service promotion and service delivery at the moment.

EFFORTS TOWARD DIVERSITY AND INCLUSION WITHIN THE FIELD (COUNSELLORS, PROVIDERS, CLIENTS)

Diversity and inclusion in the workplace has experienced major growth in the level of attention in recent years. When it comes to having a team with different talents, we placed more efforts on enriching the cultural competence of our counselling team. We expanded our counselling teams by including counsellors with different cultural backgrounds and understandings, such as counsellors who have living experiences in the United States, Canada, United Kingdom, Europe, Mainland China, etc. We have also recruited several counsellors who were born and raised in the Western countries and are native in English. Also, recurrent communication was made with our global partners in order to commit to a consistent focus on cultural diversity.

LGBTQ+ is another important area to address with our counsellors and clients. Last year, we amended our process of obtaining information in relation to gender categories of our clients. We educated our counselling team in discussing with their clients about how they prefer to be identified. Clients can also choose their preference of pronouns in the counselling form in creating an inclusive service. In addition, we developed wellness programs to work jointly with our serving companies in raising diversity and inclusion awareness of LGBTQ+ in the workplace.

Neurodiversity is a new way of thinking that has evolved since the last decades. To pioneer this concept and practice it in local companies, we designed and gave out the HR Sharing session with the Human Resource Personnel of our serving companies in early 2023. By introducing the model of neurodiversity awareness and inclusion, we encouraged the employers to adopt a style of management that emphasises placing each person in a context that maximizes their contributions. Some training programs are designed to facilitate our serving companies to develop a positive workplace for embracing the talents of neurodivergent people.

As the leading EAP provider in Hong Kong, we are happy to share that we are resilient enough to fight side by side with the employers and employees from all walks of life to tide over many challenges together. Our vision is that every employee in Hong Kong will be able to enjoy EAP services to enhance their psychological capital and work efficiency, enable them to face work/life with a positive attitude, and ultimately facilitate corporations' and society's sustainable development.

ABOUT THE AUTHOR

Ms. Natalie Cheung (General Manager), M.Soc.Sc., Adv. Dip. (Aging & Health), B.S.W., Registered Social Worker, Certified Happy Coach (Advanced), Certified DISC Consultant. She is the General Manager of Four Dimensions Consulting Limited. She is one of the founding members of Employee Development Service, the predecessor of Four Dimensions Consulting Limited, since its inception in 1991. She has over 30 years of experience in social services and management.

Natalie specializes in enhancing companies' capabilities to become a positive organization through various means, such as assessing the positivity level of the organization, designing the systematic pathways based on the organization's strengths and strategic goals, and promoting positive psychology amongst employees through tailor-made management and staff development programs, etc.

ABOUT FOUR DIMENSIONS CONSULTING LIMITED & EMPLOYEE DEVELOPMENT SERVICE OF HONG KONG CHRISTIAN SERVICE

Four Dimensions Consulting Limited (FDC) is a private limited company set up by Hong Kong Christian Service (HKCS) in 2005. Employee Development Service (EDS) of HKCS is the first EAP provider in Hong Kong since 1991 As a pioneer of the Employee Assistance Programme in Hong Kong, we are dedicated to providing comprehensive EAP services in accordance with the international standard of the Employee Assistance Professionals Association (EAPA) of the United States.

Our mission is to partner with employers in building positive organisations and leading positive social change. We offer total solutions to assist employees with work/life issues, develop strengths/potential, and increase work engagement and positivity at work, which ultimately enhance organizational excellence and sustainability.

INDIA

Ummul Ranalvi

INTRODUCTION

Growing up in a one-room tenement, we lived cheek by jowl. There were very thin walls separating families. Family fights, temper outbursts, displays of human emotions, sorrow, pain, death, celebrations, and joys were all experienced unadulterated, by children, elders, and the young. I grew up to listen to others, to talk and share. I was the one who would reach out to one and all, to make friends. When I was 16, I remember my cousin brother had come from the village into the city. He was living with us in our small home. We had a great connection. He was shy but friendly. But soon he became reclusive and went into his shell. He would not talk, eat, or go to college. We were all at a loss for what to do. Years went by with my cousin's condition worsening and no one really knowing or understanding him and his problems. In between, the physician would treat him for his delusions with sleeping pills and other drugs. I could see that slowly, he was deteriorating. After almost 10 years of this, he was taken to a psychiatrist and was diagnosed as schizophrenic. It was too late. We lost my lovely cousin. The complete ignorance and helplessness I faced at the time was perhaps the reason I decided to study psychology and chose to major in it in college.

It was my constant search for answers and solutions to mental health problems that somehow led me to EAP services. The stigma and ignorance about mental health in India in those days was stark. As luck would have it, a colleague's mother who was a certified counselor shared an affiliate contract she had received from an International EAP service provider to empanel her as a counselor in India. This conversation opened up an opportunity for me to explore—until then, I had not even heard of EAP. This was in the year 2006.

As I started my research about EAP, I looked for opportunities to work in this area. I wrote to a few international providers, showing my interest in providing EAP services in India. ICAS International was the one who showed interest in offering their license to operate in India. It was just about then that many multinational companies were keen on extending EAP services to their employees in India. I decided to go ahead and took the license to operate in India in 2006, kicking off a long, interesting journey.

The last 17 years have been a roller coaster ride. For a country in which EAP was unheard of, it took a minimum of two years of negotiations with a company before they considered offering EAP services for their employees. Many companies were of the mindset that they should not be stepping into the personal lives of their employees. That was considered personal.

Today, ICAS India services more than 200 companies, of which 35% are local clients.

THE IMPACT OF EAP SERVICES DURING THE PANDEMIC: TRANSFORMING MENTAL HEALTH SUPPORT IN INDIA

The COVID-19 pandemic not only posed significant challenges to public health but also shed light on the oft-ignored topic of mental health. In India, where mental health services were largely overlooked and stigmatised, the pandemic became a game-changer in bringing mental health discourse to the fore and underlining the need for accessible services. Employee Assistance Programs (EAPs), in particular, were previously undervalued but gained recognition as companies realised the urgent need for comprehensive support, including mental health services, during these unprecedented times.

The pandemic affected various segments of society differently. Women faced increased workloads, managing household responsibilities, children, and work pressures simultaneously. Domestic violence cases surged, leading some companies to run awareness sessions on the issue. Parenting became a significant concern, particularly as children experienced stress, anxiety, and exposure to domestic violence due to prolonged school closures. A large section of youth, too, got very badly affected. They missed their college education, experienced restlessness and loneliness, feared their exams and the future of their careers. The biggest setback to the youth was the psychosocial development, which happens at that stage of their lives. Migrant workers were also among the worst affected, losing their livelihoods and returning to their hometowns in rural India. Doctors, nurses, and frontline workers faced overwhelming workloads, impacting their physical and mental health.

In the wake of all of this, the pandemic inadvertently transformed the landscape of mental health, and of EAP services, making them an essential part of employee support programs.

CHALLENGES PRIOR TO THE PANDEMIC

Before the pandemic, mental health services in India were often considered Western concepts and culturally unacceptable. Stigma surrounding mental health was prevalent, and there was a lack of awareness and understanding. This was reflected in government spending on mental health care, which is abysmally low and leaves a significant portion of the population without access to care . In 2022, the mental health budget was 0.8% of India's health budget, and this year, it went up to 2.18%. The decriminalisation of suicide in 2017 was a significant step toward addressing mental health concerns, but much more needed to be done.

In workplace settings, any mental health issues were considered personal. Companies hesitated to offer EAP services, questioning their usefulness and value. Doubts whether EAP services would actually be used by employees and be worth the investment were often voiced.

The arrival of the pandemic, however, forced CEOs and HR heads to recognise the critical importance of mental health support. Companies quickly realised the acute need for EAP services, both in terms of medical and mental health support. What would have taken over a year to convince companies to invest in suddenly became an urgent requirement.

The turnaround time was very quick—although companies negotiated for good rates, they were quick in making decisions. It was worth the wait. The pandemic validated the need for our services and gave a huge impetus to our organisation's work.

EFFECTS OF TECHNOLOGY AND SOCIAL MEDIA AND ONLINE/VIRTUAL COUNSELING

The pandemic was also able to accelerate the adoption of online/virtual counseling services in India. It helped us, service providers, adapt to online/virtual counseling very swiftly and very willingly. Telephony was the preferred choice—there was a considerable uptake of telemedicine services during COVID-19, with the government promising a "National Tele Mental Health Programme." But online counseling also became the norm. The ease with which the shift occurred was remarkable, and it continues to be the most preferred approach today. The availability of technology enabled EAP services to reach and support individuals more effectively. Technology played a huge role in helping us to reach out to people and support them. We adapted to technology very well, and the ease at which we started doing business using technology was amazing. In India, telephony worked the best and, fortunately, just before we closed our offices for the lockdown, we had a business continuity plan in place, which helped us to service our growing number of clients seamlessly. Social media played a significant role in the dissemination of information about the importance of mental health and seeking help when needed and how to find help immediately.

The first 10 years of building ICAS India were tough, and we were barely able to sustain ourselves. It was my sheer patience, perseverance, and belief that mental health is critical that has paid dividends. It was always my dream to contribute to the space of mental health. We could not help my own cousin with his mental health issues, but today I feel very satisfied that I have been able to contribute to helping many others.

The first big breakthrough was when a very large consulting firm with more than 10,000 employees signed up with us. Since then, there has been no looking back.

DIVERSITY AND INCLUSION IN MENTAL HEALTH

ICAS India was not the first EAP service provider in India, but today, ICAS India is a leading and highly reputed quality EAP services provider. ICAS has been very innovative, creative, and is constantly working on developing material and creating solutions that will help people.

One of our unique selling points has been to ensure there is good utilisation of the services, understanding the varying needs of our employees and tailoring our responses accordingly. We have launched special new services under the EAP umbrella, like a Maternity Coaching Program, Menopause Assistance Program, and Return to Work Program for women.

Mental health professionals are also being trained to work with diverse populations, considering the unique challenges faced by different communities. This includes sensitisation programs, workshops, and training modules focusing on cultural competency, diversity, and inclusion in mental health care. Efforts are being made to understand and incorporate cultural beliefs, values, and practices into mental health interventions. This helps in creating more inclusive and relevant treatment approaches for diverse communities. For instance, caste-affirmative and queer-affirmative therapists and support groups have been on the rise in the last few years.

Professionals and organisations are recognising the need for diverse representation among counselors, providers, and clients. These efforts aim to ensure that mental health services are accessible and relevant to people from different backgrounds, including marginalised communities. By embracing diversity and fostering inclusion, EAP services can better cater to the diverse needs of the population.

Community-based mental health programs have also been initiated to address the specific needs of marginalised groups. These programs involve collaborations with local community leaders, non-profit organisations, and grassroots initiatives to provide accessible and culturally appropriate mental health support.

Apart from this, there has been a general increase in awareness and advocacy. Our work, as stakeholders in this space, not only becomes about providing services but also about helping to raise awareness of mental health issues and promote inclusivity.

In India, despite mental health discourse having gained momentum, the rural-urban divide still poses many barriers for widespread adoption of services. According to the World Health Organisation (WHO), out of the 20% of the country's population who suffer from mental illness, only around 12% seek aid or support, and they are likely to be located in urban areas and have socioeconomic privilege. Around 75% of India's 3,800 psychiatrists work in urban areas where just 31% of the country's population lives. Clearly, there is a need for more health infrastructural development, greater budgetary allocation toward mental well-being in rural areas, campaigns to spread awareness, employment of medical professionals, and making treatment accessible in these locations. The uptake of technology, as seen with EAP services, can also provide solutions. In a research paper titled "Mobile mental health care—an opportunity for India" by Peter Yellowlees and Steven Chan, published in the Indian Journal of Medical Research, mobile applications may be a viable solution to rural India's mental health care problem. They are low cost, enable real-time collection of data and feedback, can be scaled, and are location agnostic.

The Mental Healthcare Act, 2017, emphasises the rights of individuals with mental illness and mandates the provision of quality mental health services for all. The act also prohibits discrimination on the basis of gender, caste, religion, or other identities. But there is still a long way to go.

ABOUT THE AUTHOR

Ummul Ranalvi is the Managing Director and Partner and oversees the running of ICAS India. She has a Master's in Clinical Psychology from Mumbai University and has been working in the space of corporate training and counseling for more than three decades.

IRELAND

Lucy Dennehy

Many large organisations have a service in place to assist staff who may be dealing with personal or familial difficulties. In the Irish Defence Forces, this is known as the Personnel Support Service (PSS). The Personnel Support Service was established in 1992 in response to the Gleeson Commission on Remuneration and Conditions of Service Report (1989). The commission sanctioned independent civilian professionals to deliver a counselling service to serving members and their families when requested from the military chaplaincy service (Fallon et al., 2021). The purpose of the PSS is to deliver a support and social work service to Permanent Defence Forces, serving members and their families, civilian staff employed at military installations, veterans, and military reserve personnel on duty. The PSS consists of military personnel who are qualified as Employee Assistance Practitioners, and this service also has an Occupational Social Work service within the structure. The Occupational Social Work team consists of seven Social Work posts that provide support to all serving members of the Permanent Irish Defence Forces and their families. Each Social Worker has completed their professional training prior to working for the Irish Defence Forces and, therefore, are civilian employees. A number of military organizations have uniformed professional social workers recruited from within the military to perform the professional role of Social Work, e.g., United States military, South Africa military, and Canadian military (Forgey & Green-Hurdle, 2022).

Although the Irish Occupational Social Workers are not part of the military structure, they have good insight into its operation and function and find that often, staff value having the option to discuss things through with a civilian member of staff outside the constructs of the chain of command. The service deals with a range of personal, familial, mental health, and occupation-related issues through provision of direct counselling support. Additionally, many of the Occupational Social Workers and Barrack Personnel Support Service Officers (BPSSOs) have complementary qualifications. For example, I am a practising cognitive behavioural therapist. It is important to note that from a service-delivery perspective, as essentially lone social work posts, the Occupational Social Workers are co-located with the BPSSOs in the Brigades & Formations. Therefore, each social worker covers a designated geographical area where they are based and solely responsible for. The social workers carry out their casework interventions with clinical practice responsibility to the Principal Social Worker.

As noted previously, support within an occupational setting is available for a wide variety of reasons and situations that may be causing distress and affecting one's ability to work safely and function. For example, grief, addiction, mental health difficulties, and financial problems. As Occupational Social Work is associated with social work provision in the employment context, it adopts a wide variety of roles and methods to include counselling interventions, mediation, restorative interventions, brokerage, advocacy, problem-solving, programme development, training, education, and consultancy (Iverson, 2001; Thompson & Bates, 2007; Porast & Niya, 2015). Trust and confidentiality are an integral part of the service, and therefore, confidentiality is taken very seriously and a service users' details are only disclosed if permission has been given or in circumstances where mandatory reporting is required by law. Fallon et al. (2021), in their article on Occupational Social Work in the Irish Defence Forces, listed the range of problems/issues addressed by the occupational social workers, including "Mental Health Disorders, such as Depression and Anxiety" (Fallon et al., 2021).

As an Occupational Social Worker, it's essential to enact a best-practice approach to service delivery within the organisational context while upholding adherence to policy and legislation. It is also necessary as a lone post staff member to demonstrate the ability to work autonomously while recognising that particular casework interventions require practice expertise in consultation with the PSW. Therefore, as the pandemic progressed, a large population of clients was unable to engage in face-to-face interventions due to health conditions, travel, geographical location, etc. This forced many practitioners across a variety of disciplines to re-evaluate service provision and brainstorm ways in which service users, in particular, service users with compromised immunity, could access services and do so safely. Inadequate access to quality, timely, and appropriate mental health services is a longstanding, well-acknowledged deficit in the Irish health care system. As the pandemic progressed, I was receiving a large amount of Cognitive Behavioural Therapy referrals from the medical corps and found that a large amount of contact made with the service was in relation to grief, anxiety, depression and suicidality. Many service users reported high levels of stress, fear, anxiety, sadness and loneliness or worsening of pre-existing mental health disorders. Research findings by Smyth & Nolan (2022) complement my experience and note that there has been a stark impact on the mental health of young adults due to experiencing a global pandemic.

"They experienced massive disruption to their education, employment and day-to-day lives and their rates of depression increased as a result. The study shows the importance of providing adequate mental health supports for young adults as a matter of urgency" (Smyth & Nolan, 2022:48).

From discussions with clients, I learned that many felt this was due to the extensive information overload, misinformation and scaremongering on social media, making people feel a huge loss of control and feel anxiety about how to react.

Cognitive Behavioural Therapy (CBT) is a well-known therapy that has been used for the treatment of a number of psychological disorders since the 1980s and has developed a great deal over the past thirty years. For example, alongside pharmacological recommendations, Cognitive Behavioural Therapy has been recommended by the NICE guidelines (2011) as the gold standard treatment of choice for GAD sufferers. Weaver et al (2014), citing Gambrill (1995), discuss social work encompassing behavioural psychotherapy as far back as the 1960s, noting that scholars at the University School of Social Work in Michigan—Edwin Thomas, Richard Stuart and Gambrill, began applying behavioural approaches to social work practice. They discuss the notion that Gambrill (1995) attributed this innovative development to the fact that CBT was compatible "with social work, as well as their commitment to a scientific approach, including the use of empirical research, to guide practice" (Weaver et al., 2014 p20). CBT is also very popular due to the large array of outcome research demonstrating the effectiveness of CBT for a wide variety of psychological disorders. Due to the flexible nature of the therapy, it has been adapted in a lot of different ways to address different problems, so there are lots of versions of it.

Research by Kennerley et al. (2017) mirrors the prior statement and advises, "Many of the distinctive characteristics of CBT mean it is easily generalisable to clients from different cultures and backgrounds, and it allows a good working relationship to be maintained. For example, CBT aims to adopt a non-judgmental stance; it is a collaborative approach where the clients perspectives on and knowledge about his problems are respected and valued" (Kennerley et al. 2017 p.54).

As a social worker qualified as a CBT therapist during the pandemic, I felt the need to research how and if CBT could be delivered online: Was it effective and, therefore, could it be an alternative way of offering support and increasing accessibility to services for serving personnel and their families?

Online therapy, specifically internet-based CBT (ICBT), has existed for over two decades (Andersson et al., 2019; Guo et al., 2020; Păsărelu et al., 2017), and the COVID-19 pandemic saw many health services transition to online delivery. ICBT facilitates therapists reaching out to clients safely and effectively and provides greater accessibility for people with long-term illnesses, living in isolated areas, and it increases the capacity of staff caseloads (Guo et al., 2020). If one deciphers Clark et al. (2009) research regarding the NHS mental health strategy to improve access to psychological therapy via ICBT while also promoting client change, the findings solidify the concept that some accessibility, albeit a low-level, protocol-driven treatment, is effective with the research stating that patients (attended three online sessions or more) were found to have a 55 to 56% recovery rate (Clark et al., 2009).

Reflecting on the global pandemic, which has led to a large increase in depression and anxiety presentations, online access was and continues to be a very important aspect of service delivery from an economic perspective (Hyland et al., 2020). Several studies have provided the efficacy of ICBT, but many of these papers discuss the validity of ICBT via quantitative means for those experiencing anxiety and depression in general (Andersson et al., 2019, 2014; Guo et al., 2020). While this is somewhat limiting, Miller et al., (2021) carried out a multiple baseline study exploring whether ICBT was feasible in terms of engagement, commitment, satisfaction and safe practice. "Overall, 70% of participants no longer had clinically significant symptoms of anxiety and 40% no longer had significant sleep difficulty post-intervention" (Miller et al., 2021, p3). Echoing Clark (2009), Westbrook et al. (2017) research, similarly, acknowledges that reducing the amount of therapist contact per client through computerised, short-term CBT results in the capacity to take on more clients and therefore offers a more cost-effective, faster treatment.

Kuckertz et al. (2014) notes that ICBT allows patients to access to evidence-based treatment and promotes their understanding and learning about their own mental health. Another advantage is that therapists can access and monitor clients' presentations online and provide opportune treatment. This means clients who attend ICBT can gain quicker access to therapist support than patients who receive weekly face-to-face sessions (Guo et al., 2020).

Probst et al. (2020) were the first to investigate how psychotherapists and patients experienced the transition to ICBT during COVID-19. The research found that incorporating training modules to provide remote therapeutic interventions might help therapists to become better acquainted with online interventions and boost client confidence in ICBT. This is significant, as most of the quantitative research broadly discusses anxiety disorders from the clinician perspective only. These findings very much resonated with my experience and also provided clients with confidence and rationale in accessing online therapy supports. However, despite the positive outcomes, Peynenburg et al. (2019) qualitatively found that face-to-face therapy is still the preferred choice by clients, followed by medication and online treatment (ICBT). However, an important thing to note in this study is that on contemplation of delayed access to face-to-face services, a greater percentage of patients chose ICBT, which signifies hope regarding its growth in popularity.

ABOUT THE AUTHOR

Lucy Dennehy is a Clinical Social Worker with the Irish Defence Forces.

ITALY

Laura Sinatra

THE IMPACT OF SERVICES (MENTAL HEALTH, SUBSTANCE ABUSE AND EAPS) DURING THE PANDEMIC

The pandemic hit hard on Italy. The number of fatalities. The pressure on the Public Health System and the Hospitals. Doctors and nurses who could hardly meet with the number of people daily hospitalized. Medical equipment that, at times, was not available. Also, Italy experienced one of the most rigid interpretations of the anti-COVID-19 measurements.

Except for workers and employees of essential services who would go to work, the rule was "stay at home" for all the other ones. The schools were closed on 24 February 2020, playgrounds and parks were not accessible, any sort of shop that wouldn't sell essential products was closed, and grocery shops and pharmacies could be entered only by one person per family. Companies reorganized their workforce with remote work. A country that traditionally had a very low use of remote work found itself thrown, almost within minutes, into a work organization to which it was not used, not prepared, not organized, nor trained for. Employees moved PCs, monitors, and sometimes even printers from the office to the kitchen table of their homes. The lockdown also forced schools to grant *distant learning*. These two words still trigger some uncomfortable reactions in parents, students, and teachers. No school had ever thought before how to structure and deliver distant learning.

There was no time to think, to plan, or to get organized. How this sudden, dramatic collective change and its duration impacted mental health has been clearly demonstrated by statistics that are still in the process of being studied and are still under observation after the end of the pandemic emergency. Eapitalia has recorded a significant peak of counseling requests in 2020–2021, about a 60% increase in counseling support and management consultation. After a first moment of creative resilience and collaborative optimism, it was clear that the pandemic would not just go away. The first wave of adrenaline and a let's-do-this-together attitude were soon replaced by a bewildering reality: some families split in separated homes, some families in too-small arrangements, some people totally alone, some people with too many significant others to care about without the usual supports and activities. Either alone or in forced co-living, desperately apart, or perched between long pixeled-working days and constant demands from family members, unemployed or overemployed, everyone had to confront with themself and life/work conditions. Whatever the experience people were going through, it made them focus a lot more on themselves and their specific needs, and it altered their perception of safety, satisfaction, and relational regulation. In many cases, the perception of a lack of choice and freedom strongly triggered an incredible amount of stress, frustration, anxiety, anger, sadness, worries, impatience, depression, helplessness, and a sense of guilt. In addition to all the prior presented issues that triggered the requests for support, Eapitalia recorded a significant number of demands related to outbursts of issues or worsening mental health conditions that could no longer be contained by a social life that used to help set boundaries or grant control and supervision. In fact, it's been acknowledged that these outer circumstances amplified *prior vulnerabilities* regarding mental health issues that worsened consistently in all age ranges and genders. Also, the increase in requests started to draw attention to the younger age ranges. Notwithstanding that there were some dramatic cases of substance abuse and domestic violence, the number of requests that reached the EAP wasn't so significant. This is typical because when the problem is deemed as such, it's already too late for the EAP and must be addressed and treated throughout the public services in the first place.

The more the measurements would start to loosen up and people were allowed to conduct their fuller life options, the more those typical lockdown-pandemic requests started to decrease. Nevertheless, it has taken more than two years to reach again an average utilization that is closer to pre-pandemic figures, and a significant category of people and workers are still struggling. For example, mental health still impacts a lot of the younger age range who are presenting a fragile functioning either if still at school or university or already at work. At work, managers are coping more and more with very open challenges related to personal issues, motivation, and engagement, and with clear disclosures about health conditions and related needs. Children, adolescents, and young adults who experienced the pandemic during a very delicate moment of their growing might now suffer from severe depression, anxiety, and disorders and vulnerabilities that impact school or their career choices and performance.

As the request topics varied across 2020–2023, reflecting the environmental uncertainty caused by the Ukraine war, the energetic crisis, climate-related events such as the recent flooding in Italy, etc., organizations are now facing the need to develop robust soft skills, engagement and motivation, and sense-making processes. A multidisciplinary approach that addresses multifactor complexity will help to incorporate the pandemic into a wider overview and culture that is able to foster hope, resilience, and identity as pillars of its sustainability and success in the future.

THE EFFECTS OF ONLINE/VIRTUAL COUNSELING

The online/video counseling granted both immediate assistance to a wide range of issues (multi-service) and continuity of service delivery from day one of the pandemic. Virtual counseling has proven to be an impressively efficient way to reach everyone who needed support. Being its use is so pervasive and widespread, it proved that even critical and severe cases could be addressed in the realm of a first consultation and while bridging to long-term interventions.

When Eapitalia reviewed its processes right at the beginning of the pandemic, we decided that we would assign local affiliates to local requests, even if the sessions were virtual, as if they were face-to-face assignments. This regional background sharing allowed an easier "connection" between the two stakeholders: experiencing lockdown in a major city was different than being in the country. Local nuances would help an immediate need. Nonetheless, clients and cases sometimes presented specifics to which we decided that a different matching based on the background of the affiliate rather than on the location would best address the issue, even in those areas where we had different options of affiliates. We integrated the matching with further criteria. The virtual counseling allowed us to widen the possibilities of the strategic and specialistic assignments. This is still, as of today, a chance that is deemed as an incredible takeaway from the unfortunate experience of the pandemic. Also, it helped for many months to reach clients in their most private environment—their homes—and therefore focus without resistances on the heart of some issues, such as fatigue or discomfort, by tiding up a desk, cleaning dirty dishes and accumulated trash, and then showing it to the counselor. This eased clients into setting healthier boundaries. Allowing the two-year-old child to sit without stress on the lap of a parent while in a call and having an interaction that would open the mind allowed mums and dads to actually *feel* their sense of guilt and cope with it by introducing "slots" not only with their line managers but also with their children. Video counseling remained a preferred option for many until 2022. Not necessarily for counselors, but clients would appreciate the fact that it allowed "smarter" time management and a better integration in a hybrid world.

The affiliate network of Eapitalia consists of specialized psychologists. This choice of professionals took place at the beginning of 2000, so when the pandemic hit the country, the affiliates were prepared to deliver clinical assistance within a robust EAP framework. At the same time, each of them was able to adapt to emergency requests that started to demand face-to-face counseling. This flexibility was possible mainly because this type of professional typically has their own or a shared practice. Today, the choice as to whether to opt for virtual sessions or face-to-face sessions is up to the client. Now, clients can choose what they feel is better for them when they ask for help.

The request for help should be eased by different channels and options. This is one tangible proof of how inclusive an EAP can be. The pandemic has clearly shown how the client experience demands *personalization* in ways that were not even imaginable before the pandemic. Today, clients know they can choose and rely on the fact that we can match their requests to special professionals that might not be present in a specific area but can best meet their requests.

THE ROLE OF TECHNOLOGY AND SOCIAL MEDIA

The prior details are strongly entangled with the fast-paced development of technology and social media. The media have strongly affected people's minds and peace throughout the pandemic. Eapitalia has invested efforts into training hours dedicated to the infodemic and lately into bullyism and cyber-bullyism addressed to parents within a program about youth discomfort. These topics might not seem connected, but they are. A new trend is to "believe" more in what the *internet* states, in what *virtual* judgments state, rather than in robust information or even real relationships with people you hang out with. Technology (smartphones), social media (any kind), and in general, even browsers convey the possibility to be "understood" easily, without efforts and endeavor, to be classified in standards that the virtual world labels, to provide an identity without the struggles to conquer it. This is also having an impact on the expectations some of our clients raise: Within minutes, they wish to have a magic sentence that helps them out of trouble. The counselor or affiliate is summoned to be available at any minute and willing to provide those life-changing tips within the first session. Instead, EAPs can offer a psychoeducational opportunity to learn about how human beings, emotions, and behaviors function. Social media and artificial intelligence have surely changed the way clients approach their personal development and how they cope with issues. Nonetheless, there is still a long way to go toward a culture that is able to properly balance the opportunities of technology, social media, and artificial intelligence and how human beings function and need to address their potential, their weaknesses, and their strengths. EAPs can truly make a difference here.

THE EFFORTS TOWARD DIVERSITY AND INCLUSION WITHIN THE FIELD (COUNSELORS, PROVIDERS, CLIENTS)

In conclusion, which should rather sound like "last but not least," Italy's public schools have a robust system of inclusion of children with disabilities or specific learning disorders. Plus, they address parents to initiate certifications where reasonable. Later, larger companies are to integrate a certain number of protected workers. Notwithstanding, Italy is still a country where gender equality is an issue, where outcomings are a process, where LGBTQIA+ is an acronym difficult to understand, and where motivated workers with disabilities struggle to be taken seriously. The EAP is here and adds value. Among the affiliate network, you can count on specialists who are specialized in the prior listed topics and know what happens in organizations. Trainings, counseling, management consultations, group coaching, and even HR consultancy help to strengthen organizational endeavors.

ADDITIONAL POINTS:

1. What role do you see for artificial intelligence in the EAP field?

It would be a temptation to polarize the thoughts around AI, especially in the fields of human-to-human services. Instead, Eapitalia is looking at ways of integration and evolution with curiosity and a tentative approach. What we have learnt so far: We need more robust tools that allow access to services and contents by an increasingly diverse client population; there are a number of ethical and risk management issues that we will need to address. Contents that are openly generated by AI need to be framed in a specific moment of the user experience, which leads to the need to design an environment that balances and combines human and digital. Nowadays, we are in the process of studying the long-term impact of remote working and how distance requires relational skills that need to be strengthened in order to better integrate the options of AI. The challenge we face is to support companies to integrate very diverse and opposite needs and cope with complexity.

2. Has the Ukrainian-Russian war had an impact on the EAP/mental health/substance abuse field in your country?

As the request topics varied across 2020–2023, reflecting the environmental uncertainty caused by the Ukraine war, the energetic crisis, and climate-related events such as the recent flooding in Italy, organizations are now facing the need to foster a culture that can cope with uncertainty and complexity. Eapitalia is increasingly asked to provide a multidisciplinary approach that addresses multifactor challenges of client organizations. We are asked to be a comprehensive partner of the businesses in order to grant variety, coherence, and consistency of services delivered and provide a reporting that helps a sustainable and strategic understanding of the organization. In fact, with the Helpline as the first emerging hotspot for issues, the requests for support confirm how difficult it is to foster hope, resilience, and emotional stability. Individuals report the difficulty of making decisions or feeling confident that their commitment is really meaningful. There is an overall worsening of all types of disorders and abuse as a result of the combination of the environmental risk factors related to the pandemic, war, climate, and economy, and for many companies, even organizational factors.

3. Would you comment on the prevalence of substance abuse (alcohol and drugs) in your country?

Numbers report that Italy remains one of the European countries that counts the highest percentage of cannabis, cocaine, and heroin abuse. In 2021, figures say that 40% of adolescents, mainly male, report to have used, at least one time, some sort of illegal drug. Having access to cheap drugs also allows a persistent and widespread abuse. Adolescents and young adults are, in this respect, signaling a social vulnerability, and we register this through parenting requests, i.e., parents who start to sense or are faced with addressing worsening issues and need extra support through a psychologically safe environment as the EAP to clarify a variety of doubts and hesitations related to these issues and address them with long-term treatment.

Alcohol abuse is sometimes more difficult to detect as it is socially acceptable to drink. As mentioned before in this article, these cases do not often reach the EAP because when the issue gets out of control, it needs to be addressed through the public health system in the first place.

ABOUT THE AUTHOR

Eapitalia World was founded as a result of a multidisciplinary merge of its founding partners. On the one hand, a robust legal background with a focus on ADR and collaborative practice, and on the other hand, a proven expertise in the field of EAPs and HR consultancy. The author of this article is Laura Sinatra, who represents the latter experience. She is one of the founding partners and has gained her international experience in the business during her 15-year career in the field before co-founding Eapitalia World in 2015. The company currently serves small, medium, and large organizations in Italy and Switzerland. The core business of Eapitalia includes full EAPs with a 24/7 Helpline, training and webinars, talent assessment programs, individual and group coaching programs, topical events, and critical incident interventions.

RESOURCES

YEES Employee Assistance Programmes Iberia
Sagasta 15, 28020 Madrid

EAP-Institut management consultancy GmbH
A-1010 Wien, Hegelgasse 19/10
Web: www.eap.world

JAPAN

Koji Mori and Kaoru Ichikawa

This article explores the types of stress that working people suffered during the three years of the pandemic in Japan, the mental health and Employee Assistance Program (EAP) services offered during the pandemic, as well as the perspective of EAP service providers for the post-pandemic workplace. We will also report on EAP program accreditation and a new certificate program.

Though the Japanese government officially ended the isolation and quarantine requirements for COVID-19 cases together with the indoor mask-wearing and social-distancing policies on May 8, 2023, the mental health consequences of these policies are still being felt and will remain an important counseling topic for EA providers for the foreseeable future. The number of people working from home or from other mobile spaces increased from 14.8% in 2019 to 27% in 2021. Since a hybrid workstyle has proven to be more effective and convenient, many corporations are keeping it. Working from home has its pros and cons. About 80% of telecommuters report being satisfied working remotely, with 60% of them claiming to be more productive at home than in the office. However, at the beginning of the pandemic, some workers felt increased anxiety due to the sudden transition to telecommuting, such as, "I worry about how my performance will be evaluated," "I cannot get advice from my manager when I need it," and "I feel lonely and isolated." Worker stress has increased during the pandemic; 39.9% of corporations reported that their employees' mental health worsened during the pandemic. The top three stress factors were changes in communication, increased telework, and changes in interpersonal relationships with coworkers.

According to the roundtable discussion of EAP Talk Japan in 2021, the issues raised in counseling sessions were: 1) stress regarding COVID-19, such as the fear of catching COVID-19 and of any stigma from having had COVID-19, 2) anxiety due to changes in work style, such as difficulty managing on and off time, lack of communication with coworkers, and feelings of isolation, and 3) family conflicts due to more time together at home and uncovering issues that were unnoticed prior to the pandemic.

In June 2020, Dr. Myron Scholes, a Nobel Laureate economist, was interviewed by NHK, a Japanese public television network, and he stated, "The COVID-19 crisis will change the economy and society in ways we never thought possible. Transformation accelerates [change] … Resilience is the most important thing in the event of a shock." According to Resilie Laboratory's research, resilient individuals are less depressed or anxious. Significant improvement in average resilience scores were observed following coaching.

Coming out of the pandemic, EA professionals should add resilience coaching as a key competency to help employers and employees build on personal strengths, increase wellness, and become more engaged at work.

For the safety of employees and counselors, most EA professionals transitioned their service delivery modality from face-to-face to online video counseling, using tools like Zoom and Microsoft Teams. Thus, there was a change in the peak hours for EAP services. Counseling sessions were scheduled primarily in the evenings after work or on weekends prior to the pandemic. Now that employees are working from home with more privacy and easier access to online video counseling, mid-day sessions during the week have increased in popularity. Although the pandemic has ended, almost all EA providers have continued to provide web-based video counseling since most employees prefer it to in-person counseling. Chat and text counseling via smartphone apps emerged during the pandemic primarily in the public domain, such as for the teenage suicide hotline. However, some EA providers also started offering chat counseling and saw some success.

In order to achieve the United Nation Sustainable Development Goals (SDGs), Japan's SDGs through 2030 target diversity and inclusion as areas needing improvement in the workplace. However, it is still rare to find EA providers who have expertise in assisting the LGBTQ population as a professional development, and continuing education opportunities surrounding diversity and inclusion within EAP are still in the development stage.

Workplace harassment prevention training is required for all companies. Smaller companies that outsource EAP services often look to their providers to facilitate the mandatory trainings and to open hotlines for employees to call if they are experiencing harassment. Agile EA providers will be prepared to offer these additional services.

Quality control systems have been insufficient as many EAPs are too small, lack organizational awareness, or are ill-equipped to implement quality management norms and protocols. To compound the problem, end users regularly fail to verify the quality management status of EAPs and are themselves not held accountable by supervisors and employees for their choice of provider. The same issues exist in other employee health services, such as government-mandated health checkups and other government-recommended health promotion programs.

Two organizations in particular, UOEH and EAPA, are working to help employers, occupational health physicians, and other stakeholders identify reliable and trustworthy EAP providers through EAP accreditation and through formal certification of EAP counselors.

The University of Occupational and Environmental Health, Japan (UOEH), with its medical school and school of occupational health, was established in 1973 with government funding from workers' compensation insurance premiums, providing reduced tuition to students in exchange for a nine-year commitment to work as occupational physicians. Since many of UOEH's graduates work for corporations, the university is continually seeking to improve the quality of EAP from the user's perspective. In 2003, to celebrate its 30th anniversary, UOEH chose to further its initiatives to address mental health in the workplace by launching Japan's first and only EAP accreditation program based on a contract with the US Council on Accreditation (COA).

COA's accreditation standards consist of administration and management, service delivery administration, and service standards. Of these, only the service standards needed to be adjusted to conform to the actual state of mental health services in Japan. However, the procedures are the same as COA's, which are based on self-study, on-site inspection, accreditation, and renewal every three years.

Only two EAPs are accredited, and these institutions have consistently renewed their accreditation. Since the program's inception, UOEH has held information sessions on the accreditation and lobbied major institutions; unfortunately, those EAPs judged that the benefits were not sufficient to justify the burden of accreditation.

Improving the quality of EAPs is a matter of interest to the government. Since it is difficult for the national government to accredit providers, the Ministry of Health, Labour, and Welfare started a self-assessment registration system. Registered EAPs must: 1) have full-time consultants with sufficient experience; 2) disclose the services they provide, fee structure, names of consultants, their qualifications, and past consultation records; 3) have a psychiatrist with expertise in workplace mental health support the organization and refer clients to a medical institution when necessary; and 4) have a private consultation room. This registration system is not very reliable due to limited standards, especially the lack of standards for administration and management, and the inherent limitations of relying on self-assessments.

Fortunately, Employee Assistance Professionals Association (EAPA) – Japan Branch has just launched a new online certification program, Certified Employee Assistance Professionals (CEAP®), to replace the pen-and-paper test from 2008 that was impractical and not culturally adapted. This new online certification program has been designed for candidates to gain and maintain skills through interactive exercises, selected readings, case studies, and online self-assessments. The contents are in Japanese and have been culturally adapted to fit Japanese EAP practice. Growth of the CEAP population since 2008 has been slow with about only 100 CEAP-holders. With the launch of online CEAP courses, which make it easier for candidates to access content from anywhere, EAPA Japan expects the CEAP-holding population to grow to 1,000 over the next three years.

ABOUT THE AUTHORS

Koji Mori, M.D., Ph.D.
Professor, University of Occupational and Environmental Health, Japan
President, Japan Society for Occupational Health

Dr. Koji Mori is a leader in occupational medicine in Japan with a high level of practice and research accomplishments. He was involved in the introduction of the COA-style mental health service accreditation system operated by the University of Occupational and Environmental Health, Japan and is currently the chairman of the accreditation committee.

Kaoru Ichikawa, Ph.D., CEAP
President, Employee Assistance Professional Association Japan Branch
President, EAPA Japan Branch
President, Asia Pacific Employee Assistance Roundtable (APEAR)
CEO, Resilie Laboratory Inc.
Kaoru.ichikawa@resilie.co.jp

Dr. Kaoru Ichikawa is a globally well-known employee assistance consultant, researcher, and educator. She introduced the concept of EAP to global corporations in Japan and other Asia-Pacific countries. She has been promoting employee well-being, EAP, and resiliency as core human resources and management strategies.

RESOURCES

EAP Professional Organizations

- Employee Assistance Professionals Association (EAPA) Japan branch Office – https://www.eapatokyo.org/
- MH Accreditation (COA Japan) Office – https://www.uoeh-.ac.jp/medical/hoshms/mh.html
- Lawyers Employee Assistance Program Association – https://l-eap.jp/
- EAP Providers (in alphabetical order)
  - Adecco Ltd. – https://www.adecco.co.jp/client/service/hr-solution/eap
  - Advantage Risk Management Co., Ltd. – https://www.armg.jp/english/#
  - Counseling Street Inc. – https://counseling.st/
  - E Partner Inc. – https://www.epartner.jp/
  - Fuji EAP Center Co., Ltd. – https://www.fujieap.com/
  - Hokendojin-Frontier – https://www.hokendohjin.co.jp/ja/index.html
  - Ikiikishokubazukuri Kenkyujo – https://www.ikiikilab.com/
  - Japan EAP Systems, Inc. – https://www.jes.ne.jp/
  - Junpukai – https://junpukai.or.jp/
  - MD.net – http://www.md-net.co.jp
  - Mejiro Psychological Assistance Association – https://www.m-paa.org/
  - MHC Research & Consulting Inc. – https://mhc-randc.or.jp/
  - Peacemind – https://www.peacemind.co.jp/en
  - Resilie Laboratory Inc. – https://resilielab.org/en/
  - Tokio Marine & Nichido Medical Service Co., Ltd. (TMS) – https://www.tokio-mednet.co.jp/service/counseling.html
  - T-Pec Corporation – https://www.t-pec.co.jp/
  - Well Link Co., Ltd. – https://welllink.co.jp/
  - WorkWay Inc. – https://www.workway.co.jp/
  - World Life Mapping – https://www.worldlifemapping.com

KENYA

Selina Kemama Njeri

ABSTRACT

This essay explores the impact of services offered through Employee Assistance Programs (EAPs) during the pandemic in Kenya. EAPs provide various support services to employees to enhance their mental, emotional, and physical well-being. The essay delves into the challenges faced by employees during the pandemic and highlights the effectiveness of EAPs in addressing these challenges. It also discusses the specific services offered and their impact on employee productivity, job satisfaction, and overall well-being. Lastly, the essay highlights the importance of EAPs in promoting resilience and providing support to employees during times of crisis.

INTRODUCTION

The COVID-19 pandemic had a profound impact on individuals and organizations worldwide. Employees in Kenya, like in many other countries, faced numerous challenges during this period, including increased stress, depression, anxiety, isolation, and work-related issues. According to BioMed Central, the COVID-19 pandemic wave caused a surge in domestic violence and excessive alcohol consumption among Kenyans countrywide. It does not help that Kenya has less than 500 mental health workers supporting a population of 53.77 million persons.

Having observed the impact of the pandemic, many organizations implemented EAPs to support their employees. A 2020 study conducted by the National Alliance of Healthcare Purchaser Coalitions, a nonprofit employer group, discovered that 53% of companies surveyed (a total of 256) offered specific programs focused on emotional and mental well-being of employees as a response to the impact of the pandemic. Organizations in Kenya set out on a similar mission, determined to support their employees using holistic approaches. This essay examines the impact of these services in mitigating the negative effects of the pandemic on employees in Kenya.

Some of the challenges faced by Kenyan employees during the pandemic included:

- Increased stress and anxiety due to health concerns, future uncertainties, and job insecurity
- Isolation, loneliness, and lack of social support
- Balancing work and personal life in a remote work environment
- Lack of access to mental health resources

IMPACT OF EAPS ON EMPLOYEES

a. **Mental Health Counseling and Therapy:** EAPs provided access to counseling therapy services. Qualified counselors and/or psychologists offered confidential support to employees dealing with mental health concerns. Counseling sessions were conducted remotely through video calls or telephone to ensure the safety and well-being of employees.

b. **Crisis Helplines and Emergency Support:** EAPs established immediate response services to employees during challenging situations. These helplines, including toll-free lines, were available 24/7 and offered confidential support for various crisis scenarios such as emotional distress, family conflicts, domestic violence, and suicidal ideation. Therapists provided psychological first aid, emotional support, and referrals to appropriate resources.

c. **Virtual Wellness Programs and Resources:** The EAPs organized virtual systems that provided accessed resources aimed at promoting overall well-being. The programs included webinars, workshops, and online training sessions on topics such as stress management, mindfulness, resilience, and healthy lifestyle habits.

d. **Financial and Legal Consultations:** EAPs availed financial and legal consultations to support employees' concerns in these areas. Financial experts provided guidance on budgeting, debt management, and financial planning during uncertain times. Legal consultations addressed law-related issues like employment, family matters, housing, etc.

e. **Work-Life Balance Support:** EAPs recognized the need for work-life balance, especially during the pandemic when boundaries between work and personal life seemed blurred. It has provided support and resources to help employees manage their responsibilities effectively, including time, boundaries, prioritizing self-care, and remote work challenges. EAPs also provided resources to maintain work-life balance and overall well-being.

f. Employee Assistance Programs have significantly mitigated the impact of the pandemic on employees in Kenya by providing crucial support at a time of need and by positively influencing employee well-being, productivity, and job satisfaction. It is important for organizations in Kenya to recognize the value of EAPs and seriously invest in the programs to support their employees during times of crisis.

WHAT WERE THE EFFECTS OF ONLINE/VIRTUAL COUNSELING?

According to Kenya's Ministry of Health, one in 10 Kenyans suffer from a given mental disorder. These statistics surged during the pandemic. Online therapy, for Kenyans, was a lighthouse during a dark time.

Here are some of the key positive impacts of online counseling:

1. **Increased Accessibility:** Online counseling has made mental health support more accessible to individuals who faced challenges about traditional in-person counseling. Geographical limitations, transportation issues, highly packed work schedules, and mobility challenges are no longer obstacles when accessing therapy.
2. **Convenience and Flexibility:** Online counseling offers greater convenience and flexibility for sessions. Clients schedule appointments at their convenience through ICAS Kenya online booking system, eliminating the need for travel time and allowing for more flexibility in fixing therapy sessions into daily routine and attending sessions conveniently within their busy schedules or other commitments.
3. **Privacy and Anonymity:** Some people found attending therapy without necessarily revealing your identity appealing and comforting; people can seek help without worrying about running into someone they know in a waiting room or during an in-person session. Anonymity reduced the stigma associated with counseling.
4. **Comfort and Safety:** Online sessions provided the client with a familiar and comfortable environment, such as their own home. This helped the clients to feel more at ease and open up more easily during sessions and also reduced the risk of exposure to COVID-19.
5. **Increased Reach and Diversity:** Online counseling expanded the reach of psychotherapy services, allowing therapists to work with those from different regions or even countries who seek help.
6. **Continuity of Care:** Online counseling provided an alternative for individuals who were already receiving in-person therapy before the pandemic to continue their therapeutic relationship without interruption, ensuring continuity of care during a challenging time.

7. **Utilization of Technological Tools:** Online counseling has leveraged various technological tools to enhance the therapeutic experience. These tools include video conferencing platforms, secure messaging systems, and online resources. Interactive features, such as screen sharing and virtual whiteboards, were utilized to enhance communication and engage clients effectively.

ROLE OF TECHNOLOGY AND SOCIAL MEDIA

According to a report published on December 18th, 2020, by Media Council of Kenya, a majority of respondents (55%) stated that media consumption had risen during the pandemic period. After the global population were confined in their homes to prevent the spread of the virus, people turned to technological and media platforms in order to connect with other individuals and to effectively execute their jobs.

Key roles of technology and media platforms in the lives of employees included:

1. **Remote Service Delivery:** Technology facilitated the transition to remote service delivery for EAPs. Through video conferencing platforms, employees could access counseling and therapy sessions from the comfort of their homes, thus professionals continued to provide counseling and support in a safe and confidential manner.
2. **Online Resources and Tools:** Technology and online platforms allowed EAPs to share a wealth of online resources and tools to support employees' mental health and well-being, including educational materials, self-help guides and materials, webinars, and articles through websites and email newsletters. This ensured that employees were empowered with relevant information, coping strategies, and wellness resources at their fingertips.
3. **Communication and Outreach:** Networking platforms played a crucial role in communication and outreach efforts by EAPs. The online channels were used to disseminate important updates, share tips for managing stress, promote upcoming webinars or workshops, and engage with employees. Social media facilitated real-time communication and allowed EAPs to reach a broader audience, increasing awareness of available services and resources.
4. **24/7 Helplines and Chat Support:** EAPs leveraged technology to provide round-the-clock helplines and chat support where employees could access immediate assistance and guidance through phone calls or an online chat platform, thus supporting employees' access to real-time help during crises or when they needed support outside of regular business hours.
5. **Data Collection and Analytics:** Technology facilitated the collection and analysis of data related to EAP services; for example, surveys on stress vulnerability in the workplace.

EAPs used digital platforms to track employee engagement, usage patterns, and satisfaction levels. These insights helped formulate individualized services, identify trends, and make data-driven decisions to enhance the effectiveness of their programs.
6. **Confidentiality and Privacy:** Technology played a crucial role in maintaining confidentiality and privacy in EAP services. Secure video conferencing platforms and encrypted communication channels ensured that employee information and counseling sessions remained confidential. EAPs implemented robust cybersecurity measures to protect employee data and comply with privacy regulations.
7. **Feedback and Evaluation:** Technology enabled EAPs to gather feedback and evaluate the impact of their services. Online surveys, feedback forms, and data analytics helped EAPs assess employee satisfaction, measure outcomes, and identify areas for improvement. The feedback loop facilitated continuous improvement and allowed the adoption of services to better meet employee needs.

TECHNOLOGY AND MENTAL HEALTH SUPPORT

Technology and online platforms played a significant role in offering mental health support during the pandemic. Mental health apps, online therapy platforms, and virtual support groups emerged as valuable resources for individuals seeking emotional support and professional help.

We are aware that technology has been great during the pandemic, performing wonders in communication, working remotely, education, mental health support, and entertainment; it has also posed challenges in terms of misinformation and online safety. Striking a balance between leveraging technology for its advantages while addressing its drawbacks is crucial for a responsible and effective use of these platforms during times of crisis.

DIVERSITY AND INCLUSION EFFORTS

Here are some key efforts targeting diversity and inclusion among counselors, providers, and clients:

1. **Competence Training:** Counseling organizations and educational institutions have recognized the importance of competence training for counselors to equip the counselors with knowledge, skills, awareness, and techniques. It also promotes an understanding of different cultural perspectives, values, and experiences, ensuring culturally sensitive and inclusive services.
2. **Recruitment and Representation:** Organizations and educational institutions have focused on recruiting individuals from underrepresented communities. The increased

diversity of counselors helps create a more inclusive environment and enables clients to find professionals who understand their unique experiences and identities.

3. **Affinity Groups and Support Networks:** In Kenya, we have the Kenya Association of Professional Counselors (KAPC), amongst others that are established within the counseling field, to provide a space for counselors from different backgrounds to connect, share experiences, and support one another.

4. **Client-Centered Approaches:** Counseling approaches have evolved to adopt a client-centered approach that values and respects the individuality and diversity of clients. Therapists provide a safe and inclusive space for clients to express their identities and experiences without fear of judgment or discrimination.

5. **Accessibility and Accommodations:** Counseling services have strived to be accessible to all individuals, including those who are vulnerable, minority groups, and persons living with disabilities. At ICAS Kenya, we have counselors who provide sign language counseling. This includes providing accommodations such as sign language interpreters, captioning services, accessible facilities, and online therapy platforms that meet accessibility standards through Unconditional Positive Acceptance.

6. **Community Engagement and Outreach:** Counseling organizations and providers have engaged community empowerment; for example, by providing counseling services to inmates in Jamhuri Prisons and youths in Kawangware, Nairobi, to raise awareness about mental health and the benefits of counseling. We have specifically targeted underserved communities, conducting workshops, presentations, and awareness campaigns to reduce the stigma surrounding mental health and promote help-seeking behaviors.

7. **Continuous Education and Research:** Professionals engage in research, attend conferences, and participate in workshops to stay updated on best practices and emerging trends in providing inclusive counseling services.

ABOUT THE AUTHOR

My name is Selina Kemama Njeri, and I am the Managing Director at ICAS Kenya with over 10 years' experience working with ICAS World. I have a Bachelor's Degree in Human Resources and a Master's Degree in Business Administration. I am a firm believer of employee wellness; there is no war in history that was won by the efforts of a king or president alone. Great leaders recognize the importance of catering to the well-being of their employees.

REFERENCES

Marangu, E., Mansouri, F., Sands, N., Ndetei, D., Muriithi, P., Wynter, K., & Rawson, H. (2021). Assessing mental health literacy of primary health care workers in Kenya: a cross-sectional survey. *International Journal of Mental Health Systems, 15*(1). https://doi.org/10.1186/s13033-021-00481-z

NASCOP. (2020, October 15). *About Us | Division of National AIDS & STI Control Program.* NASCOP. https://www.nascop.or.ke/about-us/#:~:text=The%20National%20AIDS%20and%20STI

Nzuri. (2023). *Nzuri self-care portal.*

Place, A. T. (2017). *Ability Therapy Place: Home.* Ability Therapy Place. https://abilitytherapyplace.co.ke/

Quaife, M., van Zandvoort, K., Gimma, A., Shah, K., McCreesh, N., Prem, K., Barasa, E., Mwanga, D., Kangwana, B., Pinchoff, J., Edmunds, W. J., Jarvis, C. I., & Austrian, K. (2020). The impact of COVID-19 control measures on social contacts and transmission in Kenyan informal settlements. *BMC Medicine, 18*(1). https://doi.org/10.1186/s12916-020-01779-4

Ward, M. (2020, April 16). *7 companies increasing mental health services for employees in response to the coronavirus pandemic.* Business Insider Africa. https://africa.businessinsider.com/strategy/7-companies-increasing-mental-health-services-for-employees-in-response-to-the/pvqbct7

KOREA

Jimmy S. Kim

It is an honor to share stories of EAP work in South Korea. My name is Jimmy S. Kim, and I am the global network team manager at DAIN, the leading EAP company in Korea. DAIN was established as the first EAP company to professionally serve employees in different companies. DAIN has the largest number of counseling infrastructures with the largest number of counselors that cover 99% of the country to make it possible to provide in-person counseling services anywhere in the country, and this is the key for high customer satisfaction. Today, DAIN is recognized as a leading EAP company in Korea, serving the largest number of clients with over a 95% re-contract rate.

During the pandemic period, the world innovated faster than ever, which left a significant impact on different aspects of Korean people's lives. First, social distancing and the fear of such a virus have had a tremendous impact on mental health. During this period, we all became familiar with the term "corona blues." From the research, we found that everybody experienced feelings of depression during the pandemic, especially females and people in their 30s who reported experiencing more severe depression than other genders and age groups. Suicidal ideation was high among males and people in their 20s and 30s, with a significant difference between the age group of 50 or above and the age group of 19–39. As an EAP provider, we have noticed that this list of usage is identical to the usage of EAP counseling. The usage of female clients and people in their 30s is significantly higher than other groups.

Currently, there is a 420% increase in counseling usage compared to 2019. We attribute this increase to people paying more attention to their own personal needs due to isolation, as well as companies and the government providing more mental health care services for their employees and the general public.

During the COVID-19 pandemic, virtual platforms for mental health care have been developed and have made great progress. However, despite many Korean mental health care providers adopting advanced virtual programs, more than 80% of clients still prefer to have their counseling sessions in person. This is why face-to-face counseling is essential. Korean people feel more secure in a face-to-face setting because they find it difficult to share their personal matters online or over the phone. However, at the same time, we have observed that younger generations find it easier to discuss their personal problems online. It can be a great experience for "first-timers," and since they don't have to travel to visit counseling centers, they find it easier to access. Therefore, it is important to have a large infrastructure of counseling centers so that people can have easy access to in-person counseling, but at the same time, we still need to focus on developing innovative, secure counseling platforms for anyone to receive the service from anywhere they want.

In today's world, social media has had a significant impact on our lives. Not only do people feel more sensitive to news media, but younger generations also tend to compare themselves with others on social media. Since most people only post good memories and pictures of themselves, younger generations tend to think that everyone is doing better than them. Additionally, during the pandemic, many people bonded strongly to get through hardships together with the mindset of "We are all in this together!" However, now that everything is rapidly returning to normal, many people feel like they will be left alone. This phenomenon can be easily observed among older generations.

Especially, the birth rate in Korea is at an all-time low, so there is a deeper and deeper gap between younger and older generations as time goes by. Even the world that we live in has changed rapidly, and we need to recognize the ones that are in the margin of this ever-changing world. How do we connect from one generation to the other? We need to build a platform that is easy to access by younger and older generations. This platform can be in an online setting or an in-person setting.

Furthermore, we are all aware that many people have been exposed to false news and social media during the pandemic period. When the tragic incident occurred in Itaewon, Korea, in 2022, where over hundreds of people were jammed in a narrow space resulting in the death of more than 100 people during a Halloween feast, many individuals were affected by harmful videos and content circulated through social media. This exposure had a significant impact on both adults and adolescents, leading to the experience of indirect traumatic effects. Consequently, there was a rise in emotional distress and the potential for psychological consequences. It is crucial for us to exercise caution when sharing content with others, as everyone has different perspectives and reactions to different types of content.

As an EAP provider, we need to actively engage in dealing with such a rapidly changing world. During this period, we also need to recognize the diversity among people. Especially in Korea, many people from the LGBTQ+ community are facing significant challenges due to the country's closed-mindedness. Korea does not grant rights to LGBTQ+ individuals, and unfortunately, this closed-mindedness is also prevalent in the counseling world. Many counselors refuse to see clients from LGBTQ+ backgrounds. Therefore, it is our responsibility to ensure that they can freely receive EAP services just like anyone else.

Many companies still require the disclosure of gender, which is limited to male and female categories only. To address this, our team decided to include the option of "Not to answer" so that anyone can feel comfortable receiving services when they are in need. As clients, we have observed that many employees do not feel comfortable sharing their gender identities in the company, and some employees have even been laid off after revealing their gender. This is a serious issue in Korea, but changing it remains challenging. As an EAP provider, we strive to create a safe space for individuals to feel secure and receive the help they need. This can be achieved through online counseling settings without identification and by distributing flyers that list counselors who can assist people from the LGBTQ+ community.

ABOUT THE AUTHOR

Jimmy Sungjoon Kim, global network team manager at DAIN EAP Korea.

Contact: globalpartners@daincnm.co.kr / sungjoonman@gmail.com

RESOURCES

DAIN EAP – dain@daincnm.co.kr / +82-2-2268-5988
Korean Diversity Lab – jihak@diversity.or.kr / +82-10-6236-4684
Mind Touch Counseling Center – +82-2-2268-5980

REFERENCES

https://www.korea.kr/news/pressReleaseView.do?newsId=156490972

https://health.chosun.com/site/data/html_dir/2022/06/14/2022061400901.html

LATVIA

Diana Fridrihsone and Ayrat Khabibov

The goal of this article is to provide information on funding and delivery of medical and psychological assistance in the Republic of Latvia.

In Latvia, people have access to various mental health services, including counseling and psychotherapy, psychiatric care, psychological assessments and testing, support groups, and workshops and seminars, as well as online and telephone helplines. These services aim to address a wide range of mental health issues and can be obtained through referrals from general practitioners, local medical centers and hospitals, or specific service providers.

The reimbursement options for these services vary depending on whether they are funded through the public health care system, private insurance, or out-of-pocket payments.

As a result, services that professionals would identify as Employee Assistance Program (EAP) interventions, such as those related to substance abuse, stress conditions, emotional distress, health care/health literacy concerns, and relationship issues, have providers from various professional backgrounds and are funded from different sources.

The reimbursement options for these services vary depending on whether they are funded through the public health care system, private insurance, or out of pocket. In most of the EU Member States, either government schemes or compulsory schemes/accounts are by far the most important source of health care financing. However, since the latter does not exist in Latvia, the two other sources contribute a relatively modest share (60.8%) among the total current health care financing. Thus, household out-of-pocket payments, whose share averaged 15.4% in the EU in 2019, played an important role in Latvia at 35.6%.[30]

Employee Assistance Programs (EAPs) may be available in Latvia, particularly for employees working in multinational companies or larger organizations that have a global presence. If an EAP is not available through their employer, employees may still be able to access support services through private insurance, public health care facilities, or local NGOs and community organizations.

In the public health care system, psychiatric care, including diagnosis, medication management, and ongoing monitoring, is generally covered. Counseling and psychotherapy services may also be partially covered for specific patient groups or conditions, such as severe mental health conditions. However, the availability and scope of these services may vary, counseling for psychiatric patients is insufficiently covered, meaning that there is a long waiting time for the service and service is provided only for a limited time, and patients may need to pay out-of-pocket or use private insurance for certain services. Patients can access psychiatric care through public health care facilities such as hospitals and outpatient clinics.

The COVID-19 pandemic has challenged the ability of health care systems to ensure the continuity of health services for patients with non-communicable diseases (NCDs). The issue of remote consultations has emerged. Before the COVID-19 pandemic, remote consultations were not routinely provided or covered by public health funding in Latvia, but now remote health care services are widely accessible and reimbursed from the state budget.[31]

Private insurance is available to approximately 28% of the Latvian population (2022 data). Private insurance policies in Latvia may offer coverage for counseling and psychotherapy, provided by specialists who are licensed as health care professionals, psychiatric care, psychological assessments and testing, and participation in support groups. In the latest years, partially explained by the influence of COVID-19, the demand for such services has increased and has led to the inclusion of counseling and psychotherapy coverage schemes in most health insurance plans provided to employees. However, the coverage of these services can vary significantly depending on the insurance company and policy.

---

30 Šteinbuka, I., Austers, A., Barānovs, O., Malnačs, N. COVID-19 Lessons and Post-pandemic Recovery: A Case of Latvia. Front Public Health. 2022 Apr 7;10:866639. doi: 10.3389/fpubh.2022.866639. PMID: 35462839; PMCID: PMC9021441.

31 Kursīte, M., Stars, I., Strēle, I., Gobiņa, I., Ķīvīte-Urtāne, A., Behmane, D., Dūdele, A., Villeruša, A. A mixed-method study on the provision of remote consultations for non-communicable disease patients during the first wave of the COVID-19 pandemic in Latvia: lessons for the future. BMC Health Serv Res. 2022 Feb 26;22(1):263. doi: 10.1186/s12913-022-07634-x. PMID: 35219328; PMCID: PMC8881750.

In the last two to three years, there has been a rise in remote consultations and e-health services. It can be explained by the influence of COVID-19 and limited access to health care in the lockdown times. Currently, some private insurance companies provide the possibility of arranging remote consultations and even provide technical solutions to hold the consultations.

For refugees in Latvia, psychological support services can be accessed through public health care facilities, NGOs, and specialized programs. Refugees generally have access to the same health care services as Latvian citizens, including mental health services covered by the public health care system. Some NGOs and specialized programs provide psychological support services specifically for refugees, and the services may be reimbursed or provided free of charge. Additionally, Latvia receives EU funding to support the integration of refugees, which may include funding for psychological support services.

It is important to note that the availability and scope of psychological support services, as well as the percentage of reimbursement from the public budget and out-of-pocket expenses or private insurance coverage, may vary depending on specific factors such as the patient's needs, health care provider, and location.

ABOUT THE AUTHORS

Drs. Fridrihsone and Khabibov are partners and project leaders for the development of Lifestyle Medicine practice in the Republic of Latvia, a country in the Baltic region of Northern Europe. It is one of the Baltic states, bordered by Estonia to the north, Lithuania to the south, Russia to the east, and Belarus to the southeast, and sharing a maritime border with Sweden to the west.

Dr. Fridrihsone is an experienced pediatrician with a demonstrated history of working in the marketing, medical, and market access areas in the pharmaceutical industry. diana.fridrihsone@gmail.com

Dr. Khabibov is an experienced occupational health professional leading the implementation of health and productivity management and workplace wellness implementation practice in international companies. khabibov@hotmail.com

REFERENCES

Interviews with human resources directors and sustainability directors of LIDL supermarket chain, Riga Seaport.

Interviews with private psychologists – contractors of global EAP service providers and members of the Baltic Association for Psychological Counselling.

Interviews with lecturers of the Department of Psychiatry and Narcology Riga Stradins Medical University.

LEBANON AND JORDAN

Alexandru Manescu and Mohamed Lamaa

In recent years, there has been an increase in awareness of the value of mental health services and employee assistance in the workplace, in the Middle East region generally. However, it is critical to examine the state of Employee Assistance Programs and mental health services in countries like Jordan and Lebanon, where getting access to mental health treatment might be challenging. The main obstacles to effective mental health services in Lebanon and Jordan are stigma and a lack of access to mental health facilities and to qualified clinicians who can offer solutions that respect and integrate patients' cultural norms. In addition, many other obstacles will be discussed in this article, such as a lack of resources allocated to meet the high needs for mental health support. In this article, we will explore the benefits of Employee Assistance Programs (EAPs) as a solution to bridging the gap in mental health services in Lebanon and Jordan. We will also delve into the challenges faced and the key considerations for implementing EAPs in these countries.

MENTAL HEALTH BURDEN IN LEBANON AND JORDAN

Lebanon and Jordan are countries that have experienced significant challenges due to limited natural resources and recent crises. Lebanon's economy severely collapsed in 2020. According to the World Bank, the economic crisis in Lebanon is listed as one of the three worst worldwide since the middle of the nineteenth century. In addition, the COVID-19 pandemic and a massive refugee crisis since the Syrian war started in 2011 have added pressures. All of these were exacerbated by the Beirut explosion on August 4, which was discovered by the United States Geological Survey, that had a seismic event of magnitude 3.3 and is considered one of the most powerful artificial non-nuclear explosions. Even though Lebanese people have been used to dealing with continuous crises and ongoing civil unrest following the end of the civil war in 1991, nevertheless, the recent events have added to the burden of mental disorders in Lebanon. As an overview to the mental health burden in Lebanon, according to the most recent prevalence research in Lebanon dating to 2006, roughly one in every four people in Lebanon suffers from at least one mental disorder at some point in their lives, with anxiety and depression being the most common.

The suicide mortality rate in Lebanon is predicted to be 2.8 per 100,000 people (as of 2019). In Lebanon, one person commits suicide every 2.1 days, and one person attempts suicide every six hours. However, due to underreporting caused by inadequate surveillance systems, these data do not represent the true number of suicide cases due to stigma.

Jordan, on the other hand, is one of the safest and most stable countries in the Middle East region. However, the country has its own set of different serious challenges that have had a profound impact on the mental well-being of its population. Jordan is considered one of the countries most affected by environmental changes, especially those caused by the climate crisis and the resulting drought, desertification, and loss of arable lands, and the large influx of multiple refugee populations from neighbouring countries that have impacted the country's economy and depleted its limited resources. All of this has been exacerbated by the COVID-19 pandemic and its impact on the local population, economic status, and well-being. It is estimated that following the COVID-19 lockdown, the national GDP fell by 23% and employment losses to over 20%, which increased the burden of mental health issues and the level of stress and incapability for people to afford basic services including mental health support. According to the World Health Organization (WHO), Jordan's mental health system requires considerable reorganization, with more than 25% of Jordanians experiencing mental health symptoms. According to the World Health Organization (WHO), only 305 Jordanians out of 100,000 seek care for mental health concerns, a problem that must be addressed.

MENTAL HEALTH SERVICES CHALLENGES IN LEBANON AND JORDAN

Despite the burden of mental health that impacts both countries, several factors contribute to the challenges in accessing mental health services in Lebanon and Jordan. First and foremost is the **stigma** surrounding mental health. Many individuals in these countries hesitate to seek help due to fear of being judged or marginalized. This stigma hinders progress in addressing mental health issues and perpetuates the existing gap in services. The most significant barriers to mental health care in both Lebanon and Jordan are a lack of mental health literacy and persisting stigma. Poor mental health knowledge and poor attitudes toward persons suffering from mental illness significantly restrict help-seeking behaviour. Negative interactions with health care providers and mental health services can also be a deterrent to continuing treatment. Moreover, there's a fear of harm or criminalization for people suffering from addiction or suicide ideation, or for minorities such as LGBTIQ people in need of mental health care. In April 2022, Jordan criminalized suicide, threatening prison time and fines for those who attempt self-harm in public. While in Lebanon, drug consumption is criminalized, and persons who suffer from drug addiction are detained with the convictions of drug abuse leading them to be the victim of additional social stigma.

Both Lebanon and Jordan have low tolerance for the LGBTI community, which makes it very difficult for those from the community to access support safely and with dignity.

Additionally, **access to services and the geographical distribution of mental health facilities and professionals are uneven**, with urban areas having more resources compared to rural areas. This disparity in access further exacerbates the challenge of reaching individuals in need.

In Lebanon, the many compounded crises have had a significant negative impact on the country's health care sector. The health care sector has suffered because of the currency devaluation in 2020. Due to the government's inability to pay private and public hospitals the money it owes them and the ensuing inability to pay personnel and buy necessary equipment, hospitals have been straining to provide service users with lifesaving surgery and urgent medical care. Furthermore, due to currency restrictions, basic and lifesaving pharmaceuticals have been in short supply, severely limiting the importation of necessary medication and medical items. Given the substantial inflation and currency depreciation in Lebanon, the cost of medical services, including mental health and pharmaceuticals, has risen significantly.

In Jordan, the country's mental health public service is mainly based on psychiatric services in a few hospitals; however, it is limited in capacity and quality of service. Public mental health services are not available in more remote sites and in less populated governates, which makes access challenging for those not residing in big cities. Based on the latest statistics of the ministry of public health in Jordan, there are only a few mental health institutions. Jordan has just three adult mental health hospitals, one specialist psychiatric hospital for children, and 64 outpatient facilities. In Jordan, there are just two psychiatrists, 0.27 psychologists, and 0.04 nurses for every 100,000 people.

In addition to the challenges related to accessibility of mental health services in Lebanon and Jordan, there is a **shortage of mental health qualified professionals**, and the existing services often lack the capacity to meet the growing demand, leaving many individuals without the support they desperately need. In Lebanon, the World Health Organization (WHO) reports that about 40% of qualified medical professionals and 30% of registered nurses have already left the nation, either permanently or temporarily. The flight of human capital will not only restrict society's access to the services offered by these professions, but it will also increase the economy's downfall and hinder its recovery.

ACTIONS TAKEN TOWARD MITIGATING CHALLENGES PRESENTED IN THE MENTAL HEALTH SECTOR IN LEBANON AND JORDAN

Despite the tremendous burden of mental illnesses in both countries, Lebanon and Jordan lack comprehensive mental health policies and have poorly financed mental health services. Moreover, the COVID-19 pandemic has further highlighted the need for prioritizing mental health. This played an important factor that led both ministries of public health in Lebanon and Jordan to increase collaboration and efforts with the World Health Organization (WHO) and create The National Mental Health Strategy for Lebanon (2023–2030) and The National Mental Health and Substance Use Action plan (2022–2026) for Jordan. Both national plans focus on different major points, such as:

- Updating the national health policy to be in line with international standards and human rights instruments.
- Strengthening the role of the existing bodies and the Ministry of Public Health in leading the response to mental health crises.
- Enhancing the management of mental health and psychosocial human resources to meet with the needs.

Therefore, both Lebanon and Jordan allocated more funding to the public mental health sector, using support in collaborate projects with local and international nongovernmental organizations (NGOs). Both countries are putting significant effort into eliminating the stigma about mental health and are creating clear policies in different layers of the health and educational systems. More effort is being put in public and private education institutions to support majors related to mental health, making it more attractive to increase the number of specialized, well-trained counselors to respond to the high demand. In addition, the licensing process of mental health providers has been established in both Lebanon and Jordan, supervised by both ministries of public health, the Lebanese Psychology Association for Lebanese psychologists, and the Jordanian Psychological Association to ensure a standardized form of service provided with easy access and no harm.

EMPLOYEE ASSISTANCE PROGRAMS IN LEBANON AND JORDAN

Employee Assistance Programs (EAPs) have emerged as a promising solution to bridge the gap in mental health services in Lebanon and Jordan. These programs offer free and confidential counseling, crisis intervention, and referral services to employees and their families. Following the Beirut explosion in August 2020, CCS provided support to a good number of Lebanese located in Lebanon and in other countries, which they have found to be a great benefit to help with their mental health issues while the public and private health sector was overwhelmed with the response to the crisis. CCS has also been serving a good number of Jordanians through the EAP supplying high levels of professional Arabic-speaking counselors responding to the Arabic-speaking hotline. EAPs in Lebanon and Jordan have been serving as a valuable resource for individuals who are hesitant to seek help outside of the workplace due to stigma. By integrating mental health support within the workplace, EAPs reduce barriers and make it easier for employees to access the care they need. Moreover, EAPs provide a holistic approach to employee well-being, addressing both personal and work-related challenges that may contribute to mental health issues.

BRIDGING THE GAP: ENHANCING MENTAL HEALTH SERVICES THROUGH EMPLOYEE ASSISTANCE PROGRAMS IN LEBANON AND JORDAN

Mental health services play a crucial role in supporting the well-being of individuals and communities. In countries like Lebanon and Jordan where limited natural resources and recent crises have posed significant challenges, the need for effective mental health services is more pressing than ever. Employee Assistance Programs bridge the gap in mental health services in Lebanon and Jordan by providing accessible and confidential support to employees. Through EAPs, individuals can access professional counseling services without the fear of stigma or financial burden. EAPs also offer flexibility in terms of scheduling appointments, making it easier for employees to seek help without disrupting their work responsibilities.

Moreover, EAPs promote early intervention and prevention by offering proactive services such as stress management workshops, mental health awareness campaigns, and resilience training. These initiatives help individuals build coping skills and resilience, reducing the likelihood of developing more severe mental health issues.

KEY CONSIDERATIONS FOR IMPLEMENTING EAPS IN LEBANON AND JORDAN

While implementing Employee Assistance Programs in Lebanon and Jordan, there are several key considerations to keep in mind:

- Cultural Sensitivity: In a multicultural region, tailoring EAPs to be culturally sensitive and respectful of the local customs and traditions is essential to enhancing their effectiveness and acceptance.
- Language Accessibility: Ensure that EAP services are available in multiple languages (Arabic, English, and French) to accommodate the diverse workforce in Lebanon and Jordan.
- Partnerships and Collaborations: Establish partnerships with local mental health organizations and local professionals to maximize the impact and reach of the EAP.
- Affordability and Accessibility: Explore options to make the EAP services affordable and accessible to all employees, regardless of their financial situation or location.

CONCLUSION: THE FUTURE OF EAPS IN IMPROVING MENTAL HEALTH SERVICES

Employee Assistance Programs have the potential to play a transformative role in enhancing mental health services in Lebanon and Jordan. By addressing the challenges in accessing care and providing support within the workplace, EAPs can bridge the gap and improve the well-being of individuals and communities. As these programs continue to evolve and expand, it is crucial for employers, policymakers, and mental health professionals to collaborate and invest in creating a supportive and inclusive environment that prioritizes mental health. Through such collective efforts, Lebanon and Jordan can pave the way for a brighter future in mental health care.

ABOUT THE AUTHORS

Alexandru Manescu and Mohamed Lamaa both work with Corporate Counselling Services (CCS), which serves 50 countries across Europe and the MENA regions. Alexandru is the International Director of Clinical Services, and Mohamed is the Clinical Lead and Regional Coordinator: Middle East.

LUXEMBOURG

Eliane Bucher

THE IMPACTS OF THE PANDEMIC ON EAP SERVICES IN LUXEMBOURG

ICAS provides telephone and chat counseling services for psychological issues in Luxembourg through its central Support Center in Switzerland. However, legal services and face-to-face or video counseling sessions are delivered locally in Luxembourg.

An interesting observation specific to Luxembourg during the pandemic is that clients have experienced a greater impact in terms of loneliness and concerns for their family members compared to other countries. This can be attributed to the significant proportion of expatriates among the working population in Luxembourg. According to Statec, the national statistics office of Luxembourg, non-Luxembourgish residents accounted for approximately 48% of the total employed population in 2020.

During the pandemic, especially during lockdown periods, expatriates in Luxembourg felt a heightened sense of isolation and reported experiencing profound loneliness. Furthermore, with travel restrictions in place, many expatriates had family members residing in other countries, which increased their concerns for their loved ones' health and well-being. The absence of personal support, exchange, and mutual assistance from their families further amplified the challenges faced by these employees.

The unique circumstances faced by expatriates in Luxembourg highlight the importance of providing comprehensive support tailored to their specific needs. EAP providers have to address these challenges by offering accessible counseling services remotely, while also recognizing the importance of in-country services for legal matters and face-to-face or video counseling sessions. By understanding the impact of loneliness and familial concerns on expatriate employees, EAPs can provide the necessary support to help alleviate their distress and enhance their well-being.

For the remaining effects of the pandemic, we have not been able to detect any difference compared to the six other countries we serve (refer to the chapter about Switzerland).

THE EFFECTS OF ONLINE/VIRTUAL COUNSELING

At our centralized support center in Switzerland, we provide assistance not only to Switzerland but also to Luxembourg, Germany, France, Italy, and Austria. Regarding online/virtual counseling, we have not observed any distinct variations in its effects specifically in Luxembourg. Therefore, we would kindly direct you to the relevant information pertaining to Switzerland for further insights on this matter.

THE ROLE OF TECHNOLOGY AND SOCIAL MEDIA

At our central support center in Switzerland, we extend our services to several countries, including Luxembourg, Germany, France, Italy, and Austria. However, we have not observed any discernible variations in the role of technology and social media specific to Luxembourg. Therefore, we kindly refer you to the information pertaining to the role of technology and social media in Switzerland.

THE EFFORTS TOWARD DIVERSITY AND INCLUSION WITHIN THE FIELD (COUNSELORS, PROVIDERS, CLIENTS)

At our centralized support center in Switzerland, we are proud to offer assistance to a wide range of countries including Luxembourg, Germany, France, Italy, and Austria. As we focus on the importance of diversity and inclusion, we have not identified any notable deviations in the effects specific to Luxembourg. Consequently, we kindly suggest referring to the relevant information regarding Switzerland for further comprehensive insights on this matter.

ABOUT THE AUTHOR

My name is Eliane Bucher, and I am the managing director for ICAS in Luxembourg, Switzerland, Germany, France, Italy, and Austria. I have been with ICAS since 2005. We are part of ICAS International, a leading global provider of EAPs, health and well-being services, and critical incident support. ICAS is supporting 2,400 companies with more than 6.5 million employees in 155 countries.

With a dedicated team and a commitment to excellence, we were able to position the ICAS Switzerland/Luxembourg Group as one of the leading companies in the industry, meeting the evolving needs of our customers and clients. We are deeply committed to driving growth, fostering a culture of collaboration, and empowering employees to excel. Our strategic vision and ability to navigate complex market dynamics have been instrumental in ICAS's continued success.

RESOURCES

ICAS Schweiz GmbH
Hertistrasse 25
8304 Wallisellen
+41 44 878 30 00
info@icas.ch
www.icas.ch

SOS Détresse
Tél. 454545
www.454545.lu

CCS Corp. Counselling Services
2, Rue du Kiem,
8435, Steinfort
+35226976032
office@ccsint.com
+35226976032

Kanner-Jugendtelefon (KJT)
Tél. 161 11
www.kjt.lu

MALAYSIA

Wilson Tee

INTRODUCTION

Employee Assistance Program (EAP) is a comprehensive, worksite-based program designed to help identify and facilitate the resolution of behavioral, health, and productivity problems that may adversely affect employee well-being or job performance. In Malaysia, EAP provides various services including counseling, consultation, psychological assessment, crisis management, and psycho-education for learning and development to assist employees in dealing with a wide range of issues such as stress, anxiety, depression, relationships, and work-related problems. These services generally incorporate short-term counseling approaches as part of the intervention.

This paper explores several aspects of the Malaysia EAP, including the impact of EAP services during the pandemic, the effects of online/virtual counseling, the role of technology and social media, and efforts toward diversity and inclusion within the field of EAP consultation and counseling.

THE IMPACT OF MALAYSIA EAP SERVICES DURING THE PANDEMIC

Malaysia reported its first COVID-19 case on 25 January 2020, and the nationwide Movement Control Order (MCO) was imposed on 18 March 2020 as part of the measures to curb and mitigate the spread of the COVID-19 virus in the community. The implementation of lockdown was later relaxed to Conditional MCO (CMCO) until 10 June 2020. This chapter explores the impact of Turning Point throughout the pandemic, as it is one of the EAP pioneers in Malaysia. So as to better understand the impact that COVID-19 has had on Malaysia EAP, here are utilization trends for Turning Point's EAP customers from March 2019 through February 2022 with three different stages of the pandemic: pre-COVID-19, during COVID-19, and post-COVID-19.

Stages of Pandemic	Duration
Pre-COVID-19	Mar 2019 - Feb 2020
COVID-19	Mar 2020 - Feb 2021
Post-COVID-19	Mar 2021 - Feb 2022

Table 1: Turning Point's EAP customers' utilisation in percentages throughout the pandemic

Utilisation (%)	PRE COVID-19	DURING COVID-19	POST COVID-19
	27%	39%	34%

Table 2: Trend of utilisation for legal and financial consultations

Type of Issues in EAP Utilisation		
Top 3 Issues at Pre Covid	Top 3 Issues During Covid	Top 3 Issues Post Covid
Family/Interpersonal Relationship	Medical/Psychiatric	Family/Interpersonal Relationship
Medical/Psychiatric	Medical/Psychiatric	Medical/Psychiatric
Organizational Change (Work Related)	Organizational Change (Work Related)	Organizational Change (Work Related)

Table 3: Top three EAP issues throughout the pandemic

Below are the details on the impact of Malaysia EAP:
a. **Increased Demand for Mental Health Support:** Malaysia EAP experienced a surge in demand for their services as employees grappled with the uncertainties and challenges brought about by the pandemic. The pandemic has resulted in increased EAP utilisation,

especially related to medical and psychiatric issues like stress, anxiety, and depression. This is reflected by Turning Point's EAP customers' utilisation: there was an increase by 7% during COVID-19 and subsequently a sharp increase by 48% as compared to pre-COVID-19 (Table 1). The top three issues that consistently appeared throughout the pandemic are Family/Interpersonal, Medical/Psychiatric, and Organizational Change. Medical/Psychiatric was the top-ranked issue during COVID-19 (please refer to Table 3). This further aligned with the Malaysia government's psychosocial hotline data that recorded 37,709 calls between April and September 2020; half of them were related to emotional distress worsened by the pandemic and the Movement Control Order (MCO). The Royal Malaysian Force has also published an alarming figure of 468 suicide cases in Malaysia in just the first five months of 2021, which is a huge surge compared to the annual total of 631 cases in 2020 and 609 cases in 2019.

b. **Financial Well-being and Legal Consultation:** The economic impact of the pandemic has also influenced the utilization of EAPs in terms of financial and legal consultation and assistance. Many employees have faced financial hardships due to job losses, reduced income, or increased financial pressures. EAPs have provided financial consultation, budgeting guidance, and some legal consultation to help employees manage their financial and legal challenges throughout the period of uncertainties. Table 2 shows an increase of 7% in utilisation for legal and financial consultation with Turning Point EAP customers, and the usage subsequently heightened up to 48% as compared to the pre-COVID-19 period.

c. **Impact on Work-Life Balance:** The pandemic has led to a significant shift in the way employees work, with many working from home and facing changes in their work environment. There has been a significant shift toward computer-based working styles, and the majority of tasks have been digitised, which can be stressful to some. Those who were working from home sometimes needed to work more hours than usual; some even reported working 15 hours a day compared to their usual eight hours. In addition, working parents now had an additional responsibility to monitor their children's participation in remote learning activities when at home, which resulted in multitasking and an increased amount of effort. This has led to challenges in maintaining work-life balance, which can impact an employee's mental health and productivity. Table 3 shows work-related stress from organisational changes has remained in the top three before, during, and after the pandemic.

d. **Impact on Relationships:** Due to the Movement Control Order, distancing required lots of new adaptation and effort among family members to further improve family well-being. While working from home heightened more frequent interactions among family members, thus creating quality time and intimate interactions among family members, but it also led to intense conflicts, occasionally domestic violence, and even divorce triggered by past unresolved issues with poor communication and unclear boundaries management. This is reflected in Table 3 with family and interpersonal relationship issues remaining the highest or second highest throughout the pandemic.

e. **Collaborations and Partnerships:** EAPs in Malaysia have collaborated with mental health organizations, health care providers, and government agencies to enhance their support services during the pandemic. These partnerships have facilitated the sharing of resources, expertise, and best practices, allowing EAPs to provide comprehensive assistance to employees. For example, in August 2022, AIA launched a mental health employee insurance programme in Malaysia in collaboration with ThoughtFull, a digital mental health EAP provider. The insurance plan offers unlimited daily digital one-on-one therapy with professionals, a 24/7 wellness hotline, and mental wellness programmes. It includes coverage for employee consultations, medication and treatment as provided by a psychiatrist ("Mental Health Protection for the Workforce," AIA, August 16, 2022).

f. **Expanded Services and Resources:** EAPs in Malaysia have expanded their offerings to address the specific challenges posed by the pandemic. This includes providing resources and guidance on managing stress and anxiety related to COVID-19, coping with remote work, maintaining work-life balance, and dealing with job uncertainties or loss. EAPs have also increased their focus on providing information about vaccination, COVID-19 testing, and safety protocols.

g. **Focus on Mental Health Awareness and Education:** The pandemic has brought mental health to the forefront of discussions, and EAPs in Malaysia have played a significant role in raising awareness about mental health and providing education to employees. EAPs have conducted mental health awareness campaigns, webinars, and training sessions to educate employees about mental health, self-care, stress management, and other relevant topics. These efforts have helped reduce the stigma around mental health, encourage help-seeking behavior, and promote a culture of well-being in the workplace in the long run.

In conclusion, the role of EAPs in supporting employees during the pandemic has highlighted the importance of mental health support in the workplace and has further emphasized the value of EAP services in Malaysia.

EFFECTS OF ONLINE/VIRTUAL EAP SESSIONS

Due to social distancing restrictions, many EAP providers in Malaysia have turned to online/virtual sessions so as to continue providing services to employees; thus, they have significantly impacted the mental health landscape in Malaysia.

The effects of online/virtual consultation sessions in Malaysia EAP are as follows:

a. **Increased Accessibility and Convenience:** Online/virtual consultation has made mental health services more accessible and convenient for Malaysia EAP. Through online platforms, individuals can now access consultation services from the comfort of their own homes, eliminating the need for travel and reducing geographical barriers. This has particularly benefited individuals in rural or remote areas who may have limited access to mental health services.

b. **Expanded Reach and Increased Outreach:** Online/virtual consultations have expanded the reach and increased the outreach of mental health services by Malaysia EAP. Through virtual platforms, individuals can connect with consultants/therapists beyond their immediate geographical location, allowing for a wider range of options in terms of specialty, expertise, and cultural relevance. This has helped to bridge the gap between individuals seeking consultations and the availability of qualified consultants/therapists, particularly for specialized or niche areas of mental health.

c. **Flexibility in Scheduling and Confidentiality:** Online/virtual consultations have provided individuals with greater flexibility in scheduling appointments, making it easier to fit EAP sessions into their busy lives. This has been particularly beneficial for those who may have work or family commitments that limit their ability to attend in-person consultation sessions. Additionally, online/virtual consultation has also ensured confidentiality and privacy, as individuals can seek sessions without the fear of being recognized or stigmatized in their workplace.

d. **Enhanced Comfort and Safety:** Online/virtual counseling has created a safe and comfortable environment for individuals to share their thoughts, emotions, and concerns. Being in a familiar environment such as their own homes can help individuals feel more at ease and open up more freely during sessions. This has facilitated the therapeutic process and promoted a positive therapeutic relationship between clients and therapists, thus encouraging those who hesitate to try EAP sessions to reach out for support.

e. **Technological Challenges and Ethical Considerations:** Online/virtual sessions have also presented some challenges in Malaysia. Technical issues such as poor internet connectivity, disruptions, or privacy concerns can impact the quality and effectiveness of consultation sessions. Ethical considerations such as ensuring client confidentiality, informed consent, and maintaining professional boundaries also need to be carefully addressed in the online/virtual session context.

f. **Increased Acceptance and Integration:** Over time, online/virtual consultations have gained increased acceptance and integration into the mental health landscape in Malaysia EAP. Many individuals now view online/virtual consultations as a legitimate and effective form of mental health support. Mental health professionals and organizations have also embraced online/virtual sessions as a viable mode of service delivery, with many incorporating it into their practice models.

In conclusion, the effects of online/virtual sessions in Malaysia EAP have been significant and become an accepted and integrated form of mental health support, expanding the options and opportunities for individuals to access EAP services in Malaysia.

THE ROLE OF TECHNOLOGY AND SOCIAL MEDIA IN MALAYSIA EAP

Technology and social media have permeated Malaysian society, shaping how people connect, communicate, and access information. This has significantly impacted various aspects of EAP services in Malaysia, and their roles can be further elaborated as follows:

a. **Enhanced Service Delivery:** Technology has revolutionized the way EAP services are delivered in Malaysia. Through digital platforms, EAP providers can offer a wide range of services, including virtual consultations, webinars, self-help resources, and mobile applications. These technological advancements have enabled EAP services to be delivered more efficiently and effectively, reaching a wider audience and providing timely support to employees.

b. **Improved Communication and Engagement:** EAP providers in Malaysia are leveraging social media platforms to disseminate information, share resources, and engage with employees in a more interactive and engaging manner. Social media has also provided a platform for employees to express their concerns, seek support, and engage with EAP services, leading to increased awareness and utilization of EAP services. In 2023, WhatsApp, Facebook, and Instagram are Malaysia's most-used social media platforms for EAP engagement with employees, with WhatsApp being the most-used platform.

c. **Increased Accessibility and Convenience:** Technology and social media have made EAP services more accessible and convenient for employees in Malaysia. Through online platforms and mobile applications, employees can easily access EAP services anytime, anywhere, eliminating the need for physical presence or appointments. This has facilitated the utilization of EAP services, particularly for employees who may have time or location constraints.

d. **Enhanced Data Collection and Analysis:** Technology has enabled EAP providers to collect and analyze data to gain insights into employee needs and preferences. Through digital platforms, EAP providers can collect data on employee utilization patterns, feedback, and outcomes, which can be used to inform program improvement and decision-making. This data-driven approach has facilitated evidence-based practice in the EAP market in Malaysia, leading to more effective and targeted interventions.

e. **Challenges and Ethical Considerations:** The role of technology and social media in the EAP market in Malaysia also presents challenges and ethical considerations. Data privacy and security, confidentiality, and ethical use of social media are critical considerations that EAP providers need to address. Ensuring that technology and social media are used ethically and responsibly in the delivery of EAP services is crucial to maintain trust and confidentiality with employees. In Malaysia, the Personal Data Protection Act (PDPA) is an act enacted by the government and was established on 15 November 2013 to protect individual personal data and sensitive personal data in commercial transactions. In order to bring the PDPA in line with global data protection standards and also to address issues arising from the emerging ways of using and processing personal data, the Malaysian Government planned to table the proposed amendments to the PDPA by the end of 2023.

In conclusion, the role of technology and social media has had a significant impact on the EAP market in Malaysia; however, challenges and ethical considerations need to be carefully addressed to ensure responsible and effective use of technology and social media in the delivery of EAP services in Malaysia.

EFFORTS TOWARD DIVERSITY AND INCLUSION WITHIN THE FIELD OF EAP

Diversity and inclusion have gained increasing attention in the Employee Assistance Program (EAP) market in Malaysia, where the population is diverse and multicultural made up by different types of ethnic groups and religions, including Malays, Chinese, Indian, and the local native. Efforts have been made to ensure that consultants, providers, and clients are inclusive and diverse in various aspects, and details can be summarized as follows:

a. **Inclusive Hiring and Workforce Diversity:** EAP providers in Malaysia are recognizing the importance of having a diverse and inclusive workforce, including consultants, therapists, and providers. Efforts are being made to ensure that hiring processes are inclusive, fair, and unbiased, and that diverse candidates are actively sought and considered for employment. This includes efforts to promote diversity in terms of gender, race, ethnicity, religion, age, disability, and other dimensions.

b. **Cultural Competence and Sensitivity:** EAP customers and providers in Malaysia are being encouraged to develop cultural competence and sensitivity to ensure that they can effectively serve a diverse client base. This includes understanding and respecting the cultural norms, ethnics, beliefs, religions, and values of different clients, and tailoring interventions accordingly. Efforts are being made to provide training and education on cultural competence and sensitivity to EAP consultants and providers to ensure that they can provide inclusive and effective services to clients from diverse backgrounds.

c. **Accessibility and Inclusivity in Service Delivery:** EAP providers in Malaysia are striving to make their services accessible and inclusive to clients with different needs and abilities. This includes efforts to provide services in multiple languages (English, Malay, Mandarin, Tamil, and some local dialects), accommodate clients with disabilities, provide alternative formats of resources, and ensure that services are available to all employees, including those from marginalized or underrepresented groups. EAP providers are also working to eliminate any barriers or biases that may hinder employees from seeking or utilizing EAP services.

d. **Tailored Interventions for Diverse Populations:** EAP providers in Malaysia are recognizing the importance of tailoring interventions to the unique needs and challenges of diverse populations. This includes efforts to develop culturally relevant interventions, resources, and strategies that are specific to different groups, such as women, LGBTQ+ employees, employees with disabilities, employees from different ethnic or religious backgrounds, and employees from other underrepresented or marginalized groups. EAP providers are also working to address issues related to discrimination, bias, and systemic inequities that may impact the well-being of diverse employees.

In conclusion, efforts toward diversity and inclusion are gaining momentum in the EAP market in Malaysia, with a focus on inclusive hiring, cultural competence, accessibility, tailored interventions, and promoting inclusive policies and practices. These efforts are aimed at ensuring that EAP services are inclusive, accessible, and effective for all employees, regardless of their background or identity. On the contrary, more effort is still very much needed for issues related to LGBTQ+, as it remains a sensitive issue in Malaysia.

ABOUT THE AUTHOR

Wilson Tee is the Managing Director and Founder of Turning Point Integrated Wellness Sdn Bhd, part of the ICAS World, a Lyra Health Company Group. He is a Malaysia Registered and Licensed Counselor (KB,PA), graduated from Universiti Putra Malaysia with a Bachelor of Honours Degree in AgriBusiness (1994) and later obtained a Master's Degree in Guidance & Counseling (2009) from Universiti Kebangsaan Malaysia. Wilson provides counseling to individual, family, workplace, and specific groups specialized in career development, and conducts training programs and public talks targeting corporate companies and the larger community. The past 16 years, he has worked with a whole range of corporate and public clients in the areas of training (including topics on mental health, stress management, mindfulness, etc.), change and transition management, crisis intervention, coaching, consultation, and EAP support.

RESOURCES

No	Detail	Name
1	Psychiatrist	Dr. Lee Aik Hoe (Klinik Pakar A.H. Lee)
2	Psychiatrist	Dr. Phang Cheng Kar (Sunway Medical Centre)
3	Psychiatrist	Dr. Ting Joe Hang (Klinik Pakar Psikiatri Ting)
4	Psychiatrist	Dr. Yeoh Seen Heng (Klink Pakar Dr. Yeoh & Dr. Hazli)
5	NGO Helpline	Talian Kasih – 15999
6	NGO Helpline	Befrienders (24/7) – 03-76272929
7	NGO Helpline	Malaysia Mental Health Association (9am-9pm) – 03-27806803
8	NGO Helpline	Buddy Bear (6pm-11:59pm) – 1800182327
9	NGO Helpline	MIASA (24/7) – 1800820066
10	NGO Helpline	Lifeline (Chinese, 10am-8pm, Saturday 2pm-5pm) – 03-42657995
11	Head, Neck & Shoulder Massage / Reflexology	Wellness Art Training Centre
12	Aroma Therapy	Lohas Association of Aromatherapy Malaysia
13	Clinical Psychologist	Loo Mei Chien, ParkCity Medical Centre
14	Clinical Psychologist	Loh Sit Fong, Silver Lining Psychology Specialist
15	Clinical Psychologist	Aina Nur Azmi, Valley Psych
16	Clinical Psychologist	Lim Maureen, Pantai Hospital Cheras

17	Clinical Psychologist	Selina Ding, Ding Child Psychological Services
18	Financial Counseling	Agensi Kaunseling & Pengurusan Kredit (AKPK) Financial Counseling
19	NGO Counseling	Bahagian Kaunseling & Psikologi, Jabatan Kebajikan Masyarakat
20	Hospice	Kasih Hospice Care Society
21	Hospice	Malaysian Hospice Council
22	Hospice	Pure Lotus Hospice of Compassion
23	HIV & STD Testing Counselling	PT Foundation - Community Health Care Centre
24	HIV/AIDS Education Prevention Care and Support Programmes Sexual Health and Empowerment Programmes	PT Foundation
25	Provide Access to Safe Spaces Support Sustainable Livelihood Facilitate Access to Health Care Services Shelter Home for Elderly Transgender Aids for HIV Patients	Seed Foundation/ Pertubuhan Kebajikan dan Persekitaran Positif Malaysia
26	Support Group	National Stroke Association of Malaysia (NASAM)
27	Support Group	National Cancer Council (MAKNA)
28	Support Group	Breast Cancer Welfare Association Malaysia (BCWA)
29	Caregiver Support Group	National Dementia Caregivers Support Network
30	NGO Addictions Centre	Malaysian Substance Abuse Council (MASAC) (Malaysia)
31	Treatment Rehabilitation Centre	Cure & Care Rehabilitation Centre (Bahagian Rawatan, Perubatan & Pemulihan)
32	Private Centre for Addiction	Serene Retreat

33	Psychiatry Department (treatment of drug and alcohol abuse and dependence, quit smoking)	Damai Service Hospital
34	Treatment, Rehab, and Training	Agensi Antidadah Kebangsaan
35	Legal Aid	Bar Council Malaysia 15 Leboh Pasar Besar, 50050 Kuala Lumpur, Malaysia
36	Shelter Homes / Domestic Violence Victims	Women's Aid Organization (WAO)
37	HIV/AIDS Women and Children Transsexuals Shelter Home for HIV Victims Counselling for Sex Workers	Women & Health Association of Kuala Lumpur (WAKE)
38	Marginalized and Disadvantage Women Counselling Guidance and Programme	Good Shepherd Services
39	Sanctuary for Abused, Neglected and Underprivileged Children Between the Ages of 5–17.	Rumah Hope
40	Foster Homes Financial Aid Poor & Needy	Malaysian Children's Aid Society (MACAS)
41	Child Protection Counselling Centre Needy Children	Suriana Welfare Society
42	Females with Mental Disabilities	Pusat Cahaya Kesihatan

43	Dyslexia Autism Cerebral Palsy ADHD Down Syndrome Slow Learners	CADS Enhancement Centre
44	Adults with Physical Disability	Damai Disabled Person Association Malaysia
45	Individuals with Physical Disabilities Children with Mental Disability	Pusat Penjagaan Kanak-Kanak Cacat Taman Megah
46	Shelter Home Children with Physical Disability Underprivileged Children Adults Old Folks	Kirtarsh Handicapped and Disabled Children's Home
47	Children with Innate Mental Disabilities	Tasputra Perkim
48	Occupational Therapist Centre	Sau Seng Lum (PJ) Paediatric Rehabilitation Centre
49	Autism	The National Autism Society of Malaysia (NASOM)
50	Autism	Pusat PERMATA Kurnia
51	Women's Shelters	Women's Aid Organisation
52	Women's Shelters / Childcare	Good Shepherd Services
53	Dyslexia	Persatuan Dyslexia Malaysia (HQ)
54	Elderly Care	Nurses At Home
55	Physiological Rehabilitation	National Stroke Association of Malaysia (NASAM)

MEXICO

Deborah Loffler

ICAS Mexico is a business unit in Intersistemas that began operations in Mexico in 2006, when ICAS International Limited partnered with Intersistemas, S.A. de C.V.

The ICAS Mexico Unit (Employee Well-being and Assistance Programs) promotes through its services not only emotional health in organizations but also employee wellness. Focused on the management of psychosocial risks, they develop programs that facilitate the balance between the personal and work lives of employees of companies of different geographical scope, activity, and size. Our programs emphasize providing tools for stress management but also extend to emotional, legal, financial, and healthy eating strategies, as well as wellness coaching and other aspects related to work.

Each program is designed to meet the needs and budget of the client. ICAS Mexico currently covers over 500,000 lives (employees) and offers a network of affiliated psychologists of more than 350 professionals, established in the Mexican Republic, countries in Central America, the Dominican Republic, and Venezuela, who provide high-quality assistance to employees of important companies, national and multinational, and leaders in their activity sectors. Our national and international coverage ensures excellent attention to our clients' employees.

ICAS Mexico has developed programs, talks, and educational workshops either in-person or online at the request of our clients with the aim of promoting health, well-being, and productivity.

Aligned with NOM 35 of the STYPS, we have content that contributes to the reduction of psychosocial risk factors such as addictions, stress management, good sleep, work motivation, equity and respect in the workplace, and emotional health, among others. Also, we generate actions and strategies that contribute to the fulfillment of norms and regulations, such as the NOM.035 STYPS. It is important to mention that Employee Wellness and Assistance Programs support the compliance of NOM.035 from the Secretary of Labor and Social Welfare in Mexico. Therefore, we have developed different tools to facilitate the implementation of initiatives in organizations that help identify psychosocial risk factors and demonstrate actions to prevent them. Additionally, we provide support following traumatic incidents in companies, with Critical Incident Management services where ICAS consultants will immediately respond to the consequences of a critical incident.

Lastly, it is important to mention that for over 20 years, Intersistemas, through the Total Well-being Unit, has had exclusive representation of Mayo Clinic content in the Spanish language. Leveraging this relationship, the ICAS Mexico Unit, together with the Total Well-being Unit, has created synergies that offer added value to our clients, such as the web app available in web and responsive versions. Its main goal is to educate and motivate employees and their families about the importance of physical and emotional health care. It also promotes the adoption of healthy habits and helps employees reduce physical, emotional, and psychosocial risks. It provides information, action plans, recommendations, tips, suggestions, and routines on adopting a healthy physical and emotional lifestyle, with a preventive and health promotion approach.

The impact of our services during the pandemic was to support our clients in the uncertainty of the situation that created stress, changes, losses, and adaptations. These types of problems were the ones that we identified as having the greatest negative impact on the general population. The fact that our programs have services that provide integrated support, not only emotional help, played a significant role for our clients.

LIFESTYLE

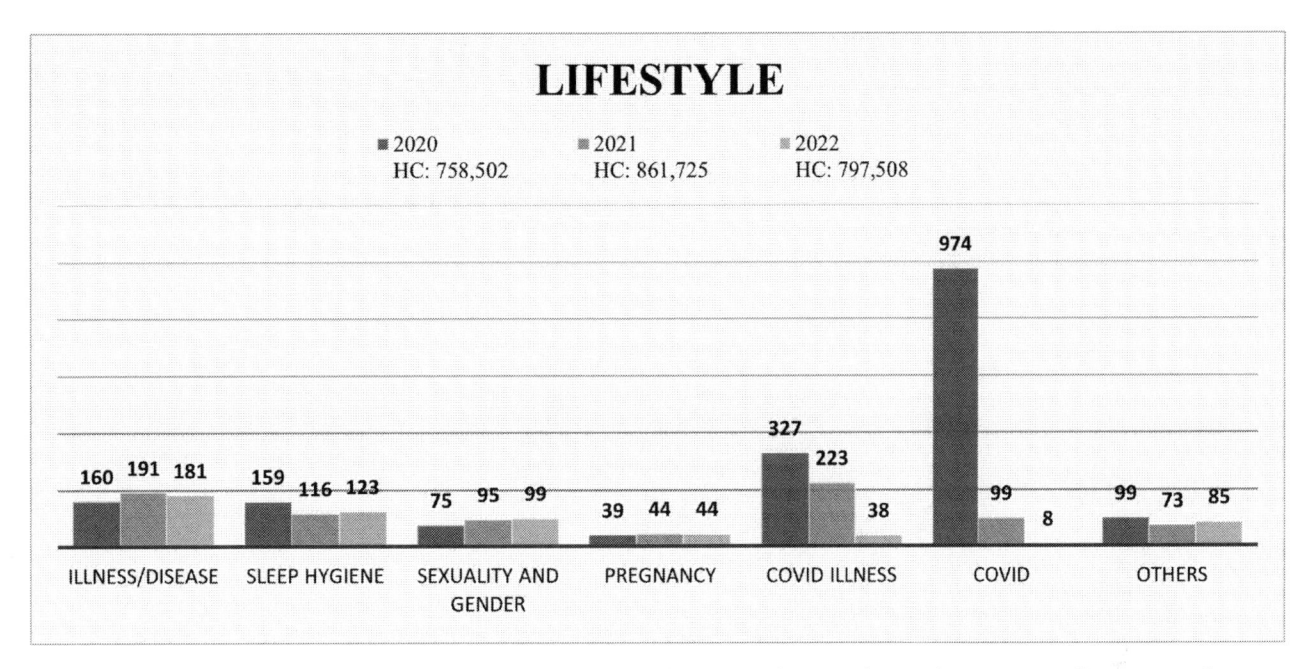

- 2020 HC: 758,502
- 2021 HC: 861,725
- 2022 HC: 797,508

Category	2020	2021	2022
ILLNESS/DISEASE	160	191	181
SLEEP HYGIENE	159	116	123
SEXUALITY AND GENDER	75	95	99
PREGNANCY	39	44	44
COVID ILLNESS	327	223	38
COVID	974	99	8
OTHERS	99	73	85

Having professional support in rebuilding family relationships during confinement, learning new ways of relating through technology, and achieving a balance between work activities at home, school, home, and family life was one of the main challenges.

Another situation where the impact of clinical support was very visible is the issue of loss. Helping in the grief process, we were able to provide support to people who experienced the loss of one or more loved ones, the loss of health, and other losses related to the rhythm of life prior to the pandemic.

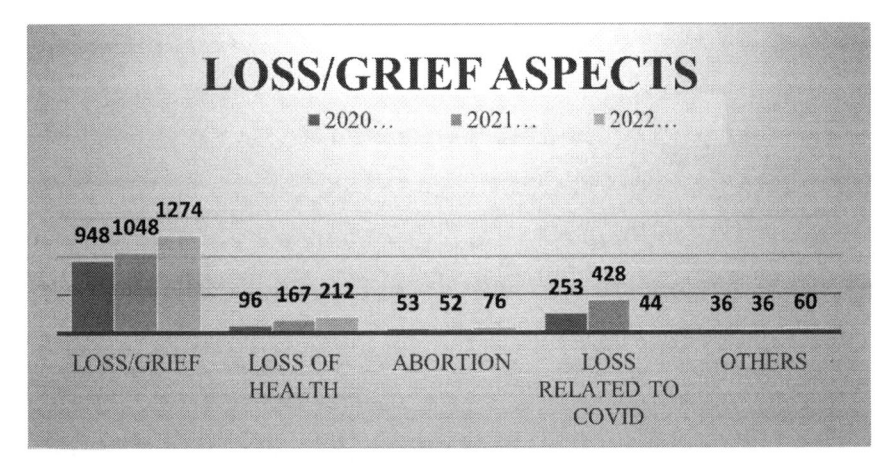

LOSS/GRIEF ASPECTS

- 2020...
- 2021...
- 2022...

Category	2020	2021	2022
LOSS/GRIEF	948	1048	1274
LOSS OF HEALTH	96	167	212
ABORTION	53	52	76
LOSS RELATED TO COVID	253	428	44
OTHERS	36	36	60

Being able to have an immediate professional response 24 hours and 7 days a week, not only for employees, leaders, Human Resources, and Health team members but also for family members, generated a support tool in different fields. Emotional help was, of course, the most requested and provided service, but the information service was also very useful. Many collaborators called to understand the procedures and requirements of hospitals, cancellation of trips, events, etc., and the service helped them reduce the stress of not knowing how to solve these issues.

During the pandemic, we were allies and partners of our clients, always looking beyond and working on digital materials to promote prevention and mental health, return-to-work protocols, and the development of topics for online talks related to what people were living at the moment because of the global health crisis.

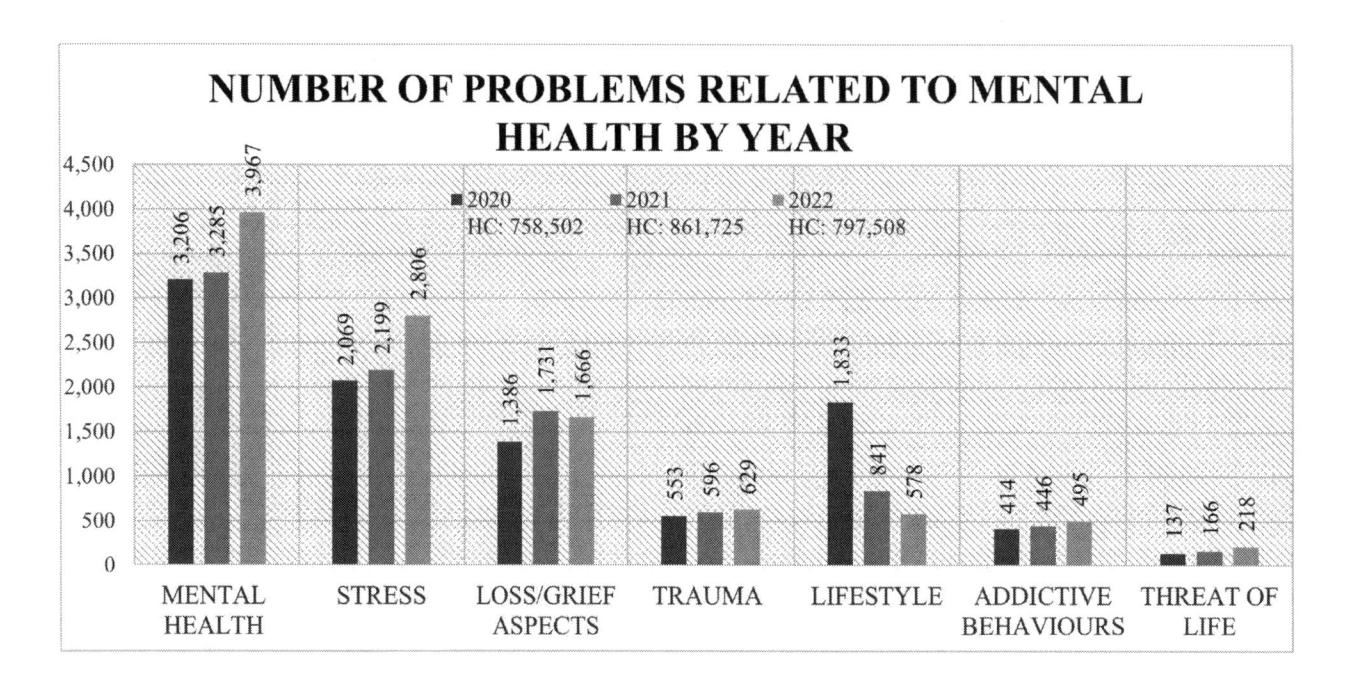

NUMBER OF PROBLEMS RELATED TO MENTAL HEALTH BY YEAR

Category	2020 (HC: 758,502)	2021 (HC: 861,725)	2022 (HC: 797,508)
MENTAL HEALTH	3,206	3,285	3,967
STRESS	2,069	2,199	2,806
LOSS/GRIEF ASPECTS	1,386	1,731	1,666
TRAUMA	553	596	629
LIFESTYLE	1,833	841	578
ADDICTIVE BEHAVIOURS	414	446	495
THREAT OF LIFE	137	166	218

THE EFFECTS OF ONLINE/VIRTUAL COUNSELING

The conditions derived from confinement led to changes in traditional care models, so incorporating virtual emotional counseling made it easier for users to access the service without the need to expose their health.

At the beginning of the pandemic, many people preferred to wait for face-to-face emotional support; however, since it was evident that the end of the pandemic would not be soon, there was a greater openness to the online help, and today, some people see virtual online emotional sessions as an advantage over on-site support, plus not having to travel.

The use of technology such as video calls had an impact to maintain constant communication with our clients. Since all face-to-face meetings were cancelled, it was important to maintain close communication to listen and attend to specific needs. In addition to this, we were able to know and implement different video conferencing platforms such as Zoom, Microsoft Teams, Skype, Google, etc. to continue facilitating conferences and educational talks on different topics.

At this moment, we do not have social networks; however, we did renovate our app as a way of contact, adding the option of contacting us by chat.

Our internal operational technology has played a fundamental role in helping us to be able to adapt our operation to the challenges that have arisen at different times during the pandemic, maintaining operations without interruptions.

With our users, it has been a support to be able to access forms of virtual attention, although it has also been a challenge since in Mexico and countries that we cover, not all people have access to technology or the adequate technology to receive the support.

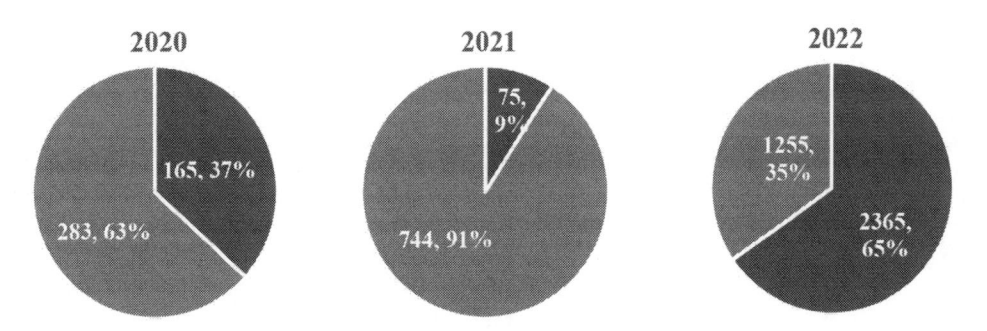

2020: 165, 37%; 283, 63%
2021: 75, 9%; 744, 91%
2022: 1255, 35%; 2365, 65%

In an environment of sudden changes such as the pandemic, being able to generate valuable materials for our clients was of vital importance, not only in traditional issues of diversity and inclusion (LGBTQ+ population, gender, etc.) but also in understanding that in times of a pandemic, the collaborators had to reintegrate into their workplace after suffering from COVID-19, and it was of great help to the clients.

In customer service, we have sought to sensitize consultants on issues of diversity and inclusion, always promoting the respectful treatment of each person.

NUMBER OF FACE TO FACE PER YEAR

■ Face to Face Counseling   ■ Virtual Face to Face Counseling

NUMBER OF SERVICES PER YEAR

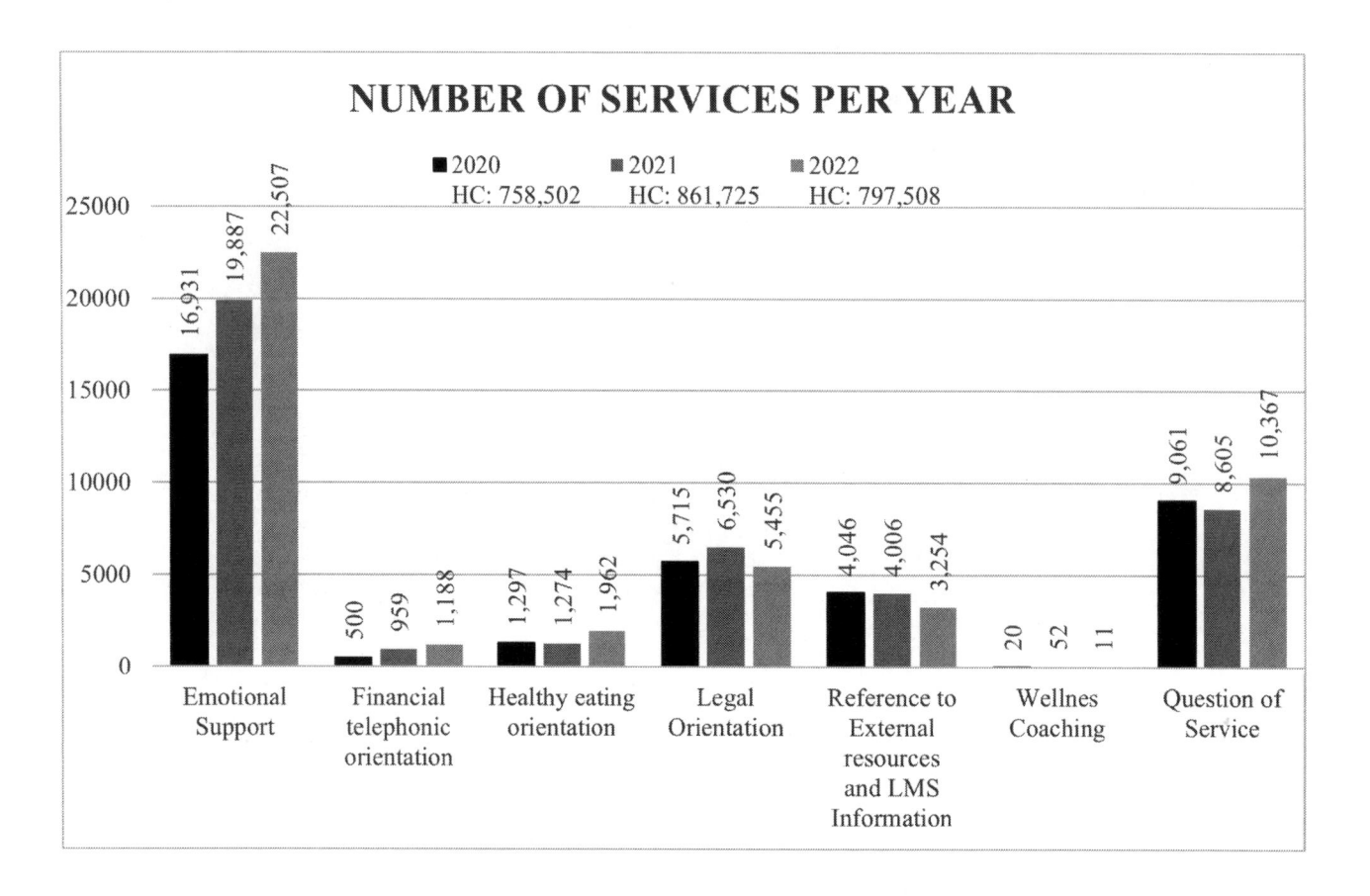

Service	2020 (HC: 758,502)	2021 (HC: 861,725)	2022 (HC: 797,508)
Emotional Support	16,931	19,887	22,507
Financial telephonic orientation	500	959	1,188
Healthy eating orientation	1,297	1,274	1,962
Legal Orientation	5,715	6,530	5,455
Reference to External resources and LMS Information	4,046	4,006	3,254
Wellnes Coaching	20	52	11
Question of Service	9,061	8,605	10,367

NUMBER OF PROBLEMS PER YEAR

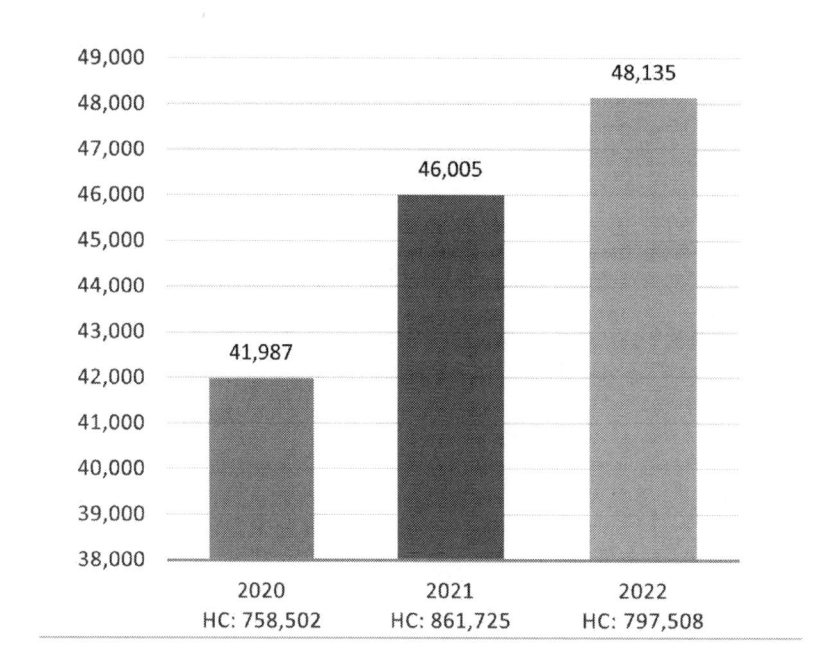

2020 (HC: 758,502)	41,987
2021 (HC: 861,725)	46,005
2022 (HC: 797,508)	48,135

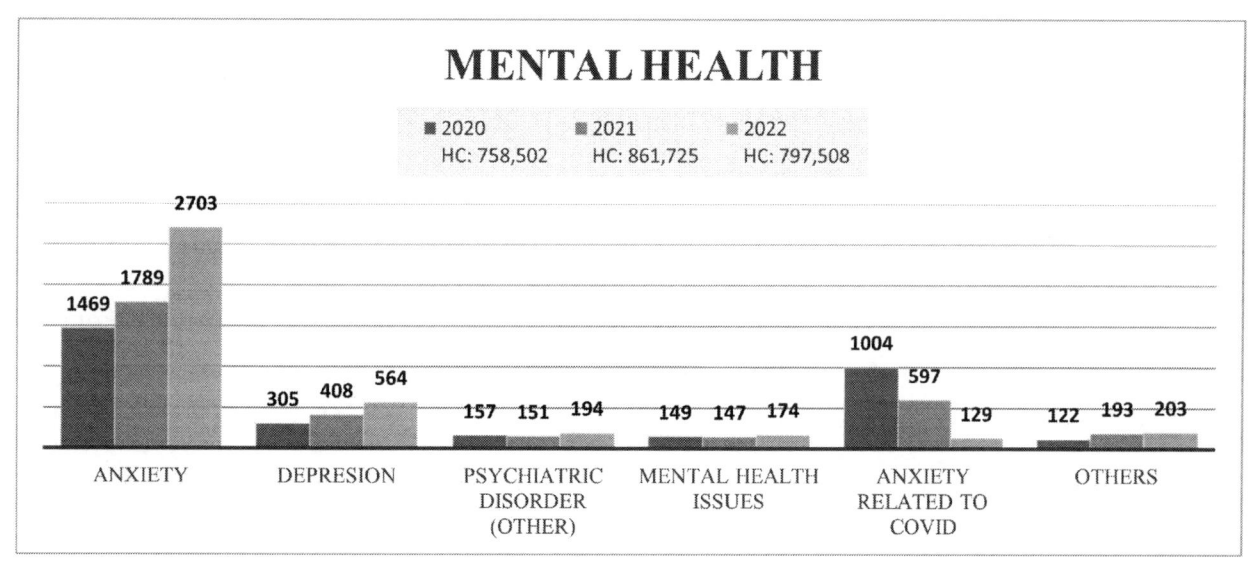

MENTAL HEALTH

2020 HC: 758,502 | **2021** HC: 861,725 | **2022** HC: 797,508

Category	2020	2021	2022
ANXIETY	1469	1789	2703
DEPRESION	305	408	564
PSYCHIATRIC DISORDER (OTHER)	157	151	194
MENTAL HEALTH ISSUES	149	147	174
ANXIETY RELATED TO COVID	1004	597	129
OTHERS	122	193	203

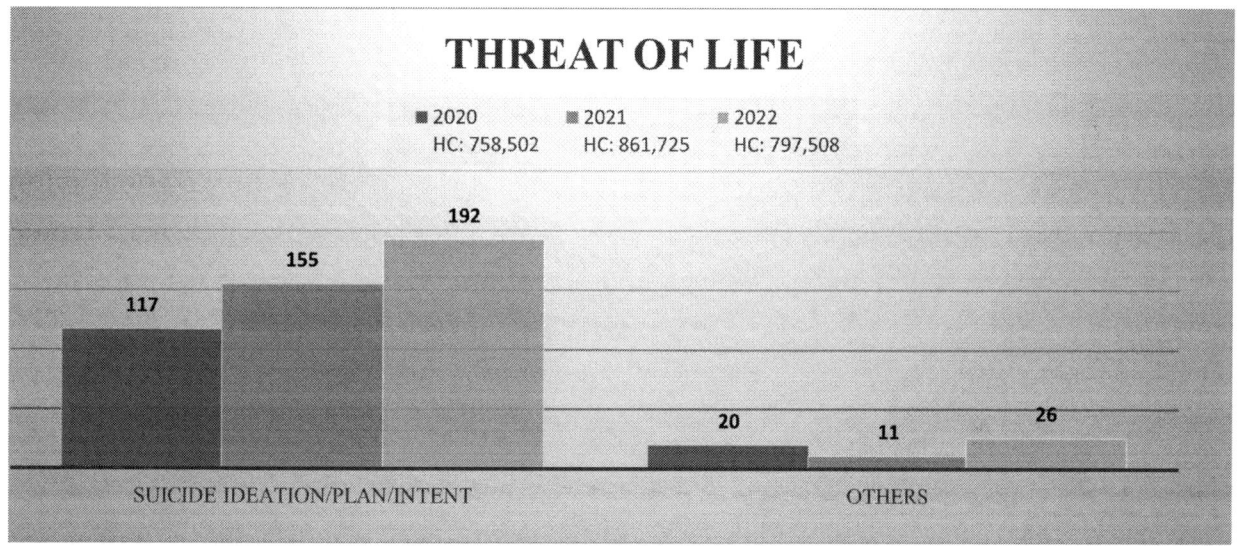

THREAT OF LIFE

2020 HC: 758,502 | **2021** HC: 861,725 | **2022** HC: 797,508

Category	2020	2021	2022
SUICIDE IDEATION/PLAN/INTENT	117	155	192
OTHERS	20	11	26

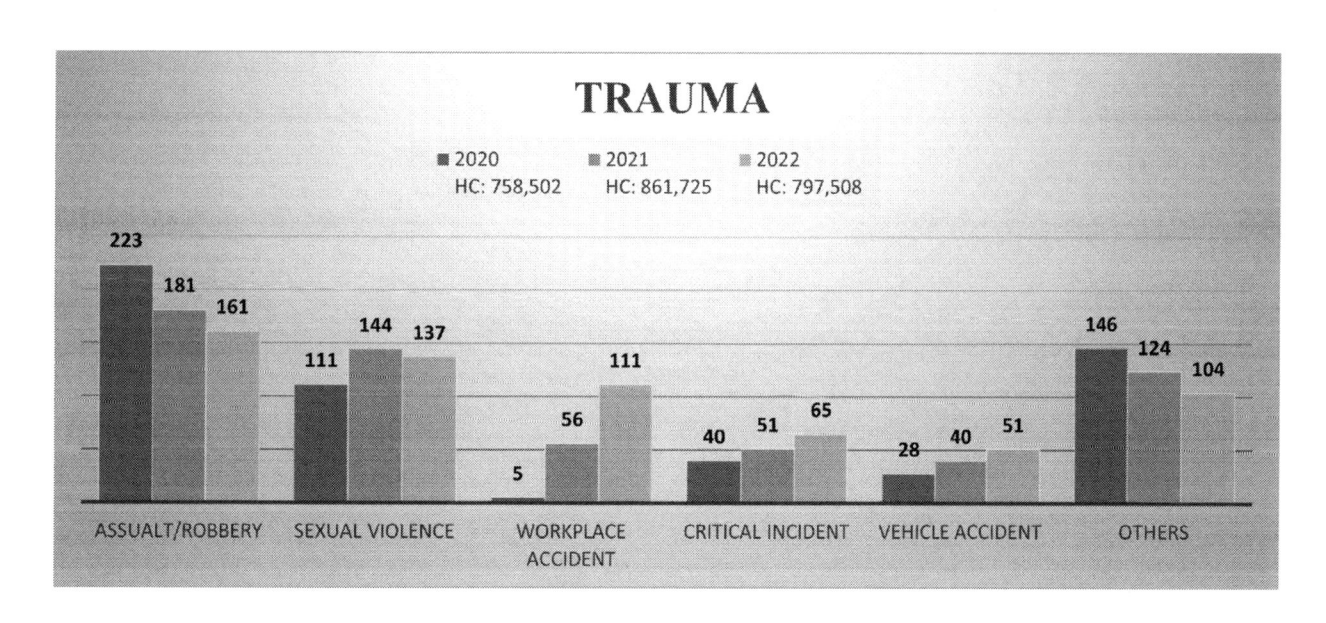

TRAUMA

2020 HC: 758,502 | **2021** HC: 861,725 | **2022** HC: 797,508

Category	2020	2021	2022
ASSUALT/ROBBERY	223	181	161
SEXUAL VIOLENCE	111	144	137
WORKPLACE ACCIDENT	5	56	111
CRITICAL INCIDENT	40	51	65
VEHICLE ACCIDENT	28	40	51
OTHERS	146	124	104

ADDICTIVE BEHAVIOURS

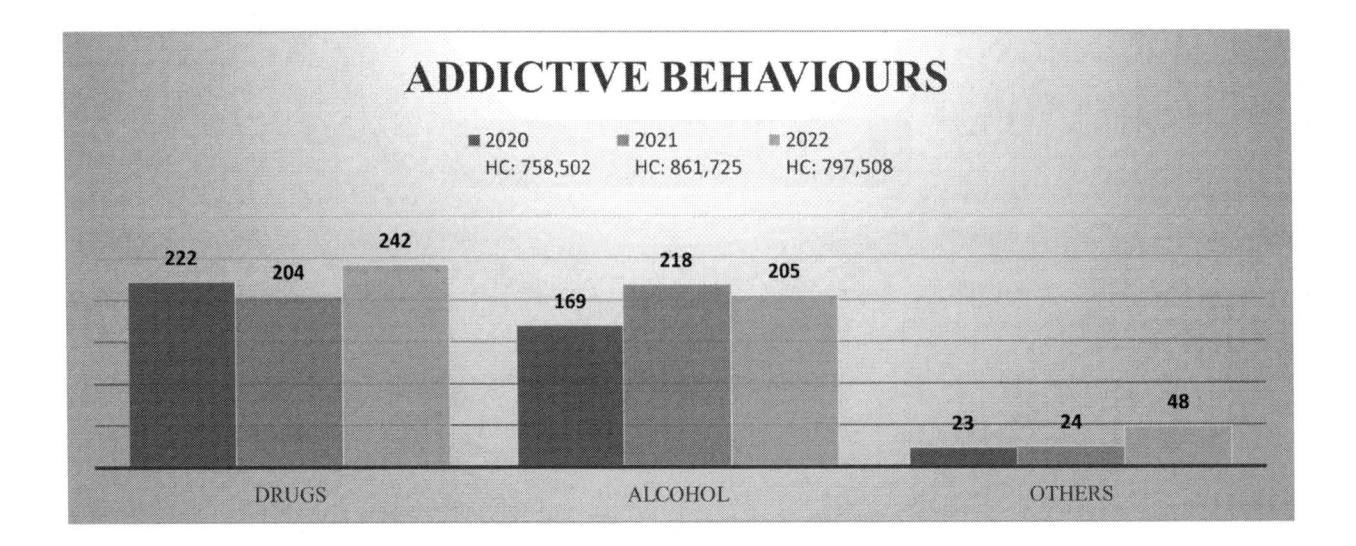

	2020 HC: 758,502	2021 HC: 861,725	2022 HC: 797,508
DRUGS	222	204	242
ALCOHOL	169	218	205
OTHERS	23	24	48

ABOUT THE AUTHOR

Deborah Loffler is based in Mexico City and has a BA in Psychology at the Iberoamericana University in Mexico and a Master's Degree in Forensic Psychology at John Jay College (CUNY) in New York. She worked in Dupont México in HR and then trained to provide EAP services. She started 20 years ago as a Telephonic Counselor at a previous EAP provider and afterward was promoted as the Operational Manager.

Since 2016, in ICAS Mexico, her role is the Business Unit director, and she has implemented Employee Assistance Programs and Managed Triple AAA Accounts of international companies in the Latin American region. She was certified as a Wellness Coach by Well Coaches Organization.

MONGOLIA

Khongorzul Amarsanaa and Enkhchimeg Purvee

INTRODUCTION

EAP Mongolia was launched in May 2012. At the time, the EAP Mongolia service was the very first service in the country run by local Mongolian psychologists. As a psychologist, I (Khongorzul Amarsanaa) was approached by Chestnut Global Partners (now Telus Health) as the local provider in Mongolia. I agreed immediately because it was the sector I had never worked in before. Then, I approached my friend/colleague, psychologist Enkhchimeg Purvee, to be a co-founder/provider with me. It was an exciting moment for us to work with employees and focus on their psychological well-being. At the time, psychological well-being was unheard of; mental health used to be stigmatised. The general public used to hold the idea that mental health issues are only for certain people, and only "insane" people seek support from professionals.

That's why our EAP service was unique in its nature. We were committed to contributing to the development of psychological care by introducing a totally new service to Mongolian employees and their family members. Attracting the Mongolian employees and their family members took us quite a few years. Before the launch, there were preliminary preparations for the Mongolian psychologists. In order to be part of the EAP, we had to complete the EAP online course. The online course was very fruitful because the curriculum was comprehensive and the discussion sessions and the homework were meaningful. Upon the completion of our online training and certification, we officially started providing EAP to companies in Mongolia.

THE IMPACT OF SERVICES DURING THE PANDEMIC

The COVID-19 pandemic, declared by the World Health Organization in March 2020, prompted governments worldwide to implement lockdown measures to mitigate its spread. Mongolia was among the earliest countries to enforce a lockdown, which included the closure of educational institutions and limited access to essential services. This unique experience significantly impacted people's psychosocial well-being, leading to psychological issues such as depression, stress, fear, anxiety, frustration, and insecurity. During the lockdown, the Employee Assistance Program (EAP) was vital in providing psychological support to management, employees, and their families. We illustrate here the response of EAP offering counseling services and psychoeducation training and the benefits of confidentiality and anonymity in encouraging employees to seek help.

The COVID-19 pandemic profoundly affected global communities, necessitating unprecedented measures to curb its transmission. Mongolia's prompt response in declaring a lockdown in January 2020 set it apart from other countries (Erkhembayar et al., 2020; Tumenbayar et al., 2020). However, policies, regulations, and restrictions were not user-friendly (Urandelger & Otgonsuren, 2021) and had adverse consequences on the psychosocial well-being of the population (Amarsanaa et al., 2021).

The lockdown measures introduced in Mongolia caused uncertainty and distress among the population. Various studies have highlighted the psychological issues experienced by individuals, including depression, stress, fear, anxiety, frustration, and insecurity (Amarsanaa et al., 2021; Yin et al., 2020). Vulnerable people, including our clients, such as those with young children, elderly family members, disabilities, or chronic illnesses, faced additional challenges due to restricted access to essential services and medical support.

Right before the lockdown, two of our counselors were working on-site for two days, and then on the day of the return, the government announced the lockdown. Thus, our providers were stuck there until further notice. Although our counselors were affected by the lockdown, they still provided services to the employees.

Despite the challenging circumstances, EAP Mongolia demonstrated resilience in continuing its services during the pandemic. EAP counselors offered 24/7 psychological counseling to employees and their immediate family members through the telephone and online. Additionally, providing psychoeducation workshops upon request proved instrumental in promoting healthy coping strategies, problem-solving skills, and effective communication among participants.

During this extended lockdown, employees worked for up to 100 days on-site. This lockdown affected their lives back home. For example, people with young children, elderly family members, disabilities, or chronic illnesses could not go home. Back home, their vulnerable family members were locked down without any help. Family members who needed medical support didn't have access to it. Also, people who were working in the depth of the mines were having horrid experiences during winter due to not seeing sunlight and being overworked for continued long days. Tragically, some experienced the loss of their beloved ones.

EAP Mongolia adopted innovative approaches to reach a wider audience. Live sessions on social media platforms were conducted regularly, focusing on various psychological well-being topics. These sessions provided a platform for participants to engage actively, share experiences, empathize with others, and learn from one another, fostering a sense of community support during challenging times.

The significance of confidentiality and anonymity played a critical role in encouraging employees to seek help. With no need to prove identity, employees felt confident in utilizing the services without fear of judgment or stigma. This anonymity facilitated an open and safe space for individuals to address their mental health concerns without hesitation.

CONCLUSION

The COVID-19 pandemic presented unprecedented challenges to the mental well-being of individuals in Mongolia. However, the timely response of EAP in providing psychological counseling and psychoeducation workshops proved to be an invaluable resource for employees and their families. The confidential and anonymous nature of EAP services further encouraged individuals to seek help and support, contributing to the overall psychosocial resilience of the population during these trying times. Moving forward, it is essential to recognize the significance of EAPs in maintaining psychological well-being and to continue prioritizing mental health support during future crises.

ABOUT THE AUTHORS

Khongorzul Amarsanaa: EAP Mongolia co-founder and national coordinator Khongorzul Amarsanaa is a qualified psychologist and has been working since 2005 with various communities on diverse issues such as personal emotional problems, anxiety, depression, cross-cultural issues, expatriates, repatriates, and family and couple relationships. She provides trauma-informed psychotherapy to survivors of domestic/sexual violence and develops/delivers capacity-building training to key stakeholders, employees, and managers. Moreover, she advocates policies to build a survivor-friendly environment. In addition, she worked to develop grassroots networks to empower and educate people involved in the local development process in both peri-urban and rural areas in Mongolia. Khongorzul Amarsanaa received EAP certificate in 2012 from Dr.

Dale Masi through American Catholic University. Currently, she is a PhD candidate at Eotvos Lorende University, Hungary. She completed a BA in Psychology at Webster University, a Master's in Counselling from Monash University through the Australian Leadership Award, and an MSc in Social Research Methods from the University of Sussex, UK, through the Chevening Scholarship. She is a member of APS Australian Psychological Society, ISSTD International Society for Study of Trauma and Dissociation, EACLIPT European Association of Clinical Psychology and Treatment, AWID International Feminist Women's Rights Organization, and AAWS Asian Association of Women's Studies.

Enkhchimeg Purvee: EAP Mongolia co-founder and local provider Enkhchimeg Purvee is a qualified psychologist and has been working since 2008 with diverse groups on issues of addictions, emotional problems, (complex) trauma, anxiety, depression, critical incident stress management, expatriates, and repatriates. She specialises in trauma psychotherapy and serves survivors of domestic violence and child sexual abuse. Enkhchimeg Purvee develops and delivers training and workshops on improving the psychosocial well-being of individuals and groups. She holds an MSc in Clinical Psychology from National University of Mongolia. Enkhchimeg Purvee completed the EAP course and received the certificate from Dr. Dale Masi through the University of Maryland. She is a member of the American Psychological Society.

REFERENCES

Amarsanaa, K., Rácz, J., & Kovács, M. (2021). *Case Study: Effects of the COVID-19 Lockdown Restrictions on Case Study: Effects of the COVID-19 Lockdown Restrictions on Eight Mongolian Single Mothers Eight Mongolian Single Mothers.* https://vc.bridgew.edu/jiws/vol22/iss12/5

Erkhembayar, R., Dickinson, E., Badarch, D., Narula, I., Thomas, G. N., Ochir, C., & Manaseki-Holland, S. (2020). Early policy actions and emergency response to the COVID-19 pandemic in Mongolia: experiences and challenges. *The Lancet Global Health, 20.* https://doi.org/10.1016/S2214-109X(20)30295-3

Tumenbayar, B., Anuurad, E., & Enkhmaa, B. (2020). COVID-19 and public health efforts in Mongolia: A lesson maybe learned? *Journal of Clinical and Translational Science.*

Urandelger, G., & Otgonsuren, Y. (2021). The Socio-Cultural Impact of COVID-19. *Global Culture Review*, *12*(1), 55–77. https://unesdoc.unesco.org/ark:/48223/pf0000374186.pdf

Yin, X., Wang, J., Feng, J., Chen, Z., Jiang, N., Wu, J., Yan, S., Li, H., Lv, C., Lu, Z., & Gong, Y. (2020). The Impact of the Corona Virus Disease 2019 Outbreak on Chinese Residents' Mental Health. *Bulletin of the World Health Organization*, *April*. https://doi.org/http://dx.doi.org/10.2471/BLT.20.258475

NETHERLANDS

Francien Resius

COMPANY COUNSELORS IN THE NETHERLANDS

At the moment, there are 252 registered Company Counselors in the Netherlands. We know there are more experts working in this field, as there is no legal obligation yet to register. But the companies I worked for, including the government, only work with registered Company Counselors.

It's a good development that more and more organizations have job offers for Company Counselors. More organizations realize that it's important to pay attention to the mental health of employees and to stimulate and offer direct support to prevent sick leave and outflow of staff. As organizations have a mission to keep employees motivated, the support of the mental health of the employees is very important. A Company Counselor can really make the difference in situations where employees need direct mental support.

HOW I BECAME A COMPANY COUNSELOR

In 1988, I finished my University Educational Sciences in Amsterdam. During my studies, I worked for a Telephone Helpline (hotline for people who needed emotional support after watching a television program with a social/emotional impact). So, my first job after university was very interesting. A big Dutch bank (later ING BANK) asked me to organize a telephone helpline for the personnel of the bank. The idea was that every person who worked at this bank was able to get mental and social support from a social expert when they experienced stress or a mental need.

This project became a success, and after a few years, I had a department with three occupational social workers. After 10 years, we worked with 20 occupational social workers (Company Counselors).

We worked with the Hotline (the telephone helpline was always open during working hours), conversations were confidential, and people could also make face-to-face appointments. Our services were offered to all managers and employees to address individual, team, and organizational problems. Our services included counseling and support for all kinds of mental, social, and work-related issues like stress management, caregiver support such as eldercare and childcare, mental health issues, bereavement, addictions, and financial problems. We always cooperated with the company doctor, HR, and other experts. We also supported the employees after, for example, a bank robbery or other crisis situation.

Besides our work as counselors, we also offered workshops that covered a variety of topics, like Social Security, dealing with changes at work or at home, stress management, strengthening your resilience, informal care, work, etc.

Yearly, we prepared an annual report for management. Our goals were always to support the employees in emotional and social needs, so they were able to work with positive energy and stimulate an open and positive company culture.

In 2019, I left ING Bank. As my department was outsourced to an external company, I decided to work as a Company Counselor for other companies. I worked for different NGOs, companies and public services. It was great to share my experience with other organizations, to learn more about other organizations, and to share my experience with other people. In December 2019, I started working as a Company Counselor for the Dutch Government (Ministry of Internal Affairs). My department is part of Health Services. The service we offer is free, and the employees can make an appointment with us without asking their managers. Besides, the service is confidential.

PASSION

I love my work. It's a privilege to support people through difficult situations in their lives, and it reminds me that work can be a medicine. My work is a big inspiration for me, and I learn from my clients daily. Naturally, I keep abreast of developments and take refresher courses in my field on a regular basis. I'm a member of the Dutch professional organization BPSW (www.bpsw.nl).

OUR WORK IN THE COVID-19 PANDEMIC

Like nearly everywhere in the world, we all started working from home in March 2020. We directly organized a Telephone Helpline for all the employees of the government to provide direct mental support. For me, working from home worked out well, but for some clients who needed more, I organized walking sessions. Although I personally prefer live/face-to-face contacts, our work continued as always, and I was surprised how well we all adjusted to a new way of working.

The main issues during COVID-19 were:

- Mental health problems because of isolation
- Coping with family issues/problems, children/relationships, and the combination with work
- Work-related stress; less breaks during the day
- Isolation/disconnection with work
- Loneliness

I started to organize online workshops called "How to get a grip on COVID stress." Those workshops were very successful because it was a good way to talk about the mental health issues in the group and to help each other.

LIFE AFTER COVID-19

Most people were happy to go back to work, and the fact that we can combine working at the office and working from home, the hybrid way, gives most people a better work-life balance.

THE MAIN ISSUES AFTER COVID-19

- People who are still on sick leave or working part time because of "Long COVID symptoms"
- Mental health issues amongst young people (remarkable: young people 20–35 years); burnout and stress
- The "Me too" movement, undesirable behavior, and how to deal with it; more and more people talk about it and don't accept inappropriate behavior (I give many workshops on this theme for teams)
- Coping with diversity at work; I organize training sessions for teams to stimulate talking about these themes; to cope with diversity and stimulate inclusive workplaces
- Work/life balance, a combination of work with children or while taking care of parents, etc. (I give many workshops on this theme for teams)
- In the beginning of the Ukraïne war, we also had more clients who asked for support because of family in the Oekraïne; it's the same now for the war in Gaza.

HYBRID WORK

Most of my colleagues work hybrid after the pandemic. For me, working in the office is the best way for me to do my work as a Company Counselor. Face-to-face contacts usually have more impact, but the combination with online services is enriching. Also, the workshops are live in the office. So in a way, I think we can say that the work-life balance after the pandemic is of higher quality. More autonomy gives us more freedom in organizing our work.

BETTER WORKPLACES, A BETTER WORLD

In the Netherlands, we can see that mental health is more and more important in the workplace. I expect there will continue to be a lot of work for the Company Counselors because they are experts who can support the employees of an organization. And even though the world is changing very fast with the digital revolution, I expect mental health support can't be replaced by computers, artificial intelligence, or robots.

I sincerely think we as Company Counselors can help to make the world a better place to live and to work by offering good mental support at the workplace. And globalization will inspire us to work more and more together as experts and learn from each other and inspire each other to contribute to a better world.

ABOUT THE AUTHOR

Francien Resius
van Breestraat 77 1071 ZH Amsterdam, Netherlands
phone 003165519269

NEW ZEALAND

Peter Finlayson

INTRODUCTION: OCP GROUP LIMITED

OCP Group Limited was established in February 2007 by Peter Finlayson. Previously, Peter was a Director and Shareholder of EAP Services Limited for 10 years.

Peter has over 25 years of experience developing and setting up companies that provide counselling support for organizations all over the world. He has an extensive marketing background and has owned several successful businesses. Being innovative and flexible and with an extremely high focus on customer satisfaction, along with the support of OCP's Business Advisory Committee, Peter can meet the needs of clients effectively and cost-efficiently with OCP Group throughout Australia and New Zealand.

OCP is one company providing and managing the service in both Australia and New Zealand. The provision of service is provided by OCP to employees and professionals contracted to OCP. Throughout New Zealand and Australia, OCP provides a seamless service to employees and management teams.

SERVICE IMPACT DURING THE PANDEMIC

New Zealand has a widely distributed number of small towns and locations that are not highly populated, and therefore, this reduces the ability to provide face-to-face counselling to clients. Despite this, OCP has an average of 80% being face-to-face counselling with the balance being shared between video and phone counselling.

For OCP, the pandemic assisted and increased the uptake of counselling. This was due to the proportion of people who would not feel comfortable with face-to-face appointments reaching out for the online option.

OCP has a very comprehensive network throughout New Zealand, and the service did not suffer for clients; in fact, if anything, it increased the number of people we could now reach. OCP increased the average number of clients accessing the service by around 10 to 15% during the pandemic. Ironically, the pandemic and its effects on the people in New Zealand increased awareness and therefore overall uptake for OCP.

THE EFFECTS OF ONLINE/VIRTUAL COUNSELLING

There were predominately positive effects for OCP due to the pandemic, and we quickly assessed that the effects were positive despite the extremely devastating effect on countries and people's lives.

OCP Group noticed:

- **Increased Accessibility:** One of the major benefits of online counselling is being able to connect people from all over the country. When people live in remote areas, virtual counselling has opened doors to quality mental health care that might have been previously inaccessible.
- **Flexibility:** Both clients and counsellors can benefit from the flexibility that online sessions offer. They can schedule sessions at times that are most convenient for them, reducing the challenges of commuting or coordinating schedules.
- **Privacy Security:** For those who might feel uncomfortable or anxious about trying mental health support, online counselling can offer an added layer of discretion, encouraging more people to seek help. OCP found that this was certainly the case.
- **Challenges in Building Rapport:** While many may feel comfortable with the online option, many also can struggle to create a connection and relationship with their professional. Sometimes, cues and body language can be missed in the online setting.
- **Technological Challenges:** Due to the geographical nature of New Zealand, not everyone has access to a stable internet connection or the necessary devices. Connection stability can also interrupt the flow of therapy, which can disrupt the sessions.

TECHNOLOGY AND SOCIAL MEDIA

- **Improves Communication:** Technology has assisted counsellors and clients to connect for support through messaging apps and video calls. Some platforms can also provide

additional resources to create follow-up notes/information and reminders to complete some actions to assist the session.
- **Awareness and Education:** Social media platforms have helped support positive actions to reach out for mental health support and removed any uncomfortable attitudes around mental health issues. This increased awareness often leads to early intervention and a broader acceptance of therapy as a standard wellness practice.
- **Potential for Misinformation:** While social media can be a source of support, it can also be rife with misinformation. It is vital that both counsellors and clients ensure the information provided online is credible and backed up by trustworthy and proven clinical professionals.
- **Mental Well-being:** Mental health professionals are challenged to provide support based on the sometimes-negative online social media content. The somewhat-doctored lives of individuals trying to create a lifestyle that is, in fact, nowhere near reality creates a false sense of real life. Clients can have unreasonable expectations about where they are at in their own situations regarding financial stability, holidays, assets, and general happiness, and therefore, they create unhealthy reflections of their own self-worth, causing anxiety and depression.

DIVERSITY AND INCLUSION WITHIN THE FIELD OF EAP

- **Representation Matters:** There has been a growing emphasis on ensuring that the field of counselling reflects the diversity of the clientele it serves. Having counselors from varied racial, ethnic, and cultural backgrounds enhances the understanding and nuances of specific community-related issues.
- **Cultural Competence:** Training programs are increasingly focusing on equipping counsellors with skills to address diverse populations. This includes understanding cultural taboos, traditions, and values that may influence one's mental well-being.
- **Inclusive Technologies:** As online counselling platforms evolve, there is an emphasis on ensuring they are accessible to everyone, including those with disabilities. Features like subtitles, voice-to-text, and multilingual support are becoming more prevalent.
- **Outreach Programs:** To address the disparities in mental health access, many organizations and platforms are focusing on outreach programs targeting marginalized or underserved communities.
- **Substance abuse trends/changes:** As of my last update in September 2021, there have been various concerns and trends related to drug and alcohol use in New Zealand.

RECENT TRENDS AND CHANGES IN NEW ZEALAND

- **Cannabis:** In 2020, New Zealand held a referendum on the legalization of recreational cannabis. The proposal was narrowly defeated, with 50.7% voting against and 48.4% in favour. Medical cannabis was made legal in New Zealand in 2018 but with strict regulations.
- **Methamphetamine:** Methamphetamine remained a significant concern, with increasing prevalence and seizures in recent years. It has been linked to a range of social problems, including crime and family breakdowns.
- **Alcohol:** While alcohol is legal and widely consumed in New Zealand, there have been ongoing concerns about the binge-drinking culture, especially among young people. There have been initiatives and campaigns to promote responsible drinking and to highlight the dangers of driving under the influence. Is there such a thing as responsible drinking? I'm unsure what that infers, as it is not working in New Zealand and is mostly driven by the enormous power and influence the alcohol industry has over a small country like New Zealand. It is, in fact, a drug not unlike cigarettes/tobacco.
- **Policy Changes and Discussions:** The New Zealand Drug Foundation and other groups have been advocating for a health-based approach to drug issues rather than a punitive one. The Misuse of Drugs Amendment Act 2019 gave police discretion to take a health-centered approach rather than prosecuting for possession and use of drugs. It's essential to keep an eye on current sources, government publications, or organizations like the New Zealand Drug Foundation for the most recent trends and updates, as the situation can change and evolve.

THE IMPACT OF THE RUSSIA/UKRAINE WAR

While it is an absolute tragedy and unnecessary invasion, due to New Zealand being so far away geographically, it hasn't had the effect on people as it has in other countries. Of course, there is a consistent attitude of disdain toward Russia's invasion, and it is often in the media. The majority of New Zealanders are supportive of the actions being taken to resolve and stop this invasion, and there have been many different initiatives for support and fundraising to assist this resolution and support the Ukrainian citizens. Unfortunately, New Zealand has a population of only 5 million and does not have the resources financially or even from a military perspective to make any major significant positive change. We can only provide as much as we are able and have done so far.

ABOUT THE AUTHOR

Peter Finlayson
Managing Director
OCP Group Limited
Australia
www.myocp.com.au
1800 319 811

New Zealand
www.ocp.co.nz
0800 377 990

International
 +64 3 595 6362

NIGERIA

Olatunji Odebiyi

The COVID-19 pandemic has had far-reaching effects on individuals' mental health and well-being worldwide, including in Nigeria. As the pandemic disrupted work routines, created uncertainty, and induced stress, the need for psychological workplace interventions and Employee Assistance Programs (EAPs) became more pronounced. This article explores the impact of psychological workplace interventions and EAP services in Nigeria during the pandemic, highlighting their significance in supporting employees' mental health.

INCREASED MENTAL HEALTH CHALLENGES

- Anxiety and Stress: The pandemic brought about anxiety and stress due to health concerns, job insecurity, and the abrupt transition to remote work. Psychological interventions and EAP services helped employees cope with these challenges (Ornell et al., 2020).
- Social Isolation: Lockdowns and social distancing measures led to social isolation, which took a toll on people's mental health. EAPs facilitated access to professional help, offering a lifeline to employees in distress.

REMOTE WORK AND BURNOUT PREVENTION

- Transition to Remote Work: The sudden shift to remote work presented new challenges in terms of work-life balance and isolation. Psychological interventions provided guidance on adapting to this new work environment.
- Burnout Prevention: EAP services offered resources for recognizing and preventing burnout, emphasizing the importance of setting boundaries and maintaining work-life balance (World Health Organization, 2020).

STIGMA REDUCTION AND AWARENESS:

- Reducing Stigma: Psychological interventions and EAPs played a role in reducing the stigma associated with seeking mental health support in Nigeria. They promoted open discussions about mental health, emphasizing that seeking help is a sign of strength.
- Awareness Campaigns: EAPs conducted awareness campaigns to educate employees about mental health issues and available resources, fostering a culture of support and understanding (Fitzpatrick, 2021).

SUPPORT FOR FRONTLINE WORKERS

- Health Care Professionals: Psychological workplace interventions and EAPs provided essential support to frontline health care workers who faced immense stress and emotional challenges during the pandemic (Nigeria Health Watch, 2020). EAPA-Nigeria collaborated with Lagos State University Teaching Hospital to provide Psychological First Aid to first responders in particular and other affected people in the health care tertiary facility.
- First Responders: EAPs extended their services to first responders, including police officers and emergency personnel, recognizing the toll the pandemic took on their mental health (Aminu, 2021).

RESILIENCE BUILDING AND COPING STRATEGIES

- Resilience Training: Some EAPs in Nigeria offered resilience training programs to help employees build the mental strength needed to navigate the uncertainties of the pandemic and its aftermath (Omigbodun et al., 2021).

- Coping Strategies: Psychological interventions focused on equipping employees with effective coping strategies to manage stress, anxiety, and other mental health challenges during the pandemic.

RETURN-TO-WORK SUPPORT

- Mental health on return: As employees returned to physical workplaces, EAPs offered support to address the mental health implications of the transition, including anxieties related to safety and hygiene.

LONG-TERM MENTAL HEALTH CONSIDERATIONS:

- Post-Pandemic Mental Health: EAPs recognized the need for ongoing support for employees' mental health, as the pandemic's effects continued to linger (The Guardian Nigeria, 2021).
- Preventive Measures: Psychological interventions focused on implementing preventive measures to address potential mental health issues that might arise in the future.

The COVID-19 pandemic brought unprecedented challenges to workplaces in Nigeria, significantly impacting employees' mental health. Psychological workplace interventions and EAP services played a vital role in providing support, reducing stigma, and fostering resilience among employees. As the pandemic's effects continue to evolve, these interventions will remain crucial in addressing the ongoing mental health needs of the Nigerian workforce.

THE EFFECTS OF ONLINE/VIRTUAL COUNSELING IN NIGERIA

The advent of online and virtual counseling, often referred to as teletherapy or e-counseling, has transformed the mental health landscape in Nigeria. Especially in the context of the COVID-19 pandemic, these remote counseling services have become increasingly popular and essential.

1. Accessibility and Reach

- Geographical Barriers: Online counseling has broken down geographical barriers, enabling individuals in remote or underserved areas, e.g., offshore oil exploration rigs, to access mental health support (Igwe, 2020).

- Increased Reach: Individuals who may have been hesitant to seek in-person counseling due to stigma or logistical challenges find telephonic/online counseling more accessible and private.

2. Convenience and Flexibility

- Flexible Scheduling: Online counseling allows clients to schedule sessions at their convenience, which is particularly valuable for those with busy work or family commitments.
- Reduced Stigma: The anonymity of online counseling can reduce the stigma associated with seeking mental health support, encouraging more people to seek help (Ogunmefun & Ukwayi, 2020).

3. Affordability and Cost-Effectiveness

- Reduced Costs: Online counseling often comes at a lower cost compared to traditional in-person therapy, making mental health services more affordable for many Nigerians.
- No Travel Expenses: Clients save money on transportation to and from counseling sessions, which can be a significant factor, especially for those in urban areas with traffic congestion.

4. Diverse Mental Health Services

- Specialized Services: Online platforms provide access to a wide range of specialized mental health professionals, allowing clients to choose a therapist who best fits their needs.
- Cultural Sensitivity: Online counselors can be more culturally sensitive by offering services that are tailored to the diverse cultural backgrounds of Nigerian clients (Yusuf, 2021).

5. Continuity of Care During the Pandemic

- Pandemic Response: The COVID-19 pandemic highlighted the importance of online counseling in ensuring the continuity of mental health care when physical distancing measures limited in-person services (Olapegba et al., 2020).
- Mental Health Support: Online counseling served as a lifeline for individuals dealing with pandemic-related stress, anxiety, and isolation.

6. Challenges and Considerations

- Digital Divide: Access to online counseling may be limited by the digital divide, where individuals in rural or economically disadvantaged areas have limited internet access and technological resources.
- Data Privacy: Ensuring the privacy and security of sensitive mental health information in online settings is a critical concern (Adebowale & Mosaku, 2020).

7. Future of Mental Health Care

- Integration with Traditional Care: Online counseling is likely to remain a significant part of the mental health landscape in Nigeria, with potential for integration into the broader health care system (Adelufosi et al., 2020).
- Research and Regulation: Policymakers and mental health organizations are working to develop regulations and guidelines for online counseling to ensure quality and ethical standards are maintained.

Online/virtual counseling has had a transformative impact on mental health care in Nigeria, increasing accessibility, reducing stigma, and providing cost-effective options for individuals seeking support. While challenges related to the digital divide and data privacy persist, online counseling is expected to continue playing a crucial role in the future of mental health care in Nigeria. Its flexibility and reach make it a valuable tool for addressing the diverse mental health needs of the Nigerian population.

TECHNOLOGY AND SOCIAL MEDIA

Technology and social media have rapidly evolved in Nigeria, playing significant roles in various aspects of society, including communication, education, business, politics, and culture. The country's large and youthful population, coupled with increased access to digital devices and the internet, has driven the adoption of technology and social media. Here, we explore the multifaceted role of technology and social media in Nigeria's context.

1. Communication and Connectivity

- Access to Information: Technology and social media have democratized access to information. Nigerians use platforms like WhatsApp, Facebook, X (Twitter), and Instagram to stay informed about local and global events.
- Connecting Communities: Social media platforms facilitate the connection of communities, both locally and within the Nigerian diaspora. Nigerians use platforms to stay in touch with family and friends, fostering a sense of belonging.

2. Education and Learning

- E-Learning: The COVID-19 pandemic accelerated the adoption of e-learning platforms and educational technology. Online learning platforms have become crucial for students of all levels to continue their education.
- Skills Development: Technology enables Nigerians to acquire new skills and knowledge through online courses and tutorials, contributing to personal and professional development.

3. Business and Entrepreneurship

- E-Commerce: The rise of e-commerce platforms like Jumia, Konga, and PayPorte has transformed the way Nigerians shop. Online marketplaces have expanded access to a wide range of products and services.
- Digital Marketing: Businesses use social media for marketing and customer engagement. Influencer marketing is also on the rise, with Nigerian influencers promoting brands and products.

4. Politics and Civic Engagement

- Political Activism: Nigerians use social media to express their political views, advocate for social justice, and mobilize for political causes. Platforms like X (Twitter) have played a significant role in political discourse.
- Election Monitoring: Social media is increasingly used for election monitoring, allowing citizens to report irregularities and share election-related information.

5. Health Care and Public Awareness

- Health Information: Technology and social media have been instrumental in disseminating health information, including COVID-19 updates, vaccination campaigns, and health promotion.
- Health Care Access: Telemedicine services have gained popularity, providing remote access to health care professionals, especially in rural areas.

6. Entertainment and Culture

- Nollywood: Nigeria's film industry, Nollywood, has leveraged technology and social media for promotion, reaching a global audience through platforms like YouTube and Netflix.
- Music and Arts: Nigerian musicians and artists use social media to showcase their talents, gain recognition, and connect with fans both locally and internationally.

7. Challenges and Concerns

- Fake News: The spread of fake news and misinformation on social media is a concern. False information can lead to panic, conflict, and misinformation.
- Privacy: Privacy concerns have arisen as personal information is shared online. Cybersecurity threats, data breaches, and online fraud are also challenges.
- Digital Divide: Despite increased access, a digital divide still exists, with rural areas having limited access to technology and the internet.

In conclusion, technology and social media have become integral parts of daily life in Nigeria, offering opportunities for communication, education, business, and civic engagement. However, challenges such as fake news and privacy concerns must be addressed to maximize the benefits of these digital tools. As technology continues to evolve, Nigeria's dynamic and tech-savvy population will play a significant role in shaping the country's digital future.

EFFORTS TOWARD DIVERSITY AND INCLUSION WITHIN THE FIELD OF COUNSELING AND MENTAL HEALTH IN NIGERIA

Diversity and inclusion are essential principles in the field of counseling and mental health services in Nigeria. Promoting diversity and ensuring inclusivity is not only a matter of social justice but also a way to improve the quality of mental health care. Here are some key efforts and initiatives aimed at fostering diversity and inclusion within the field, encompassing counselors, providers, and clients in Nigeria:

1. Diverse Mental Health Workforce

- Training Programs: Academic institutions and organizations offering mental health training have started emphasizing diversity and inclusivity in their programs. This includes efforts to recruit students from diverse backgrounds.
- Counselor Training: Initiatives to train counselors from marginalized groups have been launched to ensure that the workforce reflects the diversity of the Nigerian population.
- Cultural Competency Training: Mental health professionals are encouraged to undergo cultural competency training to better understand and serve clients from different cultural backgrounds.

2. Representation and Leadership

- Diverse Leadership: Mental health organizations and institutions are working toward diversifying leadership roles. This includes promoting individuals from marginalized groups to leadership positions.
- Representation: Efforts are being made to ensure that advisory boards, committees, and decision-making bodies include members from diverse backgrounds to better address the needs of clients.

3. Culturally Tailored Interventions

- Culturally Sensitive Approaches: Mental health providers are encouraged to adopt culturally sensitive approaches to therapy. This includes acknowledging cultural beliefs and practices in treatment plans.
- Language Accessibility: Efforts are made to provide therapy in multiple languages, ensuring that individuals who speak Indigenous languages can access mental health services.

4. Community Engagement

- Community Outreach: Mental health organizations engage with communities to

understand their unique needs and challenges. This fosters trust and encourages marginalized groups to seek help.
- Collaboration with Traditional Healers: To the extent that it is ethically feasible, collaborative efforts with traditional healers and religious leaders are promoted to bridge the gap between traditional and modern mental health perceptions/services.

5. Anti-Stigma Campaigns

- Awareness Programs: Various campaigns are conducted to raise awareness about mental health issues and reduce the stigma associated with seeking help. These campaigns target specific communities and demographics.
- Media Engagement: Media outlets, including radio and television, are utilized to disseminate mental health information and personal stories of recovery, encouraging discussions.

6. Accessible Mental Health Services

- Affordable Services: Efforts are made to ensure that mental health services are affordable and accessible to all socioeconomic groups.
- Telehealth Services: Teletherapy and telecounseling options have been expanded to reach clients in remote areas, improving access to mental health care.

7. Advocacy and Policy Development

- Policy Advocacy: Mental health organizations and advocacy groups work with government agencies to develop policies that promote diversity and inclusion in mental health care.
- Legislation: Advocacy efforts also focus on pushing for legislation that protects the rights and access to mental health services for marginalized groups.

In conclusion, Nigeria is taking strides in promoting diversity and inclusion within the field of counseling and mental health services. These efforts aim to create a more equitable and accessible mental health care system that addresses the diverse needs of its population. While progress has been made, there is still work to be done to ensure that everyone, regardless of their background or identity, can access quality mental health care in Nigeria.

Please consider the following resources:

- Nigeria Psychological Association (NPA; https://npass.org.ng) and Nigeria Association of Clinical Psychologists (NACP; https://nacp.com.ng): the professional bodies for psychologists in Nigeria. Becoming a member provides access to conferences, workshops, and networking opportunities with mental health professionals across the country.
- Nigerian Association of Social Workers (NASoW): NASoW is an organization for social workers in Nigeria. Joining NASoW provides a platform for networking with social workers involved in mental health and EAP services. Website: https://nasowlagos.org.
- Employee Assistance Professionals Association of Nigeria (EAPAN): EAPAN is an organization dedicated to EAP professionals in Nigeria. Membership offers networking opportunities, workshops, and access to industry updates. Website: www.eapa.ng.
- Local Mental Health and Wellness Events: Attend workshops, seminars, and conferences related to mental health and wellness in Nigeria. These events provide excellent networking opportunities with professionals and organizations in the field.
- Professional Development Workshops and Webinars: Participate in online workshops and webinars offered by international mental health organizations. These events often attract professionals from various countries, providing a global networking platform.
- Collaborate with Universities and Research Institutes: Universities often host mental health-related events and seminars. Collaborating with professors and researchers can open doors to networking opportunities and collaborative projects.
- Social Media Groups and Forums: Explore social media platforms like Facebook and Reddit for mental health-related groups and forums. Engaging in discussions can help you connect with professionals who share your interests.
- International Conferences: Consider attending international conferences related to mental health and EAP. These events bring together professionals from around the world and offer extensive networking opportunities. For example, EAPA-Nigeria is hosting the EAP for Africa conference between 7th and 8th November 2023.
- Collaborate with NGOs and Non-Profit Organizations: Many non-governmental organizations (NGOs) and non-profit organizations work in the mental health sector. Collaborating with these organizations can expand your professional network significantly.
- Professional Certification Programs: Pursue professional certifications in mental health counseling or EAP. Certification programs often include networking events and opportunities to connect with peers in the industry.

CHANGES IN SUBSTANCE ABUSE TRENDS IN NIGERIA DURING THE PANDEMIC

The COVID-19 pandemic has had far-reaching effects on various aspects of society, including substance abuse trends in Nigeria. Lockdowns, economic challenges, and social isolation measures introduced during the pandemic have influenced how individuals access and use substances. Here are some notable changes in substance abuse patterns in Nigeria exacerbated by the COVID-19 pandemic:

1. Increased Alcohol Consumption

- Surge in Alcohol Sales: During the pandemic, there was an increase in alcohol sales and consumption in Nigeria. With bars and clubs closed and social gatherings limited, individuals turned to alcohol as a means of coping with stress and boredom.
- Home Brewing: Some individuals resorted to home brewing of alcoholic beverages due to restrictions on movement and alcohol sales, raising concerns about the quality and safety of these homemade products (Punch, 2020).

2. Rise in Drug Abuse

- Increased Anxiety and Stress: The uncertainty and anxiety associated with the pandemic led to an uptick in drug abuse, particularly among young adults. Individuals sought refuge in drugs to cope with the emotional toll of the crisis.
- Tramadol and Codeine: Opioids like tramadol and codeine continued to be abused, with some people self-medicating to alleviate anxiety and stress. Restrictions on movement and supply chain disruptions may have affected the availability of these drugs.

3. Polydrug Abuse

- Combination of Substances: The pandemic saw an increase in polydrug abuse, where individuals simultaneously or sequentially used multiple substances. This behavior can heighten the risks associated with substance abuse, including overdose.

4. Limited Access to Treatment Services

- Challenges in Accessing Treatment: Lockdowns and restrictions on movement posed challenges for individuals seeking treatment and rehabilitation services for substance abuse. Access to health care facilities was limited, affecting those in need of support (The Guardian Nigeria, 2020).
- Telehealth Services: Some organizations and health care providers adapted by offering telehealth services for counseling and therapy, enabling individuals to access support remotely.

5. Awareness Campaigns and Education

- Public Health Campaigns: The government and non-governmental organizations conducted public health campaigns to raise awareness of the risks of substance abuse during the pandemic and to provide information on available support services (Premium Times, 2020).

6. Economic Factors

- **Economic Hardships:** The economic impact of the pandemic, including job losses and reduced incomes, contributed to increased substance abuse. Individuals facing financial hardships may have turned to substances as a coping mechanism.
- **Role of the Informal Economy:** People engaged in the informal economy, e.g., street traders and daily wage laborers, may have faced additional stressors, potentially exacerbating substance abuse issues.

It is important to note that the changes in substance abuse patterns during the pandemic are complex and multifaceted. While some individuals increased their substance use as a response to stress and uncertainty, others may have reduced their consumption due to health concerns or limited access to substances. The long-term effects of these changes to substance abuse trends in Nigeria will require ongoing research and monitoring. Addressing substance abuse during and after the pandemic will require a comprehensive approach that includes prevention, treatment, and support services. On a final note, the mass exodus of (mental) health care workers requires urgent attention to sustain the gains on mental health interventions.

ABOUT THE AUTHOR

Olatunji Odebiyi is the President of the Nigeria Branch of EAPA, the International Employee Assistance Professionals Association. https://eapassn.org/page/Nigeria

NORDIC COUNTRIES: NORWAY, DENMARK, FINLAND, AND SWEDEN, PLUS POLAND

Johannes Edberg

The background of ICAS Nordic goes back about 25 years to a company called Visavi AB that started up with EAP services in Sweden.

Louise Edberg, certified psychologist, started up Visavi. At that point, EAP was unknown in Scandinavia, and Visavi was the pioneer. After some years of successful growth, the company was bought by a competitor. After some time, old customers came back to us and asked us to re-start the service—so we did in a small version. This turned out well, and besides our other customers, we again started to work with the customers of ICAS World—first in Sweden, then gradually in the rest of the Nordic countries. Today, we have active partners working in each Nordic country and serving with local service, answering in the local language. The regulations concerning mental health, counselling and therapy are quite alike in the Nordic countries. Also the certifications for becoming a psychologist/therapist and ethical rules are quite the same. All this makes it natural for us to cooperate. I believe we have a cultural affinity and identity of common understandings. As for languages, I can understand and talk Swedish with our partners in Denmark and Norway as they speak in their languages. With Finland, it is different. Finnish has a different root of language, so we communicate in English. So all in all, I believe the Nordic countries have a lot in common that makes it natural for us to cooperate.

The background of ICAS Poland is somehow parallel and, at the same time, different. We got the proposition by ICAS World to start a local service in Poland about 10 years ago. At the beginning, we had only a very small number of contracts with a small number of headcounts. When we started the company, I already had the experience of working with EAP for several years in the Nordic countries, and when this opportunity came up, I had my doubts if this was really a good idea—the conditions in the Nordic countries are quite different from how society works in Poland. We understood that a crucial condition to work with this kind of very personal service was to have a genuine footprint in Poland.

We also understood that there was a strong need for local knowledge and experience about how the Polish society functions and what kinds of problems are relevant for the employees, both mental health services and daily life problems like tax regulations and legal issues. What kind of help was already possible to find? What cultural barriers were essential to handle in a way to build up confidence? And then we found the right person, our needed Polish footprint, in our CEO Janusz Prendota, a native Polish.

THE IMPACT OF THE PANDEMIC ON EAP SERVICES

The impact of the pandemic on our services was significant, both in Poland and in the Nordics. As the COVID-19 pandemic unfolded, it brought about numerous challenges and increased the need for support in both personal and professional aspects of employees' lives. Our EAP services played a crucial role in providing much-needed assistance during these challenging times.

First and foremost, the pandemic led to a need in mental health issues, including anxiety, stress, and depression, among employees. Our services helped address these concerns by offering accessible and confidential support through individual counseling sessions, virtual group programs, and resources tailored to the unique needs of employees. We provided a safe space for individuals to express their concerns, receive guidance, and develop coping strategies to navigate the unprecedented circumstances.

Additionally, the pandemic brought about significant changes in the work environment, such as remote work arrangements and increased isolation. Our EAP services adapted to these changes by using technology and offering virtual counseling sessions, webinars, and online resources. This ensured that employees could access support from the comfort and safety of their homes.

Furthermore, ICAS Poland actively promoted mental health awareness and well-being initiatives during the pandemic. We collaborated with organizations to develop strategies for managing stress, maintaining work-life balance, and fostering resilience. We also provided guidance to employers on creating supportive work environments that prioritize the mental health of their employees.

Overall, the impact of our services during the pandemic was instrumental in supporting employees and organizations in managing the unique challenges brought on by the crisis. We witnessed a significant increase in the utilization of our services, indicating the growing recognition of the importance of mental health support in times of uncertainty, loneliness and stress.

THE EFFECTS OF ONLINE/VIRTUAL COUNSELING

The effects of online/virtual counseling, as a result of the pandemic, differed from traditional face-to-face meetings in several ways. Virtual counseling offered convenience and flexibility. Clients could schedule sessions at times that suited their needs, without the limitations of travel time or availability of physical office spaces. It also reduced stigma. For some individuals, the perceived stigma associated with seeking face-to-face counseling was reduced through online platforms. Engaging in virtual counseling allowed people to seek help discreetly, without fear of being recognized or judged by others.

One potential limitation of online counseling is the absence of certain nonverbal cues that are more apparent in face-to-face interactions. Body language and facial expressions may be less visible, which can impact the counselling process.

It's important to note that while online counseling had its advantages during the pandemic, some individuals may still prefer the in-person experience and find face-to-face meetings more conducive to their needs. The choice between online and in-person counseling ultimately depends on personal preferences, individual circumstances, and the nature of the therapeutic relationship.

THE ROLE OF TECHNOLOGY AND SOCIAL MEDIA

The role of technology and social media in ICAS EAP is significant and multifaceted. Here are some key aspects:

- Communication and Accessibility: Technology enables efficient and accessible communication between employees and our specialists. Modern IT communication tools such as apps, forms, chat, video, and web portals are utilized to reduce barriers and create multiple channels of contact. This facilitates easy access to support services, allowing employees to reach out for assistance conveniently.
- Virtual Counseling: Technology has enabled the provision of virtual counseling services. Video conferencing platforms and secure online communication tools allow employees

to engage in counseling sessions remotely. This ensures continuity of care and broadens access to support, regardless of physical location.
- Information and Resources: ICAS Poland utilizes technology and social media platforms to share valuable information and resources related to mental health, well-being, and personal development. This includes articles, blog posts, videos, and webinars that provide education, tips, and strategies for employees to navigate various challenges.
- Web-Based Self-Help Tools: ICAS Poland also offers web-based self-help tools and applications to employees as part of their EAP services. These tools could include interactive modules, assessments, and exercises that individuals can access and utilize independently to enhance their well-being and personal growth.
- Data Analytics: Technology allows us to gather and analyze data related to employee engagement, utilization of services, and overall program effectiveness. This data-driven approach helps identify trends, measure outcomes, and continuously improve the EAP services provided.
- Social Media Engagement: ICAS Poland may maintain an active presence on social media platforms to engage with employees and promote mental health awareness. Through social media, ICAS can share relevant content, inspirational messages, and create a sense of community around mental health support.

It's important to note that while technology and social media play a significant role in ICAS EAP, the organization also prioritizes the security and privacy of employee information. Robust measures are implemented to ensure confidentiality and compliance with data protection regulations.

EFFORTS TOWARD DIVERSITY AND INCLUSION WITHIN THE FIELD

The pandemic clearly showed us that no longer could we only rely on old ways of thinking and acting. There was a huge need for breaking up closed doors and finding ways of helping in times of loneliness—individually, emotionally and also physically—as most of us as employees and counsellors were working remotely from home. The new way of working also meant a need to adapt the social communication between the employees and the companies. This change goes together with continuing complex changes in society that differ between the countries we work in. In the Nordic countries, people tend to have a quite strong confidence and trust in basic regulations and how the society is built and functions. And, in the way companies are forced to follow rules about working conditions, diversity and inclusion. In Poland, there is still a lot of suspiciousness regarding how regulations are followed by the companies. We meet a strong suspicion when we ask employees to give away personal data. Slowly, we have built up a confidence and trust.

In Poland, there are other strong tensions in the society. Confidentiality is very important for most of our employees. There is a very severe legislation about women having no right to a free abortion. Also, there is a strong impact from the leading political society against all sexual identity issues. Regardless of this strong impact from the political leadership of society, we are very proud to see more and more employees in Poland giving us trust to handle these very delicate kinds of issues that the official society denies.

The Ukrainian war, of course, has an enormous impact on the Polish society. We could see that the "normal" EAP service was, by far, not enough for handling all the refugees' problems. We needed to be inventive and find other ways of helping people. The key word was human solidarity and direct local contact. We needed to act fast and unconventionally, with a deep sense of understanding and with counsellors talking in Ukrainian.

ABOUT THE AUTHOR

Johannes Edberg is the COO for aICAS Nordic. We cover the Nordic countries—Sweden, Norway, Denmark and Finland—with EAP services. Johannes is also co-owner of ICAS Poland and work with ICAS Poland as a Clinical Director. Today, ICAS Poland is the leading provider of EAP in Poland. My personal background: I have a BA in psychology and spent many years in clinical practice.

RESOURCES

For Sweden, Denmark, Norway and Finland:
aICAS Nordic
eap@aicasnordic.com
Johannes.edberg@aicasnordic.com

For Poland:
info@icas.pl
johannes.edberg@icas.pl
www.icas.pl

Other contacts in Poland:
- Polish Psychological Association (Polskie Towarzystwo Psychologiczne): The Polish Psychological Association is a professional organization that brings together psychologists and mental health professionals in Poland. They offer networking events, conferences, and workshops where professionals can connect, exchange knowledge, and build relationships within the field. Website: http://www.ptp.org.pl/
- Polish Association for Psychotherapy (Polskie Towarzystwo Psychoterapii): The Polish Association for Psychotherapy is an organization that promotes psychotherapy and provides a platform for networking among psychotherapists and mental health professionals. They organize conferences, seminars, and training programs where professionals can network and enhance their skills. Website: http://www.ptp.org.pl/
- LinkedIn Groups: Joining relevant LinkedIn groups focused on mental health, counseling, or psychotherapy in Poland can provide opportunities for networking and professional discussions. Some recommended groups include "Polish Psychologists and Counselors Network" and "Psychotherapists and Psychologists in Poland."

PHILIPPINES

Jean Lim

INTRODUCTION

This article was written by Jean Lim, Managing Director of PowerVision EAP, Inc. in collaboration with two other EAP providers in the Philippines. Special thanks to Julian Montano, Clinical Supervisor and Head of Internal and External Support of In Touch Community Services, and Majella Tumangan-Villaroman, President and CEO of myCORD Corporation PH.

THE IMPACT OF THE PANDEMIC ON EAP SERVICES

The Philippines was hard hit by the COVID-19 pandemic, ranking among the top 20 countries with the greatest number of cases worldwide and known to have the longest lockdown as of October 2020.[32] As the pandemic extended into its second year, utilization of EAP services increased significantly in 2021 (see Table 1). In the same year, the public crisis line run by In Touch also experienced a dramatic surge in calls. And while restrictions eased up in 2022, the increase in EAP utilization was generally sustained through more active promotion and higher awareness of mental health issues.

---

[32] Baclig, C.E. (2021, March 12). *TIMELINE: One year of COVID-19 in the Philippines.* Retrieved July 24, 2023, from https://newsinfo.inquirer.net/1406004/timeline-one-year-of-covid-19-in-the-philippines

Table 1: Utilization Rates From 2019 to 2023

Metrics	2019	2020	2021	2022
Case utilization rate				
In Touch	0.7%	0.8%	1.2%	1.2%
myCORD	3.0%	5.0%	31%	5%
PowerVision	1.3%	1.6%	2.9%	3.0%
Public Crisis line calls from In Touch: % increase/decrease vs. 2019		5.6%	70.8%	6.7%

The WHO reports that the pandemic has triggered a 25% increase in anxiety and depression worldwide.[33] As can be seen in Table 2, more EAP clients from two providers have been using EAP to relieve anxiety or stress since the pandemic. However, the trend for depression and self-harm cases has not been consistent across the three EAP providers. Perhaps, this could be because the data collected is the Primary Assessed Problem and the clients' anxiety or stress may have prevailed over any feelings of depression.

---

33 World Health Organization (2022, March 2). *COVID-19 pandemic triggers 25% increase in prevalence of anxiety and depression worldwide.* Retrieved July 24, 2023, from https://www.who.int/news/item/02-03-2022-covid-19-pandemic-triggers-25-increase-in-prevalence-of-anxiety-and-depression-worldwide

Table 2: Trends of Common Assessed Problems*

Metrics	2019	2020	2021	2022	2023**
% age of cases involving anxiety or stress In Touch myCORD PowerVision	20.1% 100% 31.0%	44.0% 100% 39.4%	76.8% 68.0% 39.8%	52.1% 62.0% 39.3%	52.4% 26.0% 47.7%
% age of cases involving depression In Touch myCORD PowerVision	9.6% 0.0% 12.2%	15.2% 0.0% 8.4%	11.0% 16.0% 6.4%	13.2% 26.0% 5.7%	13.0% 20.0% 6.6%
%age of cases involving risk of self-harm In Touch myCORD PowerVision	1.2% 0.0% 16.7%	1.1% 0.0% 13.2%	0.5% 0.0% 11.3%	2.9% 2.0% 9.4%	3.4% 0.0% 17.5%

Data for In Touch and PowerVision are based on the Primary Assessed Problem tagged by counselors. Data for myCORD are based on all problem categories tagged by counselors, i.e., one case may be tagged multiple times.

** Data for 2023 represents only the first half of the year.

The pandemic also increased the public's appreciation of mental health care, pushing many companies to look for partners that can help support their struggling employees. The three EAP providers contributing to this article all experienced an increase in the number of new client companies in 2020 as compared to 2019 (see Table 3).

Table 3: Growth of EAP Clientele Against 2019 Baseline

Metrics	2020	2021	2022
% increase/decrease in # accounts			
In Touch	51.3%	32.8%	23.0%
myCORD	4%	2%	0%
PowerVision	194%	376%	555%
% increase/decrease in # employees covered			
In Touch	62%	22%	16%
myCORD	318%	110%	427%
PowerVision	31%	69%	109%

Another factor that has prompted companies to implement mental health programs is the Mental Health Act of 2018. For the workplace, this law requires employers to develop policies and programs on mental health, correct stigma and discrimination, and provide support for employees with mental health conditions. While the Implementing Rules and Regulations for the Mental Health Act was approved in January 2019,[34] the pandemic gave companies a sense of urgency to comply with the law.

Internally, all three EAP providers had to cope with new challenges during the pandemic. We had to quickly adjust our infrastructure, processes, and capabilities to provide virtual counseling, training, and hotline services in a secure work-from-home setup. Counselors had to be trained in online counseling and the use of various technical platforms. We also had to develop communications and training modules to address common pandemic-related issues promptly. The surge of cases required more from our personnel, and yet, they also had their fair share of personal struggles and adjustments. One challenge specific to our profession is the need for a quiet and private work area to conduct sessions at home, since other family members may also be working or studying at home.

To address the challenges of the counselors, the EAP organizations provided extra support to their personnel through supervision, training, support groups or "detox" sessions, fun activities,

---

[34] Official Gazette. (2019, January 22). *Implementing Rules and Regulations of Republic Act No 11036*. Retrieved July 24, 2023, from https://www.officialgazette.gov.ph/2019/01/22/implementing-rules-and-regulations-of-republic-act-no-11036/

and their own counseling. Providers emphasized self-care, support, and boundaries to prevent burnout of their personnel.

THE EFFECTS OF ONLINE/VIRTUAL COUNSELING

The move to virtual counseling during the pandemic did not encounter much resistance from clients. Many found it more convenient since they do not need to go through traffic to meet their counselor. However, the lack of a stable internet connection plus the occasional power outages were major hindrances to having a conversation without any interruptions or difficulty in hearing each other. To cope with these challenges, clients and counselors resorted to audio calls instead of video calls, and clients who did not have privacy at home made do with text messaging. Out of all the virtual counseling sessions done in PowerVision from 2020 to mid-2023, 58% were through audio call, 34% through video call, and 7% through messaging.

A major difficulty encountered by the counselors using virtual counseling is the inability to see the client's body language, particularly in audio calls and text messaging. Counselors later became more adept at detecting nuances in the voices and words of the clients. We also experienced limitations in counseling children and had to decline younger children who requested virtual counseling in PowerVision. Psychologists at In Touch endeavored to facilitate Play Therapy activities online as best as they could. To motivate adolescent clients, they did more in-session activities instead of assigning homework. They also offered flexibility for couples to share the same gadget or use separate ones, according to the client's preference. Complex, critical cases were also more difficult to handle without the physical presence of the client.

While many counselors were able to adapt to online counseling, some who were less familiar with technology experienced resistance and took more time and effort to adjust. The EAP providers helped these counselors adapt with training, resource materials, protocols, and technical support.

Many clients expressed satisfaction with the online modes of counseling, particularly for its convenience. Even clients who were overseas or in the provinces were able to access services easily. While a few clients preferred in-person meetings, we foresee that virtual counseling will still predominate even after the pandemic.

THE ROLE OF TECHNOLOGY AND SOCIAL MEDIA

The Philippines has been called the social media capital of the world, with 72% or 84 million social network users out of a population of 117 million. Filipinos spend an average of four hours a day on social media, mostly to stay socially connected, get updated with the latest news, and to express themselves.[35] Social media has played a key role in promoting awareness about mental health and was essential in maintaining a sense of community and support during the pandemic when people were isolated. Mental health professionals and organizations were offering free webinars, videos and articles that were psycho educational. Individuals also shared their mental health struggles online, and in a few cases, we received EAP referrals from supervisors or colleagues of employees who posted disturbing content in their social media accounts. However, there are also negative effects of social media experienced among Filipinos, including cyberbullying, hate speech, misinformation or fake news, addictive behavior, and negative comparisons. We also see the risk of people self-diagnosing based on content and online screening tools, without getting professional help. There were also cases of content involving suicide that triggered suicidal ideations among some people.

Aside from requesting services and making appointments online, EAP providers gave clients more options in how they can avail themselves of the services. Many companies have set up hybrid or work-from-home arrangements post-pandemic, and we foresee that we will continue to offer counseling, group sessions and training sessions virtually in the future. More delivery options should translate to more utilization, as previous hindrances such as travel time and costs are addressed by opting for virtual sessions. Virtual training offers a great opportunity to reach more people as it does not have the physical limitations of in-person training. Internally, EAPs are also using technology more to automate processes and recordkeeping, especially as transaction volumes increase.

Advances in technology have also given rise to many digital apps that range from providing educational content and screening tools, to engaging in an interactive chat using AI, to self-booking with a mental health professional. Some companies may use such apps as a supplement to an EAP service in order to provide additional support for employees. Companies may be open to digital EAPs or a hybrid delivery of EAP services. However, appropriate measures should be in place so that cases not suitable for digital interventions alone are referred to a live counselor.

EFFORTS TOWARD DIVERSITY AND INCLUSION WITHIN THE FIELD

Diversity and inclusion (D&I) was cited as a priority among the companies certified by Great Place to Work Philippines in their 2021 report. Over 90% of employees in these companies responded that people are fairly treated regardless of sexual orientation, sex, race, or ethnicity

---

35   Statista Research Department. (2023, March 15). *Social Media in the Philippines – statistics & facts*. Retrieved July 24, 2023, from https://www.statista.com/topics/6759/social-media-usage-in-the-philippines/#topicOverview

and feel psychologically safe in the workplace.[36] However, this represents only a small number of companies in the Philippines, and many of these are multinationals. A study made in 2018 by the Philippine LGBT Chamber of Commerce reported that only 17% of companies had inclusive policies for LGBTQ employees.[37] The government has been slowly responding with laws that support and protect groups that may experience disadvantages in the workplace, such as the Magna Carta for Persons with Disability, the Anti Sexual Harassment Act in 1995, Indigenous People's Rights Act in 1997, and the Anti Age Discrimination in Employment Act in 2015.[38] After several years, the Sexual Orientation, Gender Identity and Expression (SOGIE) bill is still up for approval by the Senate.[39]

The EAP providers have been partnering with our client management in advocating for D&I through various training programs and participation in events. Understanding LGBTQ+, gender sensitivity, unconscious bias, psychological safety, bullying, and sexual harassment are some topics covered in these training programs. Our counselors have varied experiences with clients coming from diverse backgrounds, with some clients reporting discomfort or discrimination in the workplace, while other clients had neutral or positive experiences in their organizations with regard to D&I. EAPs in the Philippines can play a stronger role in advocating for D&I, especially in local companies and small and medium enterprises.

CONCLUSION

The business sector can play a significant role in the country's budding efforts to build awareness of mental health and ensuring professional help is available to those who need it. There are many hindrances to help-seeking for Filipinos, including stigma, the severe shortage of mental health professionals, and the high cost of psychological services. According to a study made by an insurance company, 38% of Filipinos find the cost of psychological treatment prohibitive.[40]

---

36 Great Place to Work. (2021). *Philippines Best Workplaces 2021*. Retrieved July 25, 2023, from https://www.greatplacetowork.com.ph/resources/research-insights/philippine-best-workplaces-2021-insights-report/

37 Guillermo, J. (2020) *The Shift to Inclusivity and Diversity in the Workplace*. Retrieved July 24, 2023, from https://asiasociety.org/node/30642/shift-inclusivity-and-diversity-workplace

38 Ramos, A. (2021, October 12). *Workplace Equality and Diversity in the Philippines. 8 Laws to Protect You*. Retrieved July 24, 2023, from https://manilarecruitment.com/manila-recruitment-articles-advice/workplace-equality-diversity-philippines-laws-protect-you/

39 Sarao, Z. (2023, July 24). *Roman: Marcos unlikely to certify SOGIE bill as urgent*. Retrieved July 24, 2023, from https://newsinfo.inquirer.net/1806414/roman-marcos-unlikely-to-certify-sogie-bill-as-urgent

40 FWD. (2023, May 31*). 63% of Filipinos believe mental health as one of the most critical issues for 2023*. Retrieved July 24, 2023, from https://www.fwd.com.ph/news-press/press/2023/63-percent-of-filipios-believe-mental-health-as-one-of-the-most-critical-issues-for-2023/

But we are hopeful for the future of workplace mental health in the Philippines. The pandemic ushered in several online therapy sites that can be easily accessed by anyone. Some HMOs and other psychological clinics have also included workplace counseling services as part of their services. myCORD is pioneering the establishment of the EAP Training Institute so that other organizations can better understand EAP. As more companies implement EAPs, we can make mental health services accessible to the average Filipino employee and their families.

ABOUT THE AUTHOR

Mary Jean Lim is the Managing Director of PowerVision EAP, Inc.

RESOURCES

Mary Jean Lim
Managing Director
PowerVision EAP Inc.
Email: jean@powervisioneap.com
Phone: +(63915) 325-2575

Julian Montano
Clinical Supervisor
In Touch Community Services
Email: jmontano@in-touch.org
Phone: +(63917) 502-6992

Majella Tumangan-Villaroman
President and CEO
myCORD Corporation PH
Email: majella@my-CORD.com
Phone: +(63919) 098-5130

PORTUGAL

Manuel Sommer

MODERN CHALLENGES OF EAPS IN PORTUGUESE SOCIETY

EAPs and other workplace well-being programs have come a long way over the last 25 years. As in many other countries, the initial programs back in the 1990s were occupational alcohol and drug prevention programs that slowly evolved over the years into more holistic support responses in the workplace.

The role of international providers has been significant as they have, since the beginning of the new millennium, catalyzed the introduction of more specific counselling services and also included family members in their service offerings. However, these were mostly international companies. Traditional Portuguese companies were, at the time, not sensitive to more progressive responses to workplace prevention issues.

The international financial crisis of 2008 and the following bankruptcy of the Portuguese state was without any doubt the start of a new era.

Companies could not rely any more on public responses and needed to take matters into their own hands. This was the period when the EAP concept transpired into the local business culture and Human Resources departments started to accept a "duty to care" responsibility. Most companies at the time were still small- and medium-size companies where individual input could make a great impact and difference to employees.

The COVID-19 pandemic was another great moment for the expansion of workplace wellness programs as employees were working from home, facing new challenges with family and work under the same roof, and work meant mainly being "away" from managers, colleagues and physical workplaces. This brought along great new challenges where EAP providers had an important role of providing a transitional support and response to the new challenges everyone was facing.

Last but not least, the invasion of Ukraine in March 2022 was another moment of great upheaval in Europe. Massive emigration from Ukraine, reorganization of family support structures and the threats of a more global crisis have fueled anxiety and fear, but also dedicated responses in the workplace. For many Ukrainians who were already living and working in Portugal before the war, this meant taking up distanced family members who suddenly needed support, needing other support regarding their loved one's living in exposed areas in Ukraine, and finding other practical solutions. Many EAP programs implemented temporary counselling solutions for exposed family members in Ukraine and developed support programs for food, clothes and other urgently needed things.

Having managed to position themselves strategically in the workplace, EAPs today have managed to acquire an important role in the effective response to the multiple needs of the workplace, employees, family members and general society as a whole.

MENTAL HEALTH IN THE WORKPLACE AND OTHER TRENDS

Within the areas of EAPs, mental health/psychological support is nowadays the most required service in the workplace. The pandemic has brought down the barriers of the stigma around seeking psychological help. Overall utilization rates have gone up, leading to an increase of the perception of need within organizations. Human Resources professionals cannot separate anymore the emotional and psychological needs of their employees and family members from their workplace performance, absenteeism, reduction of presentism, burnout prevention, etc.

Almost all HR conferences in Portugal (and there are more or less five professional associations in the HR field only in Portugal) have dedicated roundtables to present cases of workplace programs that have been set up by HR departments and where individual tailored solutions have been implemented. Some of them have integrated solutions with the Occupational Health Departments, etc.

Dedicated trainings for managers have also increased. More and more managers receive dedicated training in mental health prevention and how to intervene within their teams when mental health symptoms can be observed amongst individual employees.

Some leading EAP providers in Portugal also offer within their standard service offerings free-of-charge regular webinars in the field of mental health promotion, ergonomics, mindfulness, etc., so as to proactively promote the preventative aspect of well-being.

Psychosocial risk assessments are also very popular. More and more companies wish to comply with legal recommendations to undertake assessments of current risks in the field of well-being and within the organization. Very popular is the WOD (Workplace Outcome Dynamics), a scientific tool with international European benchmarks that measures many factors for the employee and the organization, such as the level of engagement, employee satisfaction, customer satisfaction, organizational commitment, loyalty, productivity and other factors that are relevant to an effective relationship between employee, workplace and the organization. Divided into several dimensions of well-being, several driver groups and the collected socio-demographic variables, the WOD allows a flexible and customized approach to customer organizations. Also, the results are displayed on an online dashboard that allows many different viewing possibilities and factor-analysis combinations.

Employees in Portugal are very tech savvy. The more companies manage to present digital solutions and tools that allow employees to self-measure well-being, the more employees are motivated to participate in surveys, assessments and training programs and to receive individual feedback. Many tools are available in the Portuguese language, like the REBOOST, APPA tool, etc., that allow companies and employees to receive modern solutions that have a strong impact for crucial workplace indicators at their fingertips.

Another interesting trend is the connection between EAPs, the United Nations Agenda 2030 Millennium Goals and the overall goals of Europe's Inclusive Transition!

Encouraged by CSR EUROPE, the leading European business network for corporate sustainability and responsibility (members range from corporate members, national partner organizations and other associate partners), the European ESG framework reinforces the European inclusive Green Deal, meaning that many sustainable goals intend to have a very strong social component.

GRACE, the Portuguese umbrella association for CSR—Corporate Social Responsibility activities in Portugal, has been one of the leading organizations for the promotion of mental health in the workplace, also developing a Mental Health Toolkit that is in active use by organizations.

In partnership with EAP providers, wellness programs have taken up the challenge and can use this unique opportunity to be part of this magnificent change process that is currently underway.

ABOUT THE AUTHOR

Manuel Sommer is the Country Manager for Pulso Europe, Portugal.

PUERTO RICO

Marion A. Wennerholm

INTRODUCTION

As co-founder and president of Lucy López Roig EAP, Inc., I have had the privilege of being involved in the EAP field in Puerto Rico for the past 40 years. Our company was the first external EAP provider on the island and is currently the only independent, stand-alone EAP in Puerto Rico. We have seen many changes and a great expansion of EAPs over the years, and these services are now an expected benefit for employees in the public and private sectors.

This article is intended to be an update to the information provided on Puerto Rico in the *Fourth Edition of the International Employee Assistance Compendium*.

BACKGROUND

For centuries, Puerto Rico has faced great challenges, and the past 10 years have not been an exception. Natural disasters head the list, including hurricanes Irma and María in September 2017, which caused thousands of deaths (many of them from delayed medical care), devasted infrastructure and many vital services, and led to estimated damages of $100 billion. In January 2020, a series of earthquakes struck the island, including a 6.4 magnitude quake, the most powerful in Puerto Rico in 102 years. An island-wide power outage resulted, and there was severe structural damage, especially in the southwestern part of the island. In March 2020, the first cases of COVID-19 were reported. The pandemic soon brought normal operations to a standstill, as it did around the world. In September 2022, Hurricane Fiona made landfall over southwestern Puerto Rico and caused severe flooding in areas still recovering from previous disasters and emergencies.

Simultaneously with these events, Puerto Rico's economy suffered several crises and setbacks. In May 2017, the government of Puerto Rico filed for bankruptcy, the largest public sector bankruptcy in US history. In March 2023, the federal court approved the restructuring of most of the island's debt, allowing Puerto Rico to begin its re-entry to capital markets. Economic recovery is expected to be slow due to many factors such as the loss of manufacturing jobs, unreliable electric energy service, increased competition in the tourism industry and low investment credit ratings, among others.

Change and uncertainty continue to affect the political arena. In 1898, the island was ceded by Spain to the United States as part of the peace treaty ending the Spanish-American War. Since 1917, the people of Puerto Rico have been US citizens. In 1952, Puerto Rican voters adopted a new constitution, proclaiming it as a Commonwealth of the United States. However, recent decisions by the US Supreme Court have affirmed that Puerto Rico remains a Spanish-speaking, unincorporated US territory and is now widely recognized as one of the last remaining colonies in the world. Most experts do not foresee changes in the island's status in the near future, but Puerto Rico's relationship with the United States continues to be embedded in many of the challenges faced by the island.

Demographic shifts have accompanied all of the above events. According to the US Census Bureau, the population of Puerto Rico declined 12% during the 2010–2020 period. This trend has continued, due in part to a low fertility rate as well as massive migration to the US mainland stemming from a poor quality of life and high unemployment. This population loss has been associated with a significant decline in the number of school-age children, skilled workers and health care professionals. Meanwhile, an estimated 42% of Puerto Rico residents live in poverty, a poverty rate far higher than any US state. The aging of the population has accelerated, with 24% aged 65 years or older. The current (2023) population of Puerto Rico is estimated to be around 3.2 million.

STATUS OF EAPS

Most EAPs on the island are affiliated with managed behavioral health organizations as a complement to their medical-psychiatric services. Others are closely tied to health insurance companies that offer the EAP as part of their coverage.

Multinational companies, US corporate subsidiaries and federal government agencies usually contract large EAPs in the US that subcontract local providers. Some organizations have internal EAPs that coordinate direct services for their employees. Local government agencies are required by law to have EAPs.

Extremely competitive pricing has kept the cost of EAP services very low. This, in turn, has made it harder for local EAPs to recruit and retain qualified providers and to pay them fees in line with current market conditions and the increasing cost of living. One of the challenges facing Employee Assistance Programs and providers in Puerto Rico is how to continue making high-quality services available to the workforce while remaining financially viable.

Most local EAPs use licensed psychologists to provide counseling services. In recent years, there has been increased participation by clinical social workers due to the development of local graduate programs offering this area of specialization.

The Puerto Rico Mental Health and Addiction Services Administration has expanded its 24/7 telephone service staffed by mental health professionals ("Linea PAS"). This has proven to be a valuable resource in suicide prevention, crisis counseling, substance abuse and mental health service referral. In 2022, over 225,000 calls were received on this line.

NOTABLE CHANGES IN THE EAP FIELD IN PUERTO RICO

The response to hurricanes and earthquakes has increased the need for on-site services, CISDs, psychological first aid and coordination between the EAP and other sources of emergency relief. For the purpose of assisting EAPs in this area, the Puerto Rico Mental Health and Addiction Services Administration recently published its Guidelines for Crisis Intervention in the Workplace.

The COVID-19 pandemic spurred a rapid implementation of protocols to ensure the safety of clients and staff. These protocols continue to be adapted according to changing trends in disease transmission and prevention. The pandemic has resulted in the growth of remote (virtual) EAP counseling services, which are now much more common than they were prior to 2020.

Paralleling changes in the economy, the incidence of closings, downsizings and mergers of companies has required more CISD, management consulting and organizational support services from the EAP. Generational changes have shown increased demand for app-based or internet-based mental health tools as options within the program.

An article by Brenda Rivera-Garcia describes how the string of crises and emergencies has taken a toll on the mental health of the people of Puerto Rico. Although island-wide statistics are lacking, EAPs in Puerto Rico report an increase in the severity and complexity of the presenting problems (e.g., substance abuse, domestic and workplace violence, depression and anxiety). The lack of accessible, low-cost mental health services on the island often limits the referral options of EAP counselors to provide adequate long-term treatment to these clients.

CONCLUSION

The Employee Assistance Program continues to provide valuable services due to quick access, confidentiality and no costs to the employees and family members. At present, the EAP field in Puerto Rico faces several major challenges which, in turn, offer excellent opportunities for improvement and innovation:

1. Develop and promote the use of measurable outcomes and other metrics to adequately assess the scope and impact of local EAP services. The contribution of EAPs to the mental health field in Puerto Rico is not fully appreciated or valued due to a lack of published data.
2. Enhance the "identity" and visibility of the EAP field. For many employees (and even some providers), the distinction is blurred between the EAP and the mental health services provided under health insurance. Further, the focus is almost entirely on helping individual clients. There is still little awareness of how the EAP can help the customer organization to sustain a psychologically healthy workplace.
3. Promote greater sensitivity and competency when serving diverse populations. These efforts should involve broader inclusion when recruiting providers, as well as greater awareness of diversity in the outreach, educational and counseling services offered by the EAP.
4. Improve oversight, training and technologies to provide effective virtual screening and counseling services that protect client privacy. Online tools such as self-assessments, chats and educational materials are now more available and are often expected by EAP clients. However, these methodologies appear to need more effective integration with follow-up and referral services, as well as rigorous evaluation.
5. Increase readiness for future emergencies. In a study of the social vulnerability of communities in Puerto Rico in the event of a disaster, the US Census Bureau found: "Nearly half—46.1%—of Puerto Rico's population was estimated to have three or more risk factors ranging from poverty to age, more than double the estimated share (21.6%) of the stateside US population in 2019." EAPs in Puerto Rico need to be prepared for future natural or human-made disasters, with alternative plans for communications and service delivery under adverse conditions.
6. Increase communication, collaboration and networking among EAPs within and outside Puerto Rico to exchange information and share their challenges, resources and creative solutions.

ABOUT THE AUTHOR

Marion A. Wennerholm is co-founder and president of Lucy López Roig EAP, Inc., in San Juan, Puerto Rico. Website: www.lucylopezroig.com/

RESOURCES

Asociación de Psicología de Puerto Rico asppr.net
Puerto Rico Mental Health and Addiction Services Administration
assmca.pr.gov

FHC de Puerto Rico, Inc. (First Healthcare) fhcsaludmental.com/beneficiarios/productos/programa-de-ayuda-al-empleado-pae/

Inspira
inspirapr.com/pae

Lucy López Roig EAP, Inc. lucylopezroig.com

MCS Solutions (MCS Healthcare)
mcs.com.pr/en/Pages/wellness/wellness-programs/mcs-solutions

OptiMind (APS Health)
apshealth.com/aps-optimind/

United EAP Resources (San Juan Capestrano Hospital)
unitedeapresources.com

REFERENCES

Lopez Roig, L & Wennerholm, MA, Puerto Rico. *International Employee Assistance Compendium* (4th edition), Dale Masi (Ed.), Masi Research Consultants, Inc., 2010.

Guerra Velázquez GR. Hurricane María and Public Health in Puerto Rico: Lessons Learned to Increase Resiliency and Prepare for Future Disasters. Ann Glob Health. 2022 Sep 23;88(1):82. doi: 10.5334/aogh.3869. PMID: 36213729; PMCID: PMC9504014.

https://www.wsj.com/articles/puerto-rico-released-from-bankruptcy-as-economic-problems-persist-11642537090#

https://harvardlawreview.org/print/vol-136/vaello-madero/

https://welcome.topuertorico.org/history6

https://www.census.gov/quickfacts/fact/table/PR/PST045222

Ley para Crear Programas de Ayuda al Empleado y su Familia Inmediata, Ley Núm. 167 de 11 de Agosto de 2002, según enmendada (contains amendments incorporated by the following law: Ley Núm. 140 de 1 de Octubre de 2007)

https://www.assmca.pr.gov/estadisticas

https://docs.pr.gov/files/ASSMCA/Material%20Educativo/GUIA%20MANEJO%20DE%20CRISIS%20DOC.%20OFICIAL%20FINAL.pdf

https://www.cnn.com/2022/10/01/opinions/puerto-rico-mental-health-toll-garcia-rivera

https://www.census.gov/library/stories/2023/06/how-socially-vulnerable-is-puerto-rico-to-disasters.html

ROMANIA

Alexandru Manescu

The history and evolution of Employee Assistance Programs in Romania are intrinsically linked to that of psychological services in the country. Although Romania returned to its democratic path over three decades ago, in December 1989, the marks left on the country and its people by almost half a century of communist regime had a longer-lasting presence. That was predominantly visible in mental health in general, and psychological support access in particular, and the deep distrust and stigma it generated for Romanians.

Therefore, to understand the evolution of EAPs in Romania, it is important to take a short look at the background of psychological support prior to 1989.

HISTORICAL BACKGROUND

From the late 1940s until the fall of Nicolae Ceaușescu's regime in 1989, the field of psychology, psychotherapy and mental health practices were heavily influenced by the government's communist ideological and political agenda. The regime sought to control various aspects of society, including education and sciences, in order to maintain its power and suppress dissent. As such, the communist government exercised strict control over education, including psychology programs. Psychological theories and practices that aligned with Marxist-Leninist ideology were promoted, while those deemed counter-revolutionary, or capitalist, were suppressed. This had significant implications on psychological counselling, psychotherapy, and mental health treatment during the time.

Psychotherapy was greatly limited in its scope, and therapists were expected to promote principles of collectivism while discouraging individualistic or non-conformist ideas. The regime even went so far as to imprison leading psychologists of the time for refusing to conform with the imposed ideologies. That is not to say that psychotherapy was completely unavailable, as certain professionals did continue to provide appropriate mental health support, but that was usually done behind closed doors and mostly unavailable for the public.

The government also tightly controlled all mental health institutions, from hospitals to clinics, thus allowing the regime to utilise such facilities to suppress dissent and control those perceived as threats. The field of psychiatry was particularly affected. The regime used psychiatric diagnoses as a means to institutionalize and silence political dissidents. Many individuals were labelled as mentally ill simply for expressing anti-government views. These practices led to an innate rejection by the public to seek mental health support, greatly deepening an already existing stigma.

Another very visible and impactful practice that frequently occurred during the communist period of Romania was the lack of privacy. Confidentiality and privacy were often compromised. Patients could not be assured that their discussions with therapists would remain confidential, as therapists were expected to report any statements that could be interpreted as anti-government or subversive. An incredible level of distrust in professionals and even among personal connections regarding one's confidentiality was present on all levels of interactions between Romanians at that time, but that had an even more profound impact on relations with mental health and psychological specialists who, in order to perform their treatments, needed to gain access to personal and sensitive information.

Censorship of psychological literature and limited academic freedoms also greatly impacted the natural development of psychology in Romania during the communist years. Access to international psychological literature and research was restricted, limiting exposure to different therapeutic approaches and ideas. Western psychotherapeutic theories that emphasized individualism and personal growth were discouraged. Academics and researchers were often constrained in their ability to conduct independent research and express their ideas freely. As the Romanian Association of Psychologists states on its website "… especially after 1977 it (Romanian psychology) becomes increasingly isolated, as a result of difficult access to professional resource materials and international academic life."

All those details, although not the only examples that could be given, are noteworthy points when trying to understand any type of mental well-being services that were to be introduced in Romania after 1989, EAPs or otherwise, private or public. It is easy to see how it was a tremendous challenge to promote and implement them to a population that bore the scars left by the communist regime's approach to psychology for almost five decades.

EVOLUTION

As it was to be expected, Romania had a lot to catch up on in terms of openness to mental health support services, a process that is still unfolding even today as the country is ramping up its efforts to align itself with other European countries in terms of mental health delivery.

Much progress was made, and the reality is that present-day Romania does not fall short of proper academic institutions of psychology, leading experts in the field and highly qualified professionals. Compared with other scientific fields, Romanian psychology was quick to reinvent itself and invest great efforts in making up for lost years. Psychotherapy educational centres were formed, covering all major psychological schools of thought and practice. Credentialing bodies such as the Romanian College of Psychologists were established, and legal recognition was granted to professionals working in this field. The pace at which Romanian psychology, as a science, evolved after 1989 was quite impressive, so much so that one could say it was way ahead of the general population that took (and in some respects still takes) longer to embrace and access services.

ACCESS TO COUNSELLING AND PSYCHOTHERAPY

Demand for mental health support in the form of psychological counselling and psychotherapy has increased considerably in Romania, especially among the younger representatives of the population and those living in large cities. Access to care is quite facile in large urban areas but decreases considerably in rural areas, and although it is covered and available through the National Public Health system, the majority of those seeking support do so via private practices or private therapy centres.

EMPLOYEE ASSISTANCE PROGRAMS IN ROMANIA

Looking particularly at EAPs in Romania, until the early 2000s, they were almost nonexistent. Although several local clinics did provide forms of limited psychological support to employees under their general medical benefits plan, to the knowledge of the author, Corporate Counselling Services (CCS) was the first company to introduce and provide fully formed Employee Assistance Programs in Romania. It started doing so at the request of several existing clients serviced in other European countries who wanted to extend the same benefits to their Romanian workforce. In those early years, resistance was very high, and it took a lot of time for an EAP to become effective in a Romanian workplace due to the high adversity and distrust the local population had in these types of services.

It took a great deal of effort to tailor EAPs to become culturally appropriate and effective for this population. This trait can still be seen today. A key success factor in providing such services in Romania is the ability to ensure proper localisation and cultural adaption of the service. CCS internal studies (comparing 50 countries of service) show that local Romanian customers are among the first to require an increased number of proofs regarding confidentiality of service, appropriately local experts as service providers and a fully Romanian service delivery overall.

PRESENT STATUS OF EAPS

Although the last 34 years clearly saw an increase in the demand for EAPs in Romania, these services are far from being widespread in the country. Presently, their greatest expansion is visible among large multinational companies and often not as a decision of local stakeholders but as part of global or international efforts of such companies to have uniform benefits for their workforce across different countries. The number of local Romanian businesses (although the economy itself sees a considerable growth) that have implemented an EAP remains extremely small. That is interesting to look at, especially considering the cultural context of Romania, as described before, as local Romanian businesses do look more and more toward expanding medical benefit plans but less so toward psychological support or EAP services. Most frequently, they fall under the sphere of training and education rather than direct support.

This phenomenon also impacts the presence of EAP providers in the country. Generally, the established Employee Assistance companies active in Romania are mid to large international organizations that cater predominantly to their global customers that also have offices in Romania, with very little presence from fully formed local EAP providers.

Still, the COVID-19 pandemic did see the rise of local clinics and small mental health centres that do provide certain types of mental health education and counselling services for employees but with a limited scope and without branding their services as being EAPs.

Looking at the impact of the COVID-19 pandemic, it is clear that it has generated an overall increase in demand or at least interest in mental health support in both private individuals as well as companies in Romania, with many of them being more open to exploring such services, albeit still relatively slow in actively implementing them. That is also visible when looking at EAP data. CCS statistics show that utilisation rates for Romania have increased, and prior to the onset of the pandemic, approximately 50% of all clients accessed the program for legal and financial guidance with only 21% seeking mental health support. Those figures have changed for the period 2021–2022, where 39% of customers are looking for mental health and psychological assistance, 12% are in need of family support, and the number of legal guidance requests dropped to 31% in the overall figures around the presenting issue clients bring forth to the EAP.

Another visible change generated by the pandemic during the last years is a considerable change in the method of accessing EAP services. CCS internal studies show that prior to January

2020, an overwhelming 98% of all clients accessing the EAP required in-person support. The same cannot be said for figures of the last two years, where 59% of all Romanian employees accessing the program were satisfied though online or telephonic counselling. Internet-based service delivery (in the form of applications, chat support, etc.) remains low in Romania.

CONCLUSION

It is undeniable that five decades of communist regime have left a mark on the Romanian population's perception of mental health services and psychological support, and evidently, that greatly impacts the local market's openness toward Employee Assistance Programs. Major changes have happened during the last 34 years, and the overall context has improved considerably both for professionals in the field as well as the general population. Still, although we can see increased demands for private practice counselling and company-sponsored services such as EAPs, the latter have a slower growth, especially for local businesses.

The COVID-19 pandemic did generate a spike of interest in this type of service, but it remains a challenge for any provider wishing to deliver services in Romania to tailor its service delivery and EAP products to cater to a market and a population that presents the very significant cultural and historic context described in this paper.

ABOUT THE AUTHOR

Alexandru Manescu is the International Director of Clinical Services at Corporate Counselling Services International (CCS) in Bucharest, Romania.

RUSSIA

Daria Fedorova

Empatia (Ponimau) is a leading EAP provider in post-soviet Eurasia in terms of the number of corporate clients (over 1,500) and users served (over 1 million). Services are provided via an online platform and mobile application, allowing users to get consultations with psychologists, legal advisors, financial advisors, health coaches, life and business coaches, mindfulness instructors and other experts.

In recent years, businesses in Russia have faced many new and challenging questions. Save money or expand? Return employees to the office or build remote teams? Some entrepreneurs were looking for solutions and points of growth, others had to move their businesses abroad, and some gave up scaling. But in the flow of current changes, the main value for the business was and still is the employees and their mental state.

In a turbulent environment where many companies are struggling to stay afloat, competing for customers, talent, markets and resources, employee well-being has become a business priority. Classic employee benefits such as medical insurance have long since begun the journey of transformation to be replaced by comprehensive solutions when company management pays attention not only to the physical health of employees but also to their psychological comfort and social well-being. These are key factors affecting the long-term performance of each team member and, consequently, the sustainability of the business.

This is clearly visible in the increase in users and the number of consultations conducted on our platform over the past four years. Compared to pre-COVID-19, we've seen a tenfold increase in referrals in 2022. Despite the fact that business has taken a big storm in 2022 with the start of the military conflict in Ukraine, executives have continued their efforts to provide their employees with resources to improve their well-being: flexible work schedule, personal counselling support, financial and legal advice, and health coaching. All these options are designed to create a supportive work environment in which employee turnover is reduced, burnout and anxiety are prevented, and efficiency is increased as a result.

Demand for psychological counselling grew significantly throughout 2022. First, in February when the military operation was launched, the number of inquiries for support increased by a quarter. We saw the next surge in demand in September, when the partial mobilization (military draft) was announced, with a 30% increase. And so far, the level of demand for support has remained stable. Regardless of the events that occur, the top five topics for counselling do not change: these are spouse relationships, partner relationships (male-female), anxiety disorders, existential issues, and parent-child relationships.

Against the background of the announcement of the military operation and the partial mobilization in 2022, people began to seek for legal advice more often on issues related to these very events. They are interested in ways to avoid the military service, obtain social benefits and allowances, and consult about the rights of foreign nationals. The latter is also connected with the fact that over 0.5 million people relocated abroad.

The factor of uncertainty in 2022 provoked an increase in requests for financial advice on the topic of personal financial planning. So far, the focus of people's attention has shifted from investments to lending and paying taxes.

Regarding health coaching, the share of requests regarding mood improvement has increased 5.5 times compared with previous years. In a period of high anxiety, for example, after the announcement of partial mobilization, people became more interested in how to improve personal efficiency.

Mindfulness is a popular trend of becoming aware of oneself in the present moment through meditation. In a period of turbulence on our platform, the demand for mindfulness practices, taking care of yourself and your resources, has increased by almost 1.5 times.

Life coaching began to flourish as a trend. During the period of turbulence requests for sessions on the topic of adapting and living through a period of change increased almost sixfold. A key trend for the past few years can be described as a conscious approach to using a set of measures to support employees. Employers are interested in the accumulation and analysis of data for decision-making and operational research of the current situation, which allow them to maintain the flexibility and effectiveness of these programs.

What trends in the development of EAP do we expect in the future? The transition from wellness to holistic well-being will continue, and programs will be more deeply integrated into the work environment. Trends such as:

- Concern for the financial well-being of employees. The events happening in the world are leading to an increase in inflation and a decrease in employee income. Companies have a direct interest in ensuring that employees know how to build financial reserves and make the right financial decisions. Therefore, they will provide employees with education and training on personal financial management, help develop an economic mindset, and teach money strategies. After all, a financially secure employee with low levels of financial stress is more loyal and productive.
- Rehabilitation programs for demobilized employees. According to a recent survey, 47% of employers are willing to implement a corporate program to rehabilitate and adjust employees and their families who have been mobilized into the military. Companies see the need to provide them with medical care and psychological support in the first place. Also, employers agree that the needs of these employees should be discussed individually.
- Inclusion, when employees with disabilities are involved on the team. The success of such projects depends on many factors, but because of digitization, more vacancies for people with disabilities began to appear during the pandemic in those industries and professions that developed during the crisis because of the transition to online.
- Empathy as a key leadership ability. Most employees have a dopamine deficit and cognitive fatigue due to the series of crises we have seen in the last few years. In such a situation, human-centered leadership with attention to the individual needs of the employee and his or her circumstances becomes most valuable.
- Strengthening the role of HR. Such specialists are ambassadors for companies. They are not only in charge of selecting and controlling EAP and other suppliers but also of integrating well-being programs into the corporate culture and operations.
- Concern for the well-being of loved ones. The mental health of relatives has a direct impact on employee well-being. Support for elderly parents, spouses/partners and children of employees becomes an integral part of programs.
- Adapting services to demand. Companies keep track of statistics and topics of demand and adapt assistance services to the problems employees care about. For example, in 2022, we noted the demand for sexual relationship counselors, which emerged against the background of stress and anxiety of the users, so we launched it as a separate line of support.

People's need for social support and empathy to cope with the various world crises increased significantly after they faced constant fear and uncertainty.

HR trends for the future suggest that organizations must pay more attention to the needs of individuals. The focus should be on improving employees' mental health, ensuring employee safety, and using technology to provide employees with new and exciting experiences.

It used to be that only large international corporations in Russia had access to this, but every year, with the development of online services, small- and medium-sized Russian companies have the opportunity to take care of their employees, which means there is a chance that, despite the turbulence we are all going through, there will be more and more happy employees and companies in Russia right now.

ABOUT THE AUTHOR

Daria Fedorova is Co-founder and Chief Operations Officer of Ponimau Corporate Wellbeing Platform (Russia), and Co-founder and Chief Executive Officer of Empatia Corporate Wellbeing Platform (Kazakhstan).

SCOTLAND

Tony Buon

BACKGROUND

Scotland is one of the four constituent countries of the United Kingdom, along with England, Wales, and Northern Ireland. It has a devolved government and has historically maintained a distinct cultural and legal identity within the broader UK framework. Scotland forms the northern part of Great Britain and is surrounded by sea on three sides. Its only land border, to the south with England, runs for approximately 96 km along the line of the Cheviot Hills.

The latest estimate of Scotland's population (on 30 June 2021) is 5,479,900.[41] Migration was the main driver of population growth with 27,800 more people moving to Scotland than leaving. Migration has been adding to Scotland's population for the last 21 years. There is concern that Scotland's population is projected to fall by nearly 900,000 over the next 50 years.[42]

Scotland was one of the industrial powerhouses of Europe from the time of the Industrial Revolution, being a world leader in manufacturing and shipbuilding. In common with most other advanced industrialized economies, Scotland has seen a decline in the importance of the manufacturing industries and primary-based extractive industries. This has, however, been combined with a rise in the service sector of the economy.

---

41 Accessed July 15, 2023, https://www.nrscotland.gov.uk/
42 Accessed July 1, 2023, https://www.scotsman.com/news/politics/scotlands-falling-population-and-acute-pressures-set-to-hit-gdp-growth-3823973

The discovery of North Sea oil in 1966 transformed the Scottish economy, as Scottish waters consist of a large sector of the North Atlantic and the North Sea. With the growth of oil exploration during that time, as well as the ancillary industries needed to support it, the northeast city of Aberdeen became the centre of the North Sea Oil Industry. The oil boom brought new jobs, new money, new opportunities, and oil workers from around the world. It also brought new challenges to local culture, as the lives of thousands of Scots in previously remote northern coastal towns and islands were affected daily by the demands and the economic ups and downs of the oil industry.

The taxation revenue derived from oil in Scottish waters has not been devolved to Scotland but rather goes to the UK Government at Westminster. This issue forms part of the ongoing debate about the future possibility of Scotland's independence from the UK.

POLITICAL AND CULTURAL FACTORS

Before 1707, Scotland was an independent sovereign state with its own parliament and monarch. The process of union began in 1603 when King James VI of Scotland inherited the throne of England (as King James I) after the death of Queen Elizabeth I and thus "united" Scotland and England under a single monarch. This is when the term "Great Britain" came into being, and it describes the union of the crowns. Political union, however, did not occur until 1707 during the reign of Queen Anne. It was in this year that the Scottish Parliament assembled for the last time and the formal union of parliaments was enacted and the "United Kingdom of Great Britain" came into existence. The United Kingdom of Great Britain was then expanded in the 20th century to include Northern Ireland to become the "United Kingdom of Great Britain and Northern Ireland."

The Union of the Parliaments was very unpopular with the ordinary Scottish people. The Scots lost the argument for a federal arrangement but did manage to secure the continuation of the Scottish legal system, education, and church. These were important elements in allowing the country to preserve a separate cultural identity.

The concept of full independence did not re-enter the Scottish mainstream until the 1960s. The discovery of North Sea oil off the east coast of Scotland in the 1970s further invigorated the debate over Scottish independence. In 1979, the first referendum was put to the Scottish electorate to gauge if there was sufficient support to create a "deliberate assembly." This referendum was lost, and another was not to be put to the Scottish people again until 1997.

A referendum was held in September of 1997, and 75% of those who voted approved the devolution plan. The Parliament of the United Kingdom subsequently approved the Scotland Act, which created an elected Scottish Parliament with control over most domestic policy. In May 1999, Scotland held its first election for a devolved parliament, and in July, the Scottish Parliament held session for the first time since the previous parliament had been adjourned in 1707.

The King appoints one Member of the Scottish Parliament, on the nomination of the Parliament, to be First Minister. Other Ministers are also appointed by the King on the nomination of the Parliament, and together with the First Minister, they make up the Scottish Government, the executive arm of government. Scotland is represented by 59 MPs in the House of Commons of the United Kingdom, elected from territory-based Scottish constituencies, out of a total of 650 MPs in the House of Commons. Various members of the House of Lords represent Scottish political parties.

The Scottish Parliament has legislative authority for all non-reserved matters relating to Scotland and has limited power to vary income tax. The Scottish Parliament can refer devolved matters back to Westminster to be considered as part of United Kingdom-wide legislation by passing a Legislative Consent Motion if United Kingdom-wide legislation is considered to be more appropriate for certain issues.

The programmes of legislation enacted by the Scottish Parliament since 1999 have seen a divergence in the provision of public services compared to the rest of the United Kingdom. For instance, the costs of university education and care services for the elderly are free at the point of use in Scotland, while fees are paid in the rest of the UK. Scotland was the first country in the UK to ban smoking in enclosed public places.

The public and political debate continues about the pros and cons of full political independence for Scotland, which is strongly defended by some parties and individuals within Scotland, including the present First Minister, Humza Yousaf. It is important to understand that irrespective of those views about the nature of the political relationship between England and Scotland or the outcome of any future campaign for independence, the Scottish people are justly proud and fiercely protective of their separate and unique cultural, historical, and ethnic identities.

HEALTH CARE

Health care in Scotland is mainly provided by the National Health Service (NHS) Scotland, Scotland's public health care system (what is often referred to incorrectly in the USA as "socialised health care"). The service was founded in 1948, and on 31 March 2022, NHS Scotland had a total headcount of 181,723 staff, making it Scotland's largest employer.[43]

Scotland also had a distinctive medical tradition centred on its medical schools rather than private practice. The pioneers of the service believed that a national health service would reduce illness, people would become healthier, and costs would come down. It never happened.

The private sector operates in a few specialist areas including elective surgical procedures,

---

43 Accessed July 16, 2023, https://turasdata.nes.nhs.scot/media/j0vdmiul/workforce-report-june-2022-formatted.pdf

occupational health services (including EAPs), and some mental health services. Overall there is a cultural belief in the "goodness and rightness" of the NHS and a distrust of private health care. This fierce pride in the NHS and loyalty to the principle of free care for all at the point of need can be traced back to the lack of equity in access to health care before 1948, when many people went without medical care as they could not afford it.

ALCOHOL AND OTHER DRUGS

Scotland has a serious alcohol misuse problem. The majority of people in Scotland drink alcohol. Scottish people are more likely to have drunk more than twice the recommended daily benchmarks than those in England. To try to deal with these figures, the Scottish Government has introduced several strategies, including a minimum pricing of alcohol by unit and several harm-reduction measures. To date, the data has not shown any significant reduction in consumption, illness, and deaths.

Scotland has long had the highest drug-related death rate of any country in Europe. According to recent annual figures, 1,330 people lost their lives to drug misuse in Scotland in 2021. It means Scotland retains the unwanted title of Europe's drug death capital, with a death rate almost four times higher than its nearest competitor, Norway.[44]

The Scottish Government's drugs strategy is based on consensus and evidence, including many expert reports. Central to the strategy is the principle of recovery. This means that more than just reducing risk and harm, services should help people to move on toward a drug-free life. Some innovative ideas from the devolved Scottish government would require Westminster to change laws, and this is presently unlikely. This Scottish Government strategy does not make mention of Employee Assistance Programmes as part of the overall strategy and generally ignores workplace issues.

EAP HISTORY IN THE UK

The development of EAPs in Scotland parallels that of England and the UK as a whole. In the UK, there is a very long history of welfare in employment, with the first EAP program being introduced to the UK in 1981 when Control Data, an American company, began assisting their employees from their internal EAP in the States. The first external EAPs were founded in the mid-1980s. These were all based in England (normally London), with some limited services

---

44 Accessed June 13, 2023, https://www.politico.eu/article/europe-drug-death-capital-politicians-new-powers-heroin-edinburgh/#:~:text=According%20to%20new%20annual%20figures,than%20its%20nearest%20competitor%2C%20Norway.

available in Scotland. Today, all EAP providers operating in Scotland are part of the broader UK (and global) EAP providers. For more information on EAP services in the UK, see the chapter on the United Kingdom.

Over 25 organisations are providing EAP services in the UK, and most are registered with UK EAPA and abide by the EAPA UK Standards. As of December 2022, EAPA UK updated and consolidated previous documents (2018, 2015) and commenced a verification and auditing process for registered providers. This process aims to promote confidence, trust, and respect from clients (dual), enable EAPs to reflect on their services, and provide ongoing "education" for providers of best practices.[45]

UK EAPA was established in 1998 and has extended and adapted the EAPA global to suit the UK market.[46] It is worth noting that EAPA UK operates somewhat differently than EAPA in the United States, with a majority of the membership in the UK being organisational or corporate members.

In late 2007, Robert Gordon University in Aberdeen, Scotland, was contracted by the Employee Assistance European Forum (EAEF) to conduct research into the perceptions of HR Managers of EAPs in Europe.[47] And whilst this study did not look at Scotland in isolation, the results can be generalised to the Scottish market. The results suggested that Human Resource Managers (i.e., the customers) have a good perception of EAPs. They see them as professional counselling services offering valuable support to employees and are generally satisfied with the services they receive. Nearly all of the services advocated by respondents for inclusion in EAP are what might be described as traditional EAP services, e.g., face-to-face counselling for employees, critical incident, trauma support, and so on.

EAP SERVICES

So far, EAPs have made little real headway in any European country, with the exception of the UK and Ireland. EAPs in Scotland generally follow the EAP model used in the rest of the UK. That being, external services provided by private EAP providers offering employee counselling (both telephone and face-to-face) and other specialist services.

Generally in Scotland (as in the rest of the UK), EAPs are often seen as employee counselling services.[48] Given this and the general distrust in the UK of "private health care," EAPs are some-

---

45   Buon, T (2023) EAPA UK AGM Presentation: *The new EAPA standards, verification approach and next steps.*

46   Accessed July 6, 2023, https://www.eapa.org.uk/about-us-employee-assistance-in-the-uk/

47   Buon, T & Taylor, J (2008) A Review of the EAP Market in the United Kingdom & Europe. *Journal of Workplace Behavioural Health.* V23, No4, 425–444.

48   Buon, T & Taylor, J (2008) A Review of the EAP Market in the United Kingdom & Europe. *Journal of Workplace Behavioural Health.* V23, No4, 425–444.

what marginalised. All government departments and most large organisations have an EAP, but the model can range from a rarely promoted telephone assistance service through to the "full" EAP model found in many US-based organisations. EAPs are very rare in small to medium enterprises (SMEs) even though they employ most of the UK workforce.

The Certified Employee Assistance Professional (CEAP) credential is of limited interest to EAP professionals in Scotland. It is often seen as an "American" credential, and there are only a handful of CEAPs in the country. This is generally because most of the EAP counselling is provided by contract counsellors who normally hold counselling and psychotherapy qualifications and are credentialed by their respective professional bodies. That is, the British Association for Counselling and Psychotherapy (BACP) and the United Kingdom Council for Psychotherapy (UKCP).

EAP PROVIDERS

All of the EAP providers presently servicing Scotland are headquartered in England and are part of UK-wide (or global) networks. Several have EAP offices in Scotland. As of 2023, there were no Scottish-based EAP providers. However, all the major EAPA UK Registered providers offer the full range of EAP services in Scotland.

For a full list of providers in Scotland, please see the United Kingdom chapter in this *Compendium*.

SUMMARY

Scotland has been referred to as the "sick man of Europe," having some of the worst health statistics in Europe. Life expectancy in Scotland is the lowest in the UK, and there is a 10-year gap in life expectancy between those living in the most and least deprived areas of Scotland. Scotland also has the eighth-highest level of alcohol consumption in the world.[49]

While EAPs could have a major role to play in the mental and occupational health of Scotland, unfortunately, EAPs are not mentioned in any Scottish health, welfare, or even alcohol and other drug strategies.

Overall, EAPs in Scotland appear to, at least on the surface, differ little from those operating in the rest of the UK. Some providers have established Scottish offices and have targeted some Scottish markets (noticeably, oil and gas). But generally, Scotland is not viewed as an independent EAP market. This may not be a good strategy for growth, for global experiences with EAPs in Asia and Europe have shown that EAP development is best served with EAPs that are developed to suit

---

49 Accessed July 10, 2023, http://news.bbc.co.uk/1/hi/scotland/7903584.stm

the local culture. EAP services always need to be modified to this culture and the local market, and it is very important to keep in mind that Scottish culture is different from that of England, Wales, and Northern Ireland.

ABOUT THE AUTHOR

Tony Buon is an experienced Workplace Psychologist, Coach, and Author. Tony holds formal degrees in Psychology, Behavioural Sciences, and Workplace Education. He is a Certified Employee Assistance Professional (CEAP) and a Registered Civil, Commercial and Workplace Mediator (CMC-UK). Tony is the Managing Partner of Buon Consultancy. From 1985 until 2001, Tony was a director and owner of one of the global EAP providers, IPS Worldwide. Tony now consults and trains independently throughout the UK, Europe, the Middle East, and Asia. He also acts as an independent EAP consultant. Tony has served as the International Commissioner on the Employee Assistance Certification Commission (EACC).

Email: tony@buon.net

Web: www.buon.net

SINGAPORE

Elizabeth Nair

INTRODUCTION

Singapore is an island country and city-state in South-East Asia. The land area is 728.6 sq km, population size of 5.28 million. Four official languages are English, Chinese, Malay and Tamil. Singapore is a unitary parliamentary democracy. In 1967, compulsory military conscription was introduced for 18-year-old males.

THE IMPACT OF COVID-19 ON SERVICES

The Singapore Psychological Society and The Singapore Association for Counselling rallied members. Civil servants and private practitioners worked together to provide psychological support services. A government-supported 24-Hour Hotline was established, staffed by professionals who volunteered for shifts. It was extensively used by the whole spectrum of the population.

Samaritans of Singapore (SOS) reported that 2020/2021 showed a 37% increase in Hotline calls with suicide risk and a 51% increase in incoming texts expressing suicidal ideation or plans since July 2020, compared to 2019/2020. Females aged 20–29 years made the most calls, while males aged 30–39 sent the most text messages. For 2021/2022, SOS reported a 17.4% increase in the 24-Hour Hotline calls and a 120% increase in 24-Hour CareTexts compared to 2020/2021. Notably, the most prevalent concern raised by adults aged 30–59 years was employment-related and financial problems.

A cross-sectional study of health care workers (HCWs) in four public hospitals and a primary health care system over a four-week period in 2021, compared to a similar period in 2020 that coincided with a major surge in COVID-19 cases, showed that the mental health of HCWs had objectively worsened in the second pandemic year.

The total number of drug-related arrests declined from 2019 to a non-significant 4% increase in 2022 to 2,826. In 2022, 62% of new abusers used methamphetamine, and the second highest was cannabis at 21%, replacing heroin in the preceding years.

The number of EAP calls for personal counselling increased dramatically. Working from home was a hardship for many. Singles who lived alone missed going to work and socializing with colleagues. They missed their leisure activities and frequent work-related travel and overseas travel to connect with family and friends. The fear of losing their jobs was a constant. Plus the anxiety and grief and feelings of isolation and helplessness when a family member was diagnosed with COVID-19 and isolated.

Working from home meant physical and emotional family intrusions during work hours. Many did not have dedicated work areas at home. Those with young children were additionally tasked with home tutoring and helping with the home administration of the virtual classroom.

Time management was a big challenge for employees during the initial work-from-home phases in 2020. Work-related anxiety drove a haphazard work schedule, often stretching many hours beyond eight hours a day and stretching haphazardly into the night and early morning hours.

THE EFFECTS OF ONLINE AND VIRTUAL COUNSELLING

There was an upsurge in EAP requests from male employees at the start of the pandemic. Telephonic and web-based calls were both popular. However, as soon as it was allowed, a good number requested to come in person for counselling. They explained that this was one way they could actually move out of their homes, where they felt imprisoned during the lockdown. Taking public transport to arrive at the EAP consultancy for support provided a much-needed diversion and escape from the confines of home, even though there was a strict requirement to wear a mask at all times, including during the in-person counselling. Expatriate males especially obsessed about their job security. They brought up excessive workload, close virtual supervision, and long hours as challenges.

Female employees with young children and without private, dedicated workstations at home were immensely stressed. Even during the telephonic counselling, their young children would call out for their attention. Those who had pet dogs at home had pet intrusions several times during the counselling. Female employees seemed to be more impacted by the domestic intrusions. They were relieved to be able to connect with the EAP counsellor and receive undivided attention. Time management on a daily basis was a struggle, as they attempted to meet the demands of home schooling their children and household chores and deliver excellent work for their employer. With virtual counselling, they could offload their frustrations about the insufficient support from their spouses and learn how to enlist more help.

Family who lives in the same home as employees are also eligible for EAP counselling. Parents at home during the lockdown meant closer observation of how their children were spending their time. A common point of dispute had to do with recreational and social computer and mobile time, which the parents felt powerless to curb. This was a point of verbal and sometimes physical conflict between parents and school-age children. EAP counsellors chose to allocate separate individual times for parents and children in such conflicts to work out the best management strategies with cooler heads on both sides. Once the strict lockdown was lifted, parents often chose to bring their children to the EAP consultancy in person.

Managers called on EAP to seek advise on how best to supervise their staff while the whole organization was working from home. Initially overwrought themselves with their own job security concerns, many adopted a draconian approach of checking to see who had their computers logged on day and night, as well as sending work-related emails in the night and expecting a response by morning. Understandably, this meant employees were stressed out and increasingly anxious and upset with the perceived unreasonable job demands. Eventually, managers and employees benefitted from EAP virtual training to help them manage the change in work procedures, set boundaries in working from home, and understand the emotional reactions during change. Managers and line supervisors learned to identify and refer their staff for EAP counselling.

THE ROLE OF TECHNOLOGY AND SOCIAL MEDIA

The functioning of the COVID-19 Hotline was immensely supported by technology and social media. Efficiency, speed of communication, and transmission of relevant information were enabled. The professionals who signed up as volunteers to staff the Hotline were recruited by email. Signing in to their shift was by a password-accessed web page. Referral resources of multiple organizations, email and telephone details, and brief summaries of their services were updated in real time and made available through protected Google page access. Each shift comprising of different language and dialect capacities was connected by WhatsApp Group with a supervisor.

Throughout the pandemic, emails, WhatsApp, telephone, and text messages were used for quick communications between individuals, organizations, government agencies, hospitals, and employers. Pen-and-paper communications were only to confirm directives and advisories earlier communicated through speedier electronic technology. This included information on the dates and times that different polyclinics and community centres were open for free COVID-19 vaccinations and specific dates for different age-bands. The protocol to follow on arrival at the vaccination centres was also communicated, as well as how to conduct and care for themselves in the days and weeks after vaccination.

Social media, and in particular, Facebook, was a much-used popular means of COVID-19-related information dissemination. Bus routes and time schedules where free face masks were available for collection, free vaccinations were available, and when schools were closed and home schooling was in place are samples of the many COVID-19-related information shared across the board to the general public by other members of the public who felt a need to share. In that process, some misinformation was also shared on social media. This was noticed and corrected by the COVID-19 Pandemic Management Team, which conducted a daily television information broadcast.

Television was also a vehicle for public education through skits conducted by popular comedians in the different languages, as well as more serious Q&A sessions with medical experts. The global spread of COVID-19 and updated Singapore statistics of confirmed cases, hospitalization, recovery, and death were shared daily in the televised late afternoon presentation by the COVID-19 Management Team and also sent by WhatsApp messaging. Information-sharing during a crisis and life-threatening situation was identified as an important stress management strategy by Nair (1989) in her PhD thesis Stress Inoculation in Relation to War.

The G2 smartphone was introduced in Singapore in 2013. Mobile phones became the prime portable item for personal identification and security access to workplaces, supermarkets, and all public and private buildings. The mobile also displayed updated information on a person's vaccination status. Unvaccinated persons were not permitted physical access to public or private buildings, supermarkets, food courts, or their workplace. Food deliveries at home became a way of life for many. Food orders and payment were made virtually or by mobile phone with contactless delivery placed outside the front door. 2023 has seen 92% smartphone ownership and island-wide Wi-Fi connectivity.

EFFORTS TOWARD DIVERSITY AND INCLUSION

Practicing counsellors have professional training to accept diversity in sexual orientation in clients. However, some struggle with strong religious community beliefs that only an unequivocal male-female union within the bounds of marriage is acceptable. This includes older and younger counsellors. They sometimes opt, given a choice, to exclude themselves from EAP counselling where the client presents with a different sexual orientation.

EAP providers have updated training and workshop materials on sexual orientation and preferences. Companies in Singapore have opted for training on LGBTQI+ information for employees and managers to promote inclusion and workplace collaboration and productivity. EAP workshop facilitators in Singapore have therefore increased their knowledge about diversity through virtual research and a wider exposure to documentary and drama series on television.

Expatriate EAP clients with diverse sexual orientations have felt more confident talking about their challenges at work with their religious upbringing, place of worship, and close family members. EAP clients also seek counselling for a partner living with them with whom there is conflict concerning diversity issues. In Singapore, the local population has been less open in seeking EAP counselling for diversity and inclusion. This is changing with increasing openness and parliamentary and public discussions.

CONCLUSION

EAP in Singapore is predominantly provided for staff by international MNCs who engage local professionals. It is a fledgling model for local SMEs who feature as the largest employer. COVID-19 has served to alert employers of the benefits of EAP for mental health and productivity.

ABOUT THE AUTHOR

I am Elizabeth Nair nee Chacko, born in Singapore. I earned a Bachelor of Psychology as a Colombo Plan Scholar from the University of Western Australia, and a PhD in Psychology, Commonwealth Fellow, Stress Research Group, University of Nottingham, UK. My work track includes Chief Psychologist, Ministry of Defence, and an academic at the National University of Singapore.

I am the CEO/Principal Psychologist and Lead Counsellor in Work & Health Psychologists (WHP), a consultancy I established in 2004. In June 2007, the National Library of Singapore deemed my website (www.workpsych.com.sg/) to be an important part of Singapore's documentary heritage and included it in their live archives.

International affiliates are in India, Indonesia, Finland, South Africa, and China. Sixteen Singapore affiliates collectively speak Mandarin, Indian and Chinese dialects, and Malay, apart from English. WHP was a forerunner in offering EAP services in Singapore to the banking and financial sector, as well as to MNCS, SMEs, and the health and education sectors.

RESOURCES

MindFi
160 Robinson Road, #14-04
Singapore 068914
E-mail: well@mindfi.com
Website: www.mindfi.co

Work & Health Psychologists (WHP)
39B Jalan Pemimpin, #08-00
Singapore 577184
E-mail: workpsych@singnet.com.sg
Website: www.workpsych.com.sg

REFERENCES

Abhiram K, Tan BYQ, Tan M, Tan L, Sia C-H, Chua YX, Lim LJH, Suppiah CM, Sim K, Chan YH, Ooi SBS. The Effect of COVID-19 endemicity on the Mental Health of Health Workers. Journal of the American Medical Directors Association. 23(3):405-413.e3 (Mar) Original Study. Building Bonds, Transitioning Boundaries, Samaritans of Singapore Annual Report 2021/2022, Singapore.

Chia DXY, Ng CWL, Asharani P, Yong SA, Tan JW, Noor Azizah Z, Chua SKG, Low LTK, Cheok CCS, Kandasami G. Understanding Cannabis Use in Singapore: Profile of Users and Drug Progression. Singapore Medical Journal, 1-18. Doi: https://doi.org/10.11622/smedj.2022071 (June) [Epub ahead of print]

Nair, E (1989), Stress Inoculation in Relation to War, Nottingham University, UK (archived in British Library)

Overview of Singapore's Drug Situation in 2022, Central Narcotics Bureau Press Release, Singapore, 26 May 2023.

SLOVAKIA

Zuzana Podkonická

Slovak republic is a small country in Central Eastern Europe with a population of approximately 5 million people. It became a sovereign republic in 1993 after a peaceful separation from Czech Republic. Since its independence, the economy developed steadily thanks to foreign investments and an export-oriented economy. Slovakia is an industrial country with a main focus on manufacturing. The automotive industry, with several production facilities of major car companies, is based in the country and is of particular importance for economic growth.

Slovakia has also faced significant growth in the Shared Service Centers (SSC) industry due to advantages like cost effectiveness, language proficiency, geographic location, and support from the government. SSC employs a large number of employees and is increasingly turning toward EAP programs.

However, in Slovakia, Employee Assistance Programs (EAPs) are still an emerging concept. Several international EAP providers operating globally began to offer these services after the economy crisis in 2009. It was mostly offered in US-owned companies. The global EAP providers hired affiliate psychologists in Slovakia who provided counseling to employees, and all the other services would be provided mostly from abroad. This would require a long response time and lower trust of employees in the services. The management of Slovak subsidiaries soon began to prefer a local touch for the services, and this gave the possibility for Slovak EAPs to grow.

ENEF Consulting was established in January 2013 as a company providing EAP services to local clients. The company was established as a health care facility in accordance with Slovak law, which dictates that mental health services fall under a health care system. You cannot officially provide mental health counseling unless you are a health care provider. Health care providers in Slovakia have various obligations to ensure the provision of quality health care services and to meet the needs of patients. These requirements include highly qualified professionals, continuous education of counselors, privacy and confidentiality, continuity of care, and accessibility. Health care providers must comply with relevant quality standards, protocols, and guidelines established by health care authorities.

There are ways to go around this law, which is a preference of many companies and psychologists. For example, they renamed "mental health counseling" as "coaching" or "lifestyle counseling." This way, there are less obligations that need to be met. Legal changes were expected in late 2023, improving the legislation by eliminating "gray areas" and ensuring a higher quality of care.

ENEF Consulting provides standard EAP services offering psychological, legal, financial, practical, and well-being support to employees of our clients.

We are a member of EAEF and EAPA, which helps us follow the latest trends and issues in EAPs. Our first client was a local share center of a global company with only about 600 people. Since then, we have grown and now take care of about 35,000 lives, either for our local clients or for clients of the big EAP global companies as their local partner. We have recently begun to provide our services in Czech Republic, which is a bigger market with a population of 10 million people.

THE IMPACT OF THE PANDEMIC

The utilization of EAP programs in Slovakia was very low in the early years of implementation of the EAP services. Employees did not trust the program and were not used to calling for help when having mental health or other issues. We had to do a lot of education about the program and mental health as well as the issues of confidentiality. There has been and still is a strong stigma around mental health.

The interest in using EAP services among employees has grown rapidly due to the pandemic, the war in Ukraine, inflation, and energetic crises. Issues of mental health became a daily topic on news and TV discussions since more and more people have been impacted. A lot of awareness was raised around the importance of taking care of our own mental health. Although mental health is still stigmatized, there are many more people who are willing to come and at least try the services since it is given to them as a benefit.

Slovak Academy of Science did surveys for the project "How have you been Slovakia" in 2022, in which they have been monitoring the relationship between the social context, the levels of stress, and the depressive feelings in respondents. Since the beginning of the pandemic, results show that more than 25% of respondents feel their mental health had worsened over the last two years. In 2022, 34% of the Slovak population experienced intensely depressive feelings on an everyday basis.

The levels of stress and depressive feelings are significantly impacted by the war in Ukraine and climate changes.

Since the awareness of the importance of mental health has grown, organizations are looking for ways to support their employees' health and are more interested in EAP services as a solution. Many of them, especially smaller organizations, do not show interest in the whole EAP program but only for the mental health part of it. Here, we see more space for education about the services.

THE EFFECTS OF VIRTUAL COUNSELING

During the pandemic, most of the Slovakian companies applied the remote work model. Employees stayed in their home offices, not able to go anywhere during lockdown. We offered our services online immediately. Many of the employees who were using face-to-face services at that time interrupted the counseling, asking to wait until it gets back to "normal." Some switched to virtual counseling with no problem, and all the new intakes were provided online.

During the pandemic, we also provided online support groups for some of our clients, either for certain teams or just mixed groups focused on a specific topic. It was very popular among employees and, based on their feedback, very helpful in those difficult times.

After the pandemic was over, many of the clients preferred to stay in the virtual space, while others were happy to come back to face-to-face sessions. At this moment, we have about half of our services provided online and half face-to-face. Employees using virtual counseling see it as more time convenient, comfortable in their own environment, and easy to access. Employees using face-to-face usually have a lot of virtual meetings in their work and prefer the personal contact, also using counseling as a way of socializing when in their home offices.

There has been also a switch in the preferences of many psychologists. They have been providing their services only online ever since. It lowers their cost for space and travel. Thanks to the possibility of virtual counseling, there has also been a rise of several companies providing an online portal for virtual counseling. This creates a good match with the psychologists who work only online and with people who demand virtual counseling. Virtual online portals became, in a way, competitors to EAPs.

THE ROLE OF TECHNOLOGY AND SOCIAL MEDIA

Social media influences society in Slovakia in many ways. It is a great source of information but also a great source of conflict when the power of it is misused. The anxiety and fear created by the latest events offer a huge space for politicians and extremist groups to use social media for their benefit. It has been difficult for many people to distinguish between hoaxes and relevant information, which brings chaos and hate into relationships—even the closest ones. People are polarized into groups. These are the common groups: vaccinators versus anti-vaccinators, blaming Russia for the war versus blaming the US, those for gay marriages versus those against gay marriages, etc.

There are also beneficial roles of social media and technology. There are a lot of podcasts available on topics of mental health, self-development, and financial health that are regularly accessible to people. Slovak people who are bilingual also benefit from English or German apps providing resources and trainings in relaxation, meditation, or emotional regulation.

Webinars are also a good way to reach and educate people. Chat counseling became very popular among young people and is provided by a state-funded organization.

If one is interested in any topic, the information is within reach. However, a very important task is to choose the reliable source and information. The education of the population on finding and using the right information is highly needed.

DIVERSITY AND INCLUSION

Slovakia is a very traditional country. Almost 95% of the population of Slovakia is white. There are different nationalities, but Europeans prevail. About 2% of the population is Roma, and they are not very well integrated and most of them do not work. It is a huge issue that is constantly being addressed in Slovakia but with no successful results to this date.

The largest number of migrants come from Ukraine. Religion-wise, we are mostly Christians, meaning almost 80% of the population.

These facts are one of the reasons that questions of diversity and inclusion do not come up as often as in other countries. We are used to looking similar, have a similar religion, and have very low contact with diversity in Slovakia until we travel abroad. Many people are not able to relate to these topics, even when brought by their employer, since it seems so far away from their everyday life. When we meet with diversity face-to-face in Slovakia, the reactions are often very defensive. The younger generation is more open-minded regarding diversity.

The most addressed question around diversity is the question of sexuality. This topic was opened last year after the brutal shooting attack by an 18-year-old boy in front of a gay bar. He killed two people who were gay, and one was wounded. Discussions about attitudes and the treatment of homosexual people in Slovakia were given space. Many homosexuals or other sexuality-oriented people would rather go live abroad since the environment here is very unfriendly and discriminating.

As an EAP provider, we had several requests from employers to come and educate employees on topics of diversity and inclusion. We find it useful when employees have been previously exposed to diversity themselves, either privately or at their workplace. It is less impactful when it is just ordered as one of the program's topics with no real previous experience of the employees. There is a high need for education and awareness to rise in this area.

ABOUT THE AUTHOR

I am Zuzana Podkonická, the founder of Enef Consulting and qualified as a clinical psychologist and psychotherapist in the gestalt modality. I studied and worked in the USA as a mental health counselor and then gained more clinical experience in Slovakia as well as experience as a consultant and soft skills trainer in the organizational environment. I have worked as an affiliate psychologist for several global EAP companies, which enabled me to acquire considerable knowledge and experience about the EAP and helped me to grow my company.

RESOURCES

Please contact info@enefconsulting.sk if you are looking to find a specific professional.

Zuzana Podkonická, MS Clinical Psychologist, Enef Consulting s.r.o. zpodkonicka@enefconsulting.sk

SOUTH AFRICA

Navlika Ratangee

INTRODUCTION

South Africa, a nation of extraordinary diversity and profound historical significance, stands as a beacon of resilience and transformation on the African continent. Nestled at the southern tip of Africa, this country has traversed a complex path from its tumultuous past to its present role as a dynamic and vibrant nation on the global stage.

South Africa, split into nine provinces, celebrates a rich tapestry of cultures. The country is home to a multitude of ethnic groups such as Zulu, Xhosa, Sotho, Afrikaner, and many other vibrant communities, with sign language being one of the 12 official languages. South Africa's history is marked by pivotal moments, including the end of apartheid in 1994. The nation's first democratically elected president, Nelson Mandela, and Archbishop Desmond Tutu played instrumental roles in the peaceful transition to democracy.

The developing country boasts a diversified economy, with thriving industries in mining, agriculture, manufacturing, finance, and technology. Johannesburg, often referred to as the "City of Gold," is the economic hub of Africa and home to the Johannesburg Stock Exchange. South Africa actively engages in regional and global diplomacy. It is a founding member of BRICS (Brazil, Russia, India, China, and South Africa), playing a key role in shaping emerging economies' policies.

Currently, South Africa, with a population of 59.3 million, faces many challenges including high unemployment rates (32.6%), corruption, violent crime, "loadshedding" (scheduled power outages due to insufficient power supply), HIV/AIDS, and gender-based violence (GBV), and it is the most unequal society in the world (Gini coefficient of 63%).

Employee well-being programmes have gained prominence in corporate South Africa; however, they are not common in small- to medium-sized enterprises (SMEs). Larger organisations recognise the importance of supporting the physical, mental, and emotional health of their employees. These programmes are designed to enhance job satisfaction, reduce stress, improve overall employee health and productivity, and more recently, serve as a proactive way to enable employees to thrive. Programmes typically include counselling support (via different modalities), financial well-being support, and legal advice. More advanced programmes would include a holistic well-being approach with diversified services, such as absenteeism management, musculoskeletal care (including ergonomics), disability and incapacity management, occupational performance, occupational health, learning and development, and executive support.

INTRODUCTION TO ICAS SOUTHERN AFRICA

ICAS Southern Africa is part of ICAS World, a Lyra Health company—the world's leading provider of behavioural risk management services to the business community. Since its local launch in 1999, ICAS has established itself as Africa's foremost specialist in the provision of behavioural risk management and employee well-being programmes, contributing to the health and performance of employees and organisations in all sectors of the economy. With operations spanning the continent, ICAS Southern Africa supports more than 940,000 employees (over 1.2 million members) in over 1,200 companies, 24 hours a day, 365 days a year.

ICAS's services are provided through sophisticated, high-tech call centres and a large, multidisciplinary team of highly qualified professionals, trainers, and consultants. ICAS strives to make a difference in employees' and their dependents' lives by advocating for positive mental health and overall improved well-being, employing advanced technology, developing and adopting international best practices, and maintaining the highest standards of ethics and professionalism. The company values innovation, quality, and integrity and is driven by its commitment to achieving results for clients.

THE IMPACT ON SERVICES (MENTAL HEALTH, SUBSTANCE ABUSE, AND EAPS) DURING THE PANDEMIC

The COVID-19 pandemic has had a profound impact on mental health, substance abuse, and Employee Assistance Programs (EAPs) in South Africa. Overall there were four main themes that were evident on the impact of services during this time.

1. An increase in demand and more focus on well-being as a strategic objective.
2. Telehealth and digital well-being expansion
3. Increase in maladaptive coping mechanisms
4. Normalisation of mental health concerns

Increased Demand: In South Africa, the pandemic triggered a surge in demand for mental health services. The stress, uncertainty, and emotional toll of the virus, coupled with lockdown measures, led to increased fear, panic, anxiety, depression, and other mental health issues. South Africa, like many other countries, faced a mental health crisis exacerbated by the pandemic, with particular challenges among health care workers, first responders, and vulnerable populations. Organisations in South Africa responded by acknowledging the importance of providing well-being support and looked to offer additional mental health support, which became part of the organisation's strategic objective.

Telehealth Expansion: To ensure the continuity of care while adhering to social distancing measures, mental health providers in South Africa expanded telehealth services. This allowed individuals to access therapy and counselling remotely, addressing some of the challenges posed by lockdowns and restrictions and the limited in-person care that was available. Even when in-person care became more available, there was hesitation to book appointments with high rates of postponements or cancellations due to illness or fear of exposure. Digital well-being apps started mushrooming as a tool to proactively support individuals on their health and well-being journey. This was in light of there being more of a focus on growing self-awareness, self-care, and staying mentally healthy.

Increase in Maladaptive Coping Mechanisms: The stress and coping challenges associated with the pandemic contributed to an increase in maladaptive coping mechanisms, which included gender-based violence and substance use in South Africa. Substance abuse treatment centers reported a rise in admissions, and so did women's and children's shelters. These facilities faced major disruptions, which included a reduced capacity or even temporary closure due to the pandemic. Awareness and teletherapy became critical tools for providing support. Virtual support groups and counseling sessions helped individuals in recovery stay connected and access needed assistance.

Normalisation of Mental Health Concerns: Since one in every three people in South Africa will struggle with a mental health concern, this opened up the door for more open conversations, particularly in the workplace, about the importance of mental health. A positive from the pandemic is the work that was done to create awareness and normalize mental health concerns. There is still a stigma that exists with mental health in general, but the pandemic has accelerated efforts to normalize the conversation. EAPs in South Africa experienced a significant increase in utilization during the pandemic. Employees sought support for various pandemic-related stressors, including remote work challenges, grief and loss, caregiving responsibilities, financial strain, isolation, gender-based violence, and mental health concerns. Anxiety was one of the top presenting problems of this time, and "languishing" became known as a common term, referring to a feeling of despair and feeling stuck and unable to move forward.

The pandemic forced a rapid transformation of mental health services in South Africa, highlighting the importance of flexibility and innovation in health care delivery. Many of these changes, such as increased telehealth options and expanded mental health support, are likely to persist as part of the "new normal" in health care and employee well-being services in South Africa.

THE EFFECTS OF ONLINE/VIRTUAL COUNSELING

There are a number of positive effects of online/virtual counselling, together with some challenges in the South African context.

The ability to access care and support virtually has resulted in an increase in service provision and ease of access. Particularly for those who were isolated, struggling with GBV in the home (we saw an increase in support via our live chat counselling services in this regard) and those who lived in remote areas or worked remotely. In some ways, this also worked to reduce the stigma associated with accessing mental health support and increase the privacy and continuity of care in dealing with mental health concerns. Another big win has been reaching the younger generation that resonates with digital tools and ways to access mental health support.

Despite the positive impact, challenges related to internet connectivity and access to devices remain. Not everyone in South Africa has reliable internet access, and data costs are high, which can limit the reach of virtual counseling services. Virtual counselling also requires the counsellor to home in on their therapeutic skills and be more culturally sensitive in serving clients from diverse backgrounds effectively. Other challenges relate to the privacy concerns regarding online care, such as data security and confidentiality. Ensuring a seamless integration between online and traditional services, along with maintaining a consistent quality of care, requires careful planning and coordination.

THE ROLE OF TECHNOLOGY AND SOCIAL MEDIA

The role of technology and social media in employee well-being and mental health in South Africa has evolved significantly in recent years. While these platforms offer opportunities for support and education, they also present challenges that need to be addressed.

Access to information on mental health, well-being and coping resources has never been easier. We have seen the positive impact technology played, especially over the pandemic, to ensure people could stay in touch with loved ones, remain connected to the workplace, continue with work, and pass necessary information along at great speed. Mental health apps blossomed the world over as tools to help manage stress, anxiety, and depression using features such as mood tracking, meditation, breathing exercises, and cognitive-behavioural or dialectical-behaviour therapy practices. The role of creating and being part of online communities became more known and welcomed. Concurrent to this, however, is the danger that technology and social media played in misinformation and information overload (digital fatigue and screen addiction), which needs to be guarded against as a contributor to increased levels of anxiety and increased levels of burnout.

There has been a rise in digital abuse and cyberbullying. Social media, unfortunately, plays a role in fostering a culture of comparison, which has a negative impact on one's mental health. Some individuals also become reliant on the online validation and likes/views/followers to affirm their self-worth. This trend is worrying and is impacting people the world over, particularly in understanding the mental health pandemic in the youth.

One focus area that South African organisations have been addressing, together with the support of their employee well-being partners, is to encourage positive digital health habits. This includes the implementation of digital detox challenges, education and awareness of the positive and negative impacts of technology and social media on mental health, privacy awareness training, critical thinking skills to help discern between credible information and misinformation, and more robust conversations on work-life integration and setting boundaries and expectations for hybrid ways of working. This also came with the recognition of the role DEIB (diversity, equity, inclusion, and belonging) plays in the space of mental health.

EFFORTS TOWARD DIVERSITY AND INCLUSION WITHIN THE FIELD (COUNSELORS, PROVIDERS, CLIENTS)

Efforts toward diversity and inclusion within the South African employee well-being field take on a unique context shaped by the country's rich cultural diversity and historical legacy. Workforces are diverse, reflecting the rainbow nation. Broad-based black economic empowerment (BBBEE) has been written into legislation committing organisations to build a workforce that mirrors the nation's diversity. This includes recruiting counsellors and providers from various racial, ethnic, linguistic, and cultural backgrounds to better serve the population's unique composition.

At the root of cultural competence within South Africa is the concept of "Ubuntu," meaning humanity toward others ("I am because we are"). South African counsellors and providers often undergo training that embraces the principles of Ubuntu, emphasizing interconnectedness and mutual respect. This cultural competence training helps professionals understand and respond to the distinctive needs and worldviews of clients in a South African context. Furthermore, South Africa has 12 official languages, thus service providers need to cater to all the languages to ensure accessibility to all South Africans.

From an organizational perspective, inclusive transformation policies are developed and implemented, addressing past disparities and promoting equal opportunities. These policies encompass anti-discrimination measures, affirmative action, and accommodation strategies for clients facing social and economic challenges. Data collection of equity and transformation metrics and analysis of employee demographics are used to identify disparities and inform tailored services. Well-being programmes, educational materials, self-help tools, and wellness resources also need to be tailored to address the specific mental health challenges faced by different communities within South Africa, including those related to race, culture, gender, and sexual orientation. Collaborating with community-based services is also common due to individuals being rooted within their communities and it being natural to seek support within the community. In addition, traditional healing practices are part of the support that needs to be incorporated to ensure inclusivity.

Efforts toward diversity and inclusion within the South African employee well-being field are integral to addressing the unique social, cultural, and historical dynamics of the nation. By fostering an inclusive and culturally sensitive environment, organizations contribute to the promotion of mental health and well-being for all South Africans, irrespective of their diverse backgrounds or identities.

ABOUT THE AUTHOR

Navlika Ratangee is the Managing Director of ICAS Southern Africa. She is a GIBS MBA graduate and clinical psychologist with diverse experience in human capital management, behavioural risk, change management, managerial consulting, global management consulting, leadership, women in leadership, employee well-being, organisational resilience, and organisational strategy. She also has a wealth of experience in dealing with mental health in the workplace and has consulted to many South African corporates in this regard. Completing her PDBA and MBA, both with distinction, Navlika was also awarded the prize as top graduate for the MBA programme. She has furthered her executive education at IODSA and Harvard Business School, Boston.

ICAS was recognised as a Top Gender Empowered Company in South Africa and was a finalist for the coveted Standard Bank Top Women Awards. ICAS has also been recognised as a finalist for Top Empowered Company for Diversity, Equity and Inclusion in the Workplace, and Navlika herself is a finalist for Top Empowered: business leader of the year award in 2023.

RESOURCES

Navlika Ratangee
Managing Director
ICAS Southern Africa
+27 82 314 1793
Navlika.Ratangee@icasworld.com
www.icas.co.za

Employee Assistance Professionals Association of South Africa
Contact: Radhi Vandayar (President)
officemanager@eapasa.co.za
+27 12 346 443
www.eapasa.co.za

SPAIN

Miguel Cristobal

There have been many changes in the Employee Assistance Programs market since Healthy Work participated last in this publication. My name is Miguel Cristobal, and I am a Clinical Psychologist. Together with my wife, Carla Boyer, we founded Healthy Work, an EAP and wellness provider in Spain and Italy in 2006. It has rained a lot since. From finding a market resistant to taking care of the employees' well-being beyond promoting healthy eating and exercising, to one fully conscious of the importance of maintaining a healthy mind and preventing and offering help with mental health. The pandemic, with the loneliness, sorrow, and difficulties working remote or in relationships with teammates and family members (among others), raised the necessary awareness of the necessity to support employees' well-being beyond the not-unimportant physical aspects.

The difference came from the fact that leaders, managers, and employees allowed themselves to share with everyone at work the struggles they were dealing with throughout the pandemic. They were able to **show their vulnerabilities**, giving examples to everyone in most organizations and allowing themselves to overcome the stigma and talk about depression, anxiety, and even suicide. The obvious need to help people with their struggles, even if just to increase productivity, was laid upon the table.

It is not that the literature was not already talking about new managerial skills that included mindfulness (being mentally present and not somewhere else in the future), avoiding narcissism to center interest not on us but on our employees, and compassion (caring about everyone). (The most used example was the change in these new skills brought to Marriott.) But, bringing these into practice was another thing.

So, the virus brought sadness, difficulties, loneliness … and it brought **awareness**. An awareness that made leaders realize that they needed to take care of employees just as they took care of clients. That as humans, we have great times, but we also suffer. That life is yin-yang and that being vulnerable to mental problems happens to most of us. That getting help in those moments is a necessity in some cases, but a luxury available through EAP programs at others. It helped the EAP market expand.

Healthy Work multiplied the number of calls accessing the program by 12 in one year, and the **increase in use** has stayed steady for over three years now. Companies are not surprised anymore about our services. They have heard of EAP programs and are convinced about their contributions to reduce absenteeism, presentism, accidents at work, etc. It is not only the multinationals that provide these services for their offices abroad.

There is such a need for these services that some have created companies to compete in the market with different models. **Low-cost therapy online** is now widely available and is sold to organizations all over Spain and Italy. The new model just provides low-cost therapy sessions that employees can access anytime from anywhere online. No need to wait or talk to any human in-person in your access to help. You can even select your therapist and choose your appointment time online. These rarely provide trainings on well-being issues, or add financial and legal well-being, or support finding household help, elderly care, or childcare. They rarely provide any information to companies on how they can improve the health of their employees. Their services are counselling-focused, making sure they reduce costs. Counsellors often need to be available 24/7 and do not get paid much because their employers find the clients/patients for them. Some people have called this the "uberization of mental health." Technology is a key to make this model work with the least number of employees serving the most clients possible. Saving costs is key. Confidentiality is always preserved.

In order to compete with these models without sacrificing quality and paying our providers a decent fee (which has not increased in the last few years), we had to include services with in-the-moment support only. Employees can access immediate help but only for some cases and sacrificing confidentiality. HR pays for extra sessions for some employees to deal with a difficult moment. Employees with not many resources or urgent intense difficulties would access longer treatments with the authorization of HR. In some cases, we have also gotten approval without giving the name of the employee. Obviously, if we do facilitate it, is with the written consent of the person who called the line. We provide quality help but are limited in time. Often, we can direct the person to the right public or private services.

The virus also brought changes in the way we provide counselling. Spain and Italy were countries with not much use, always in person, and always using all the sessions provided by their employers. It wasn't a question of how many were needed to resolve an issue; there were always other things to tackle, and all the sessions were sometimes not even enough. Now, the **use has increased** in both countries, **the sessions continue to be used in total, and employees are more readily willing to get served online**. Approximately 40% of access to counselling is now online. It works for those who do not have the time to travel back and forth to a counsellor's office with larger support systems. Not so much for people who may feel lonely or need the physical contact. Spanish and Italian cultures are traditionally effusive and contact-ready. It is hard to foresee a future without face-to-face counselling.

The requests for trainings related to mental health have also increased. There is an awareness that managers and leaders need skills to manage the wellness of the members of their teams. The demand for learning to identify people in need of help, talk to them, and direct them to the right resources, if needed, is a new and necessary skill to acquire. We are conscious of the need to build resilient workforces, and management should also help employees learn the skills to take care of themselves: to handle stress, deal with a digital world, and build a box with tools to feel good … Learning mindfulness is quite common. Although there are apps to practice mindfulness, a recent study showed that people access them 1–3 times. Online, half-hour webinars to practice together with others get hundreds of followers.

There is no doubt that the composition of workforces nowadays, with the new generations frequently changing jobs, eager to learn and easily bored, have also had an impact on the EAP field. Technology is a must in our delivery—to access information and to access the program. All of us had to develop apps to keep up, and we continue to build on them. Tests to assess happiness, stress levels, anxiety, and well-being are being incorporated as a way to not only intervene when someone needs help but to help prevent the stress and remind users of the importance of taking responsibility for our own well-being and especially mental health. Something to watch for is making sure that science is behind all these measurements, tests, and recommendations. Unfortunately, this is not always the case. Social media is also here to stay and more important every day. Instagram and TikTok are now channels to educate the public, reduce stigma, and let people know that EAP programs are here and available for your companies. Recently, our employees went out into the streets of Madrid to interview passersby about mental health and their knowledge of our programs. We were surprised to find out the familiarity with well-being solutions. We are now working on a campaign to promote saying nice things to coworkers to encourage respect, a sense of belonging, and the right environment to grow mentally healthy. We are using social media to get the message across.

In terms of including support for "respect diversity," there is still much work to be done in both Spain and Italy. Younger generations find it easier than older ones. A drastically politically divided world does not help. It seems that people are not open to different ways of thinking, and do not respect or listen. We had an intervention at a company to help employees communicate their opposing views on Catalan nationalism and to help them respect each other. We need to realize that when we all do not agree, we can provide better service to our clients. People prefer to have everyone agree from the beginning; after all, it is easier, but in the long run, it is less efficient. EAPs can help companies contribute to a more respectful world by investing in promoting diversity.

As for Healthy Work, we have included a very diverse group of counsellors to provide services, upon request, by those trained in LGTB, race, age, and gender diversity when our clients request it. It is true that there is not much demand. Any counsellor should be respectful of all differences, but sometimes an employee may feel more comfortable with a specific person.

As for professionals to network with, we would recommend the members of the Employee Assistance European Forum. The standards of quality and ethical values guarantee good services.

ABOUT THE AUTHOR

Miguel Cristobal is the co-founder of Healthy Work Spain.

RESOURCES

Stimulus
Calle Serrano Anguita 13 – Ed. Impact Hub
28004 Madrid
+34 911 92 40 74
contacto@stimulus-consultoria.com

Healthy Work
Madrid, Spain
+34915590061
contacto@healthywork.es

SWITZERLAND

Eliane Bucher

INTRODUCTION

My name is Eliane Bucher, and I am the managing director for ICAS in Switzerland, Germany, France, Luxembourg, Italy, and Austria. I have been with ICAS since 2005. We are part of ICAS International, the leading global provider of EAPs, health and well-being services, and critical incident support. ICAS is supporting 2,400 companies with more than 6.5 million employees in 155 countries.

With a dedicated team and a commitment to excellence, we were able to position the ICAS Switzerland Group as one of the leading companies in the industry that meets the evolving needs of our customers and clients. We are deeply committed to driving growth, fostering a culture of collaboration, and empowering employees to excel. Our strategic vision and ability to navigate complex market dynamics have been instrumental in ICAS's continued success.

THE IMPACT OF THE PANDEMIC ON EAP SERVICES IN SWITZERLAND

The COVID-19 pandemic had a significant impact on Employee Assistance Programs (EAPs) in Switzerland and sustainably changed service delivery. The key effects were:

- **Increased Demand for Mental Health Support:** The pandemic caused heightened levels of stress, anxiety, and other mental health challenges among employees in Switzerland. In a study conducted by the University of Basel, 18% of respondents reported suffering from severe depressive symptoms only 6 months after the start of the pandemic. With 29%, the symptoms were particularly high among 14- to 24-year-old persons.

- **Surge in Demand:** We have experienced a surge in demand for mental health support services as employees faced uncertainties, work-life balance challenges, social isolation, and concerns about their health and well-being. At ICAS, the case volume increased by 71% immediately after the outbreak. There was a greater need for counseling for emotional issues and mental well-being. The proportion of F2F counselling has more than doubled.
- **Shift to Remote and Virtual Support:** EAPs in Switzerland had to adapt their service delivery models due to remote work arrangements and physical distancing measures. ICAS transitioned to video counselling for F2F sessions to continue providing support and counseling services to employees. This shift allowed for continuity of care and increased accessibility to EAP resources.
- **Focus on Well-being and Resilience:** The pandemic highlighted the importance of employee well-being and resilience. EAPs in Switzerland placed a stronger emphasis on preventive measures, offering webinars to help employees cope with stress, build resilience, and maintain their mental and emotional health during challenging times. During the first months of the pandemic, we have conducted more than 171% of webinars.
- **Addressing Remote Work Challenges among Managers:** With the shift to remote work, EAPs in Switzerland recognized the need to address the new challenges associated with remote work arrangements. EAP providers offered guidance on managing work-related stress, setting boundaries, maintaining productivity, and supporting employee engagement in virtual environments.
- **Recognition of Mental Health as a Priority:** The pandemic brought greater attention to mental health in the workplace, and EAPs played a crucial role in promoting mental health awareness and support. There was increased recognition among employers and employees in Switzerland of the importance of prioritizing mental well-being, and EAPs were at the forefront of providing resources, counseling, and guidance in this area.
- **De-stigmatization of Mental Health Issues:** Before the pandemic, mental disorders were still highly stigmatized in Switzerland. Only half of the people would have told their friends about a diagnosis. At work, no more than 20% would talk about it for fear of disadvantages in the job. Only one in three people with a mental disease found its way into a medical or therapeutic support system. With countless media reports on the impact of the pandemic on mental well-being, the topic is much more present in society today. Other factors, such as confessions of mental health problems by celebrities, athletes, and

other well-known personalities, as well as the open approach of Generation Z, have greatly contributed to the de-stigmatization of mental health.

Overall, the COVID-19 pandemic highlighted the essential role of EAPs in supporting employees' mental health and well-being in Switzerland. EAPs had to adapt their services to meet the changing needs of employees, with a focus on virtual support, preventive measures, and resilience-building.

Although the pandemic has largely ended and lost its scare, the case volume and the proportion of F2F consultations have remained stable at a very high level.

THE EFFECTS OF ONLINE/VIRTUAL COUNSELLING

The increasing need for psychological support and the lockdowns had a major impact on EAP providers in Switzerland. Online/virtual counseling has greatly increased in importance due to the pandemic. During the lockdowns, all F2F sessions had to be conducted via video. Clients have come to appreciate this timesaving and ecological type of psychological counseling. Even now, after the pandemic, almost half of the F2F consultations in Switzerland are taking place virtually.

These are some notable impacts that video/virtual counselling have brought:

- **Unlimited Accessibility:** Online/virtual counselling has significantly improved the accessibility of EAP services, regardless of the location of the employees. Thanks to these technologies, the EAP could be accessed seamlessly and without restrictions, even during the lockdowns of the pandemic.
- **Convenience and Flexibility:** Employees no longer need to travel to physical counselling locations, making it more convenient and ecological to seek assistance. Virtual counselling allows employees to schedule sessions at times that are convenient for them, even outside regular office hours. This flexibility is particularly beneficial for employees with demanding schedules or those who prefer the privacy and convenience of receiving counselling from their preferred location.
- **Reduced Stigma:** Online counselling can help reduce the stigma associated with seeking mental health support. Some individuals do feel more comfortable discussing personal issues from the privacy of their own homes. The perception of anonymity and reduced visibility associated with virtual counseling can encourage individuals to seek help who may have otherwise hesitated. It can cater to individuals who prefer digital communication channels or who are more comfortable expressing themselves in writing. This

expanded reach allows EAPs to engage with a more diverse employee population.
- **Technical Challenges:** Implementing and maintaining online/virtual counselling services comes with technical challenges. Both the EAP provider and employees require reliable internet connections, suitable devices, and familiarity with online platforms. Technical difficulties or connectivity issues can potentially disrupt counseling sessions and create frustration for both parties involved.
- **Nonverbal Cues:** In virtual counseling, the absence or limitation of nonverbal cues can affect the therapeutic alliance between counselor and collaborator. Building trust and connection may require extra effort and creativity in the absence of a physical presence. Counselors must therefore be appropriately trained to effectively serve and support clients through online channels.
- **Confidentiality and Security:** Ensuring confidentiality and data security is crucial in online/virtual counseling. EAP providers must employ secure platforms and encrypted communication and comply with data protection regulations to protect employee privacy.

In summary, online/virtual counseling has brought many positive changes to EAPs in Switzerland. However, challenges related to technology, nonverbal communication, and maintaining confidentiality had to be addressed carefully among our counsellors to provide effective and ethical virtual counselling services.

THE ROLE OF TECHNOLOGY AND SOCIAL MEDIA

Technology has had several impacts on Employee Assistance Programs (EAPs) in Switzerland, both positive and negative. Here are some key effects:

- Increased Accessibility: Technology has made EAPs more accessible to employees. Online platforms and mobile applications enable employees to easily access support services, information, and resources at any time.
- Expanded Reach: Technology allows EAPs to reach a larger audience. Through web-based or mobile applications, EAP providers can disseminate information about mental health, well-being, and available resources to a wider range of employees. This expanded reach helps in raising awareness and reducing stigma around seeking assistance.
- Enhanced Counselling Channels: Technology facilitates more possibilities to contact the EAP, such as options like live chat, video counselling, online booking of video counselling sessions, etc. Such communication channels provide convenience and anonymity, which are particularly beneficial for younger individuals hesitant about personal interactions

by phone or face-to-face. They are also more comfortable and ecological by not having to travel to attend psychological support.
- Privacy and Confidentiality Concerns: The use of technology raises concerns about employee privacy and confidentiality. EAPs need to implement robust security measures to protect sensitive employee information and ensure that online platforms comply with data protection regulations. Employees should be assured that their personal information will be treated with confidentiality to foster trust and encourage utilization of EAP services.
- For privacy and confidentiality reasons, social media sites like Facebook, Instagram, and TikTok are not channels that EAP providers are usually using to interact the employees of their customers in Switzerland.

Business networks have a more marketing-related approach by informing potential stakeholders about the benefits of an EAP. Especially during the pandemic, YouTube was a well-admired possibility to quickly share videos on current issues with the workforce or EAP customers, regardless of their location. Overall, technology and social media have transformed the landscape of EAPs in Switzerland, making support more accessible, convenient, and personalized. However, it is crucial to balance these advantages with the potential challenges to ensure the effective delivery of EAP services and safeguard employee privacy.

EFFORTS TOWARD DIVERSITY AND INCLUSION WITHIN THE FIELD (COUNSELORS, PROVIDERS, CLIENTS)

EAP providers have to make deliberate efforts to address diversity and promote inclusivity in their services. Here are some key steps they should take:

- Cultivate a Diverse Workforce: EAP providers should actively seek to hire and retain a diverse workforce that reflects the demographics of the employees they serve. This includes individuals from various ethnic, racial, cultural, and linguistic backgrounds, as well as individuals with different abilities and experiences. Diverse EAP staff can enhance cultural competence, understanding, and empathy when working with employees from different backgrounds.
- Training and Education: EAP providers should invest in ongoing training and education for their staff to increase cultural competence and understanding of diversity-related issues. These trainings should include topics such as implicit bias, cultural sensitivity, LGBTQ+ inclusion, disability awareness, and intersectionality.

- Tailored Resources and Interventions: EAP providers should offer a range of resources and interventions that are culturally sensitive and address the specific needs of diverse populations. This includes providing educational materials, self-help resources, and counseling approaches that are inclusive and considerate of different cultural contexts. It is essential to avoid a one-size-fits-all approach and instead tailor interventions to the unique experiences and backgrounds of employees.
- Inclusive Policies and Practices: EAP providers should have inclusive policies and practices that explicitly state their commitment to diversity, equity, and inclusion. This includes ensuring that their organizational culture is welcoming and respectful to all employees, irrespective of their background or identity. EAP providers should also actively challenge and address any instances of discrimination or bias that may arise within their services.

By taking these efforts, EAP providers can create a more inclusive and supportive environment for employees from diverse backgrounds, helping to address their unique needs and enhance overall well-being.

ABOUT THE AUTHOR

Eliane Bucher is the managing director for ICAS in Switzerland, Germany, France, Luxembourg, Italy, and Austria.

RESOURCES

ICAS Schweiz GmbH
Hertistrasse 25
8304 Wallisellen
+41 44 878 30 00
info@icas.ch
www.icas.ch

Proitera GmbH
Dornacherstrasse 210
4053 Basel
+41 61 366 10 20
info@proitera.ch
www.proitera.ch

Dargebotene Hand: anonym - 24 Stunden
Tel. 143
www.143.ch

MOVIS AG
Kreuzstrasse 26
8008 Zürich
+41 848 270 270
info@movis.ch
www.movis.ch

Seglias & Partner
Talstrasse 20
8001 Zürich
+41 44 930 58 55
seglias@seglias-partner.ch
www.seglias-partner.ch

TAIWAN

Jyh-Hong Lee

EAPS IN TAIWAN

The origins of Employee Assistance Programs (EAP) in Taiwan can be traced back to various perspectives. Some attribute it to labor guidance provided by the Catholic Youth Labors Association in 1958, while others relate it to labor education specified in regulations of Export Processing Zone Administration under Ministry of Economic Affairs in 1962. Another viewpoint suggests its origin from the "Big Sister" system established by Matsushita Electric Corporation Taiwan in 1972. Early understandings of EAP in Taiwan focused on workplace social work, labor education and guidance, and issues related to social adaptation and interpersonal relationships of young workers.

In 1994, the Labor Welfare Division of Council of Labor Affairs initiated an Employee Assistance Program to promote work-life balance and effective business practices. It provided educational lectures, life counselling, and work experience exchanges, along with the publication of an "Employee Assistance Program Work Manual." In 1998, Employee Assistance Program Service Center (EAPC) was established under Hsinchu City Lifeline International, which demonstrated and promoted EAP practices. These efforts led to the establishment of Taiwan Employee Assistance Professional Association (TEAPA) in 2007, solidifying EA as a distinct profession.

TEAPA organizes annual forums, inviting various stakeholders to fully engage in extensive discussions. In 2014, TEAPA became Taiwan Chapter of International Employee Assistance Professional Association (EAPA). The association also conducts Diploma of Employee Assistance

Professionals (DEAP) training that serves as a CEAP certification accelerator. In 2017 came the first CEAP, with Dr. Lee, followed by Ms. Shu-Ting Fan in 2018. In 2019, Dr. Lee became the official instructor of Fundamentals of EA training co-work by APEAR and EAPA.

IMPACTS OF THE COVID-19 PANDEMIC ON EAPS

The COVID-19 pandemic had a significant impact in Taiwan and led to reactive and proactive developments for EAP practices and EA professionals. TEAPA organized forums in 2020, 2021, and 2022 aimed at addressing workplace stresses, crises, and changing demands to help employees, organizations, and professionals enhance workplace well-being under the pandemic and explore new perspectives of EAP in a post-pandemic era.

Taiwan Occupational Safety and Health Administration, Ministry of Labor (TOSHA), has revised guidelines to help workplaces implement preventive measures based on their specific environments and operations. These guidelines consider risk levels and reference the guidelines issued by Taiwan Central Epidemic Command Center. Workplaces are also encouraged to consult and observe international information to ensure effective management and strategies. The guidelines include early-stage measures such as spatial distancing, contact avoidance, and workplace disinfection protocols. In mid stages, they cover remote work practice, flexible arrangements, alternative leaves, and safety considerations for employees working from home. These guidelines require workplaces to establish or review practices that prioritize the physical and mental well-being of their employees. Various ministries, including Ministries of Economic Affairs, Health and Welfare, Education, and others, have also provided relevant guidance to strengthen assistance programs for safety and mental health. These initiatives highlight the evolving and crucial role of EAP in supporting organizations and employees.

The pandemic has impacted several aspects of human resource management, including remote work HRM, crisis communication, employer branding, organizational resilience, and corporate social responsibility (CSR). These challenges necessitate consultation from professionals well-versed in workplace human behaviors. Additionally, there has been a renewed emphasis on direct services addressing workplace mental health issues such as stress adaptation, occupational fatigue, job insecurity, employee anxiety, morale and engagement, social disconnection, psychological capital, and neurotic unsafety. These impacts have spurred both reactive and proactive developments in EAP practices and EA professionals.

Government has played a crucial role by providing regulatory flexibility and increased resources. In addition to promoting work-life balance, EAP, and workplace health promotion, the Administration of Physical Education introduced a "Subsidy Program for Hiring Sports Instructors in Enterprises" to encourage hiring full- or part-time sports professionals. This initiative aims to promote sports enthusiasm, foster healthy and vibrant workplaces, improve individual physical and mental well-being, and enhance interpersonal interaction and teamwork. Corporate has evolved from a reactive and fragmented service to a comprehensive framework that promotes employee safety, health, well-being, and interpersonal connection through expanded or adjusted content and methodologies.

In addressing current social and psychological challenges posed by COVID-19, EAP in Taiwan has undergone a paradigm shift in its form and focus. It now embraces a positive role in promoting and practicing workplace culture and a climate of humanistic management. EAP has expanded its scope to encompass functions such as disaster and crisis intervention, psychological well-being, positive health management, and so on. It aims to create healthier and more supportive environments that utilize personal engagement with work and life.

ISSUES OF REMOTE COUNSELING SERVICES

Remote counseling in Taiwan is still in its early stages, and there is limited scientific research or studies available. Exploratory research is scarce and not openly accessible, and relevant discussions are often based on experiences and evidence from other countries or regions.

Psychological counseling and psychotherapy differ significantly from other counseling services in terms of participants, issues addressed, legal requirements, and evidence-based practices. In Taiwan, while there are regulations under Psychologist Law that govern the practice of licensed psychologists, there is no corresponding legal basis for general counseling services and personnel. This restricts licensed psychologists to stay in medical settings such as hospitals and clinics, and keeps them from non-medical issues in personal, community, educational, or corporate settings. And other helping professionals must position themselves cautiously as "non-counseling roles" to avoid conflicts with clinical and counseling psychology professionals or associations. This lack of clarification has led to misunderstandings of counseling services, and it has caused other counseling professionals to hide.

Regarding remote psychological counseling, it was not officially approved until November 29, 2019. The Health and Welfare Ministry's Medical Affairs Bureau issued "Reference Principles for Psychologists Conducting Online Counseling Services." It allowed online counseling services to be conducted in various telecom ways and required institutions and psychologists to adhere to principles such as obtaining informed consent, confirming patient identity, ensuring patient privacy, and maintaining compliant records. This regulation marked a significant shift from traditional physical forms of clinical services and coincidentally aligned with the COVID-19 pandemic, enabling licensed psychologists to legally provide online services or therapy. However, we could see nothing from other counseling services besides of counseling and clinical psychology.

USE OF TECHNOLOGY AND SOCIAL MEDIA

According to an OOSGA report on May 23, 2023, Taiwan has a high internet and smartphone usage and high coverage rate of social media and platforms. Approximately 90% of Taiwanese use one or more social media, and everyone, on average, has around 6.5 accounts on popular platforms like Facebook and Instagram or local brands like PTT and D-card.

While corporations typically have technology resources to create official websites and social channels for business communicating, individual professionals may have a shortage of professional social accounts, including psychologists, marital and family experts, financial advisors, legal consultants, fitness trainers, and professionals focusing on work-life balance and occupational health. On this point, social media as a strategic tool has extremely low demands, yet it achieves so high. The OOSGA report emphasized the increasing integration between real-life events and social media activities, particularly in the business domain, resulting in more professionals using social media to promote their services. Those small venders and individual professionals publish posters in waves with well-crafted articles, commentaries on current news, and reports on their service footprints across Facebook, Instagram, X (Twitter), and LinkedIn to raise their personal brands and attract potential buyers.

For the EA profession, one of the core techniques involves advocating and explaining contents and procedures of certain EAP services to participants. However, the target now has to be expanded to include potential buyers. Therefore, EA professionals need to actively manage a positive, attractive, and persuasive brand to appeal to both individual clients and corporate contracts.

EFFORTS TOWARD DIVERSITY AND INCLUSION WITHIN THE FIELD

Taiwan has undergone significant social and cultural transformations since World War II. Chinese traditional culture, brought and led by KMT, aimed to evoke and unite national identity. At the same time, Taiwan embraced Western ideas through academic research and cultural exchanges. KMT's governance maintained a delicate balance between these two influences, facilitating dialogue and integration.

However, everything changed with the lifting of martial law in 1987. This marked a turning point in Taiwan's history and brought about tremendous changes in the country. Military control was reduced, and civilians were no longer subject to military trials. Political prisoners and thought criminals were no longer subjected to criminal law, leading to a society that valued freedom of speech. The Constitution granted people freedom of association, assembly, procession, publication, and speech. As a result, Taiwan transitioned from an authoritarian and dictatorial regime to a democratic society founded on principles of the rule of law and human rights.

This highly democratized society has shown a strong commitment to justice, freedom, and human rights. This commitment is evident in various legal, policy, and cultural practices, such as the Employment Service Act enacted in 1992. It aims to promote employment opportunities and economic development for citizens by ensuring equal employment services and prohibiting discrimination based on various factors, including race, class, language, ideology, religion, political affiliation, birthplace, gender, sexual orientation, age, marital status, appearance, facial features, physical or mental disabilities, or previous membership in labor unions. It echoed upon previous legislation such as the Disabled Rights Protection Act in 1980 and paved the way for subsequent laws and policies fostering diversity, fairness, and inclusivity in workplace. For example, Gender Equality in Employment Act was established in 2002, Implementation Measures for Maternal Health Protection for Female Workers was introduced in 2014, and Employment Promotion Act for Middle-aged and Elderly Workers was enacted in 2019.

In Taiwan, many companies have embraced diversity and inclusivity in their policies and practices before legislation. For example, same-sex partners and civil unions have been recognized and supported by companies for an extended period. These companies provide equal personnel rights and employee benefits to them as well. Underscoring its commitment to inclusivity and human rights, Taiwan completed its legislation on May 24, 2019, and became the first country in Asia and the 27th country in the world to allow same-sex marriage.

Taiwanese workplaces, regardless of their scale, composition, or nature, generally support diversity and inclusivity in their policies. Although implementing these values may present challenges and difficulties, Taiwan and its workplaces have rarely expressed opposition to these progressive ideals. The understanding that transforming a workplace culture necessitates ongoing practice and dedication has prevailed, even amid struggles to meet legal requirements. It serves as a manifestation of principles of diversity, inclusiveness, respect, and friendliness.

Government actively supports and advocates for EAP at both central and local levels, organizing awards, commendations, and certifications to promote and exchange creative ideas and practical experiences. Notable initiatives include "Healthy Workplace Certification" conducted by National Health Agency, Ministry of Health, and Welfare, since 2007. This certification has evolved into the "Outstanding Enterprises for Workplace Health Promotion" award, focusing on various aspects such as maternal care, friendly childcare, family support, inclusivity for vulnerable groups, and ethnic integration. Additionally, Taipei City Government has organized "Gender Equality Certification for Workplaces" since 2019 and "Outstanding Healthy Workplace Incentive Program" since 2017. Taichung City Government awarded "Happy Workplace" since 2020, while Kaohsiung City awarded "Happiness Enterprises" since 2015 and expanded by steps. These initiatives encourage local businesses to participate widely and enhance the effectiveness of corporate advocacy on D&I.

AN EAP LANDSCAPE IN TAIWAN

Taiwan provides insights into how government and professional organizations lead companies to commit to higher standards and a broader scope of EA practice. The focus is not on EA professionals in their superior expertise or competencies but on how governments drive the social and workplace change wisely, as well as how workplace leaders define and actualize themselves in the cultural perspective of a more developed and matured self in the sense of thinking, learning, reflecting, disciplining, self-cultivating, family-caring, people-leading, and world-harmonizing.

In Taiwan, EAP was seen early on as reactive, fragile services, and then, a framework of delivering resources, education, and consultation, and now, a comprehensive prevention system for workplace safety, health, supportiveness, and mutual respect committed and provided by entrepreneurs and management.

EAP contains and integrates various helping and developing practices, and it is driven by EA technology and professionals. It even yields a return on investment in terms of dollars by assessing loss due to negative behaviors like violence, accidents, withdraw and absence, and other behavioral risks, and positive attitudes and behaviors like security, engagement, morale, OCB, and so on. In addition to these facts, EAP in Taiwan shares common roots of leadership philosophy and a collectivism culture. Entrepreneurs and corporates in Taiwan tend to declare and espouse their people-oriented ideas and philosophy for a long time. And the truth is they might have no idea how to live and lead it out. More and more of them now have a superior strategy to maintain the most valuable assets in a better status, fuller efficiency, and expectable tenure.

The author defined EAP in five features: a performance management strategy, a service delivery system, a set of workplace services, a dual-client framework for both business and employees, and covering full EA technology and competency. By scrutinizing this unique landscape of EAP in Taiwan, he would love to consider an additional one, that is, a partnership to assist leaders of inquiring, designing, enacting, and assessing the lifestyle for the people he cares about. And in short, to help leaders commit into IDEAL.

ABOUT THE AUTHOR

Dr. Jyh-Hong Lee is Associate Professor of Industrial and Organizational Psychology at Asia University, Taiwan Republic of China. He is the 4th Chairman of TEAPA (2016–2019) and Honorary Chairman according to bylaws. He earned CEAP in 2017, the very first one in Taiwan. He is the moderator of the 2018 and 2019 Taiwan DEAP training, and official instructor of Fundamentals of EA training sponsored by APEAR and EAPA.

Email: someday@asia.edu.tw
Mobile: 886-916020533
LN: jyhhonglee
FB: stephen0526
Address: 500, Liu-Feng RD., Wu-Feng District, Tai-Chung City. Psychology Asia University.

RESOURCES

Taiwan Employee Assistance Professional Association
http://www.teapa.org/big.asp
E-mail: teapatw@gmail.com

EAP, Directorate-General of Personnel Administration, Executive Yuan
https://www.dgpa.gov.tw/mp/archive?uid=224&mid=223

Work-Life Balance Network, Ministry of Labor https://wlb.mol.gov.tw/

Registration portal for EA training: https://wlb.mol.gov.tw/Page/Lesson/LessonList.aspx

Application portal for subsidy: https://wlb.mol.gov.tw/Page/☒☒sContent.aspx?cid=1241

Application portal for consulting visit: https://wlb.mol.gov.tw/Page/Content.aspx?id=457&reURL=https%3a%2f%2fwlb.mol.gov.tw%2fPage%2fTutoring%2fTutoringOnline.aspx

National Health Insurance Administration, Ministry of Health and Welfare

Application for certification/awards: https://health.hpa.gov.tw/content/login/Index.aspx

Healthy Workplace Promotion Center: https://www.hpa.gov.tw/Pages/List.aspx?nodeid=334

Employee Assistance and Care Center, Taipei Municipal United Hospital https://sites.google.com/view/tpecheapcenter/%E9%A6%96%E9%A0%81

Minor Program in EAP, Department of Counseling and Guidance, National Changhua Normal University: http://gc.ncue.edu.tw/eap/index.html

Minor Program in Corporate Counseling and Employee Assistance, Tamkang University: http://www.edpsy.tku.edu.tw/course/super_pages.php?ID=course2&Sn=5

Focus and Forecast Consulting Company: https://www.ffceap.com.tw/
+882 2 3765-3313
request@ffceap.com.tw

EAPC Hsinchu Lifeline International http://www.eapcenter.org/
Contact portal: http://www.eapcenter.org/%e8%81%af%e7%b5%a1%e6%88%91%e5%80%91/

Employee Assistance Program Service Section, Teacher Chang Foundation: http://www.1980.org.tw/staff_service_show.php?staff_service_id=1
Ms. Yang: +886 2 25965858 ext. 403

Taiwan, Human Dynamic Asia Pacific Consulting Co., Ltd. https://www.humandynamic.com/
Ms. Chen: +886 2 23770993 ext. 311

EAP service, Xu Li Foundation: https://www.shiuhli.org.tw/eap
Mr. Chang: +886 2 2363-9425 #11
pcchang@shiuhli.org.tw

EAP Department, Chinese Psychological Therapy Foundation: https://www.tip.org.tw/eaphome

REFERENCES

Author's Note: All these references are published in Chinese traditional characters and could not be retrieved in English. Readers may conduct electronic retrieval based on the References List below.

1. 林桂碧，2001，臺灣地區EAPs（員工協助方案）的發展與經驗。2010.0106，檢索：http://forum.rad.gov.tw/posts/downloadAttach/4793.page
2. 經濟部加工出口區設管理條例：https://law.moj.gov.tw/LawClass/LawAll.aspx?pcode=J0050001&kw
3. 新竹生命線EAP中心，2023.0617，檢索：http://www.eapcenter.org/ufaqs/eap%E6%AD%B7%E5%8F%B2/
4. 范淑婷，2011。第五章，員工協助方案（EAPs）概論。方隆彰等，2011，職場社會工作：以員工協助方案(EAPs)為導向的實務。台灣：華都文化。
5. 潘世偉，2020.12，重返職場–新冠肺炎疫情後的調整與準備。台灣勞工季刊，64。
6. 勞動部職業安全衛生署，2000.0130，因應嚴重特殊傳染性肺炎（武漢肺炎）職場安全防護措施指引。
7. 嚴重特殊傳染性肺炎中央流行疫情指揮中心，2020.0305，企業因應嚴重特殊傳染性肺炎（COVID-19）疫情持續營運指引。
8. 勞動部，2021.05。居家工作職業安全衛生參考指引。
9. 勞動部，2021.05。居家工作職業安全衛生參考指引-三大重點。
10. 經濟部工業局，2020.0203。製造業因應嚴重特殊傳染性肺炎(武漢肺炎)指引。
11. 衛福部，2020.04，防疫期間醫療機構員工心理支持與協助建議措施。
12. 教育部，2022.0513。校園因應「嚴重特殊傳染性肺炎」（COVID-19）疫情調整防疫措施（高級中等以下學校）。
13. 康雅菁，2020.09，疫情對國內企業人力資源管理之影響與因應。台灣勞工季刊，70。
14. 康雅菁，2020.09，疫情對國內企業人力資源管理之影響與因應。台灣勞工季刊，70。
15. TEAPA，2021、2022、2023年會。
16. 林勻婷，2022，臺灣通訊諮商研究主題與研究法之分析 - 以2001-2021年為例。清華大學(台灣) 教育心理與諮商學系，碩士論文，曾文志博士指導。預計20270707開放。(A Review Study of Communication Counseling Research between 2001 and 2021 in Taiwan.)
17. OOSGA，2023.0617檢索：https://zh.oosga.com/social-media/twn/

THAILAND

Athalie de Koning

BACKGROUND: NEW COUNSELING SERVICE (NCS) ORIGINS AND EXPANSION

NCS was founded in 2001 by Johanna de Koning, a social worker and psychologist with a true heart for people in need. Johanna, together with her husband, Rex, originally provided counseling services to Thai people in their native language and quickly realized that many expats living in Thailand needed access to mental health care too. The couple began collaborations with Thai colleagues in order to expand the services and reach more people. Johanna established a regular Intervision practice in order to deepen professional relationships, provide accountability, and establish a standard of care that was lacking in the Thai mental health landscape at that time. NCS launched some of the very first Employee Assistance Programs in this region and offered everything from personal counseling to cultural consultations to crisis intervention. During the devastating tsunami of 2004, NCS was on-site within days, offering trauma therapy and practical help such as clearing destroyed areas and relocation. In the years following, NCS has been on the front lines with every major event, such as the monsoon floods of 2011, the 2014 military coup, and the 2019 pandemic, which affected all sectors, deeply impacting the EAP landscape.

In the past four years, we have seen an explosion of mental health awareness in Thai media and a significant increase in EAP utilization. Especially during the pandemic, we noticed that many EAPs that formerly operated on a small scale suddenly had to increase their offerings to meet the demands of the pandemic. Although we only had a brief official lockdown in Thailand, many clients were afraid to continue face-to-face counseling, so we adapted accordingly. The government mandated mask-wearing, and because it is difficult to read subtle facial expressions while wearing a mask, we quickly switched to transparent face shields, which helped to enhance the face-to-face experience while still adhering to government guidelines. A majority of households in this country are multigenerational, so our clients were afraid to bring home a disease that could affect the elderly in their home. For this reason, we began offering online sessions very early on in the pandemic. Interestingly, our younger counselors and clients have shown a strong preference for online counseling even after restrictions were lifted, while our senior counselors still prefer face-to-face sessions. Although many clients request online counseling and we are happy to meet this need, where possible, we do encourage at least a first session face-to-face in order to establish rapport and trust. Especially in Thai culture where seeking mental health support is still quite new, we find that initial session to be a very important factor in whether the client seeks counsel again. Meeting face-to-face at our mental health center, a calming and inviting environment, helps the client to truly focus on their well-being without distraction. We have actually had some clients come in and rest in our reception room for a while because they said it was such a welcome break from their stressful office surroundings. Personally, even with the advent of many online counseling platforms and advanced AI solutions, I do believe that the trend will eventually go back to in-person counseling, for the simple reason that human connection is irreplaceable and extremely vital in mental health situations.

AI COUNSELING: CURE OR CURSE?

Last year, we were approached by a VR software company to consult on the development of an Artificial Intelligence Counseling Chatbot. We provided them with a comprehensive list of intake questions and had many interesting discussions in our team about the impact, concerns, ethics, and practical applications of AI Counseling. While testing the chatbot, we encountered important issues such as: How should the bot respond to trigger topics such as self-harm or abuse? What are the confidentiality concerns when using an open source chat feature? What are the ethical and legal implications should a client receive ineffective advice from the bot? While we are curious to see where this will lead in the future and we are excited to stay at the forefront of innovation, we decided that, for the time being, NCS will refrain from using an AI chatbot even for intake sessions, as we truly value the initial human contact experience for our clients. However, the technology that we can use to greatly expand our reach here is social media.

Thailand is one of the largest users of Facebook in the world. Thai culture is very community-oriented, and the online platform provides a way to share news, exchange ideas, and generally entertain huge audiences. Instagram and TikTok follow closely in usage, especially with the younger demographic. This is an area where NCS can grow. We launched an Instagram account earlier this year and have already found that many people check our profile there before deciding whether to contact us. We plan to expand our reach online through short-form articles and videos on social media and long-form resources on LinkedIn, YouTube, and our website. The messages we share on social media regarding mental health awareness, our practice standards, and diversity and inclusion actively shape our clients' understanding of who we are.

COLORFUL COUNSELORS

NCS has a history of helping people from all walks of life. Bangkok is a colorful city with people from so many different backgrounds, and our team reflects this diversity. We have found that our social media presence this year has helped to attract a diverse group of applicants in terms of age, nationality, sexual orientation, neurodiversity, and beliefs. In upholding our counseling ethos, we want to ensure that everyone has access to quality mental health support. Our financial aid program is one way that we reach out to people who cannot afford counseling. Our anonymous hotline is another concrete way to provide support for those who may be struggling with shame or judgment from their surroundings. NCS makes it very clear that our offices are a safe space, free from prejudice and bigotry. Thailand is undergoing a lot of changes as the new generation parts ways with some of the more conservative values of old. We look forward to what the future holds for Thailand's youth, and although it is a long road ahead, we see great potential for a new era of integrity and equality.

ABOUT THE AUTHOR

My name is Athalie de Koning, and at the beginning of 2023, I accepted the position of Creative Director at NCS. NCS has been operating in Thailand for more than 20 years, quietly working to change the lives of thousands of people. The organization started off as a humble charity project and has since grown into a full team of qualified counselors and support staff. NCS is now a corporation that uses a large portion of its profits to champion mental health care access for all. It is the only fully licensed mental health center in Thailand, recently renewing its accreditation with the ACC in accordance with the SCopEd framework in the UK. My job as Creative Director is to guide NCS on this dynamic path as we meet the demands of increasing EAP usage, a wider variety of coverage options, and more detailed reporting requirements—all the while upholding the quality that NCS has worked so hard to establish over the past 20 years.

RESOURCES

New Counseling Service (NCS)
www.ncsbkk.com

Thai Counseling Psychology Association
https://www.thaicounseling.org/

Sati Application
https://www.satiapp.co/

Faculty of Psychology, Chulalongkorn University
https://www.chula.ac.th/en/academic/faculty-of-psychology/

TRINIDAD AND TOBAGO

Patricia Elder and Brent Pereira

IMPACT OF SERVICES DURING THE COVID-19 PANDEMIC

COVID-19 is an infectious disease caused by a virus with mild to severe, even fatal results, depending on one's health status, age, and underlying medical problems. In 2020, the Corporate Communications Unit of the Ministry of Health of the Government of Trinidad and Tobago provided guidelines and regulations for the provision of psychosocial services, medical services, and education to the approximately 1.4 million citizens nationwide. As an EAP provider, the work of Elder Associates Limited was recognized as an "essential service." As such, we continued to deliver support and care throughout the period.

Our model of service delivery was amended to accommodate the needs of our clients and customer organizations. Remote service delivery options were fortified to allow for all counseling, consultation, and training services to be provided virtually.

THE ROLE OF TECHNOLOGY AND SOCIAL MEDIA

With remote service delivery, there was an increased reliance on technology. Key components of EAP that support clinical services, previously delivered on-site, were required to be provided to the clients remotely. In addition to the platforms used to facilitate clinical contact, technology supported other necessary functions, including securing consent for treatment and authorization for release of information. The evolution of a paper-based to electronic record system meant the requirement for electronic client signatures and also encryption of client data to ensure confidentiality. Remote service delivery also meant more dependence on social and electronic media for communication of notices, updates, and changes to service delivery options as health regulations and pandemic developments changed.

A general acceptance of the use of remote EAP services by clients was noted. However, some persons were not at all comfortable using this option. This was attributed to a lack of comfort with technology; inability to secure a private, confidential space during the session, particularly when family or intimate partner relationship issues were the presenting problem; or just a preference for in-person service. In some cases, access to a reliable internet connection posed a challenge.

As an EAP service provider, we fostered enhanced cooperation with customer organizations and mental health and community agencies. Navigating the novelty of the pandemic provided the opportunity to build connections with other professional organizations and mental health agencies in sharing information regarding prevention protocols, protective equipment, and educational activities. Social media, electronic and print media, as well as in-house flyers were used to educate the public of the presence of mental health services in the community and ways to access them. We fully utilized the occasion to debunk the stigma around mental health, self-care, and EAP services.

A major factor affecting EAP service delivery during the COVID-19 pandemic was the suspension of business services due to public health policies and regulations. In response to patterns of increasing infections and the capacity of the health care system, periodic shutdowns were implemented. For many organizations in the hospitality, tourism, and other service industries, a significant loss of income was experienced.

While social support services such as food grants and rental assistance were provided by the Government of Trinidad and Tobago, the negative impact on the lifestyle and mental health of many individuals and families was significant. Increased financial stress on employers, employees, and their families alike affected the psychological well-being of many citizens. The repercussions of this trauma on persons were noted with the presence of anxiety and depressive symptoms, as well as family and relationship conflicts, both inside and outside the home.

THE EFFECTS OF ONLINE/VIRTUAL COUNSELING

The impact of services provided during the pandemic can be reviewed through the lens of the utilization data for the period as well as clients' subjective reports of the impact of services. During the period June 2020 to May 2022, Elder Associates Limited observed an increase in the request for counseling services of greater than 30%, which were provided virtually. It found that employees and their dependents more readily accessed the EAP for initial services but also were more likely than previously to maintain engagement in treatment. A reduction in missed and cancelled appointments was also noted. This can be interpreted as evidence of the need for, appreciation of, and impact of the counseling services provided.

During the pandemic, Elder Associates Limited was also able to maintain an average satisfaction rating of above 4.5 on a scale of zero to five representing very unsatisfied to very satisfied, respectively. It is noted that over a one-year period, feedback was solicited from clients specifically on their experiences with counseling in a virtual modality. While many clients indicated a preference for in-person counseling, less than 1% of clients surveyed expressed dissatisfaction with the online modality. 98% of clients expressed satisfaction with the counselor they worked with and their counseling experience.

EFFORTS TOWARD DIVERSITY AND INCLUSION

To meet the increased and diverse demand for services, Elder Associates Limited has been committed to representation in the composition of care team members and variety in our service delivery. Intentionally, care team members reflect a range of ages; ethnic, religious, and national backgrounds; and gender identities. We also offer services in seven different languages, including sign language. The involvement of varied community members and traditionally underserved populations in the assessment of our services provides invaluable feedback that informs how we can better serve our people.

ABOUT THE AUTHOR

A leader and visionary for the delivery of comprehensive mental health services in the Greater Caribbean region, Dr. Patricia Elder is a Certified Employee Assistance Professional (CEAP) trained as a Peer Reviewer for the Council on Accreditation of Employee Assistance Programmes, and a member of the Trinidad and Tobago branch of the International Women's Forum. Dr. Elder is the Regional Director for the Caribbean for the Institute for Forensic Psychology (IFP), providing pre-employment evaluations of law enforcement personnel.

Dr. Brent Pereira is a Certified Employee Assistance Professional (CEAP) and National Certified Counselor with over 15 years clinical experience in Trinidad and Tobago and the United States of America. He currently serves as the Clinical Director of Elder Associates Limited.

Elder Associates Limited provides comprehensive psychological services, specializing in the design and implementation of Employee Assistance Programmes (EAPs). Founded in 1993 by

Dr. Patricia Elder and initially established in Trinidad and Tobago, the company has expanded services throughout the Greater Caribbean region. In January 2013, Elder Associates Limited was accredited by the Council on Accreditation (COA) as an EAP Service Provider and most recently reaccredited in 2021. COA's programme of quality improvement is designed to identify providers that have met high performance standards and have made a commitment to their stakeholders to deliver the very best quality services.

RESOURCES

Trinidad and Tobago Association of Psychologists
https://psychologytt.org

Employee Assistance Professionals Association
Trinidad & Tobago
https://www.facebook.com/eapatt

Trinidad and Tobago Association of Social Workers
https://www.ttasw.org

REFERENCES

Japan Ministry of Land, Infrastructure, Transport and Tourism. Telework Population Survey. 2022.3.

Future of work after the COVID-19. McKinsey Global Institute. 2021.2.

Japan Productivity Center. 11th Survey on Workers' Attitude. 2022.10.

Japan Productivity Center. 10th Survey on corporations' mental health countermeasures. 2021.12.

Mitsunori Hirose. Advantage Risk Management EAP. Pandemic Talk Japan. EAPA Japan branch annual conference. 2021.6.27. NHK. June 5, 2020.

Miyazawa, Y., Ichikawa, K., Shimazu, Correlation of Resilience and Work Engagement. A. The 93rd Annual Conference of Japan Society for Occupational Health. May 2020.

Tomoko Sugawara, CEAP. T-Pec Inc. EAPA Japan branch annual conference. 2021.6.27.

University of Occupational and Environmental Health, Japan. Mental Health Accreditation System. https://www.uoeh-u.ac.jp/medical/hoshms/mh.html.

Japan Organization of Occupational Health and Safety. Registered mental health counseling agency. https://www.johas.go.jp/sangyouhoken.

TURKEY

Banu Mercan Öztürk

INTRODUCTION

My name is Banu Mercan Öztürk, and I work as a business excellence manager at Remed Assistance. I am responsible for customer relations, operational processes, quality management and network development. I have been with Remed Assistance for 19 years and have 17 years of experience in the EAP field.

Remed Assistance is an ever-growing assistance company providing global services. It was founded in 1993 by Selçuk Tiftik, MD. It provides services 24/7 from three alarm centres in Istanbul, Antalya and Cairo. Remed launched the Employee Assistance Program (EAP) as the first EAP provider in Türkiye in 2006, under the AVİTA brand. As of 2023, it serves more than 2 million people from several sectors such as banking, automotive, transportation, pharmaceuticals, FMCG, defense industry, manufacturing, energy, logistics and retail.

The core EAP services provided by AVİTA are as follows:

- Psychological counseling
  - Telephone counseling
  - Face-to-face / online / virtual counseling
- Legal information
- Fiscal information
- Medical information

- Back and neck pain and office ergonomics
- Newborn care information
- Healthy nutrition counseling
- General information
- Techno-support
- Veterinary counseling
- House/garden plants counseling

THE IMPACT OF SERVICES DURING THE PANDEMIC

In recent years, the number of people in Türkiye suffering from anxiety and depression has significantly increased due to factors like repeated natural disasters, migration, economic downturn, and the COVID-19 pandemic. According to data of the Ministry of Health of Türkiye (MoH), 17% of the population faces mental health issues and 3.2 million people suffer from depression. Out of a population of about 83 million, almost 9 million people seek mental health support in Türkiye each year. The outbreak of the COVID-19 pandemic brought forth unprecedented challenges to societies worldwide, including Türkiye. As the nation grappled with the physical, emotional, and economic toll of the crisis, the significance of supporting the well-being of employees became paramount.

COVID-19 has negatively affected the mental health of the population. Awareness of the impact of Employee Assistance Programs has increased during the pandemic. The number of our new customers increased by 371% in 2020, and the EAP usage rate increased by 71%. According to our utilization reports, the most common mental health issues among employees during the pandemic were anxiety and depressive symptoms. Our reports showed that there has been a 72% rise in anxiety levels and a 10% increase in depression levels. According to the report, depressive symptoms were 10% more prevalent in women compared to men, while anxiety symptoms were 2% more common in men.

Additionally, utilization patterns among employees have changed during the pandemic. Due to changing work/life conditions such as lockdowns and remote working, different support needs of employees emerged. The service of back and neck pain and office ergonomics, provided within the EAP, was mostly used by those who suffered from neck and back pain due to the lack of ergonomics in working conditions at home. The utilization rate of this service increased by 570%. Similarly, due to technical glitches encountered while working remotely, the usage rates of techno-support service have increased by 282%. We also supported our users by organizing over 500 webinars attended by nearly 30,000 people during the pandemic.

In the face of the COVID-19 pandemic, EAPs played a significant role in supporting employees' well-being and fostering resilience. By providing accessible mental health services, promoting work-life balance, and nurturing a supportive organizational culture, EAPs have made an important impact. However, it is crucial to address potential challenges and invest in the sustainability of EAPs to ensure their continued effectiveness. This includes providing access to mental health services and creating a culture of open communication about mental health issues.

THE EFFECTS OF ONLINE/VIRTUAL COUNSELING

Employee Assistance Programs play a crucial role in supporting employees. With the shift toward remote work and social distancing measures during the pandemic, online/virtual counseling has emerged as a vital tool for providing mental health support to employees in Turkey.

Before the pandemic, online/virtual counseling was not preferred much among employees. However, the use of online/virtual counseling has increased significantly since the pandemic. While only 1% of employees received online counseling in 2019, this percentage rose to 35% in 2020. At the beginning of the pandemic, we had already completed the infrastructure for online/virtual counseling, so we quickly adapted to the new situation. Employees who were already receiving counseling before the pandemic seamlessly switched to online sessions and continued their outgoing sessions with their counselors. Additionally, online/virtual counseling has facilitated the provision of ongoing support, enabling employees to address emerging challenges related to the pandemic and its associated stressors.

Online/virtual counseling has increased accessibility to mental health services for employees in Turkey, particularly those in remote areas or with limited access to face-to-face counseling. It has allowed employees to receive support without the constraints of geographical location or transportation barriers, ensuring that more individuals can benefit from EAPs.

The pandemic disrupted face-to-face counseling services, making it difficult for employees to receive consistent support. Online/virtual counseling has offered a solution by ensuring continuity of counseling.

Despite its benefits, online/virtual counseling may not be suitable for everyone. Some individuals may prefer or require face-to-face interactions. Issues related to internet connectivity, technology literacy, and privacy concerns should be addressed to ensure the effectiveness and security of online/virtual counseling services. We provide online/virtual counseling through our own platform. In order to minimize the risks, we send the client an e-mail 24 hours before the session, explaining how to log in to the system and containing the minimum technical requirements. We get ongoing feedback from clients and counselors to identify areas for improvement and optimize the delivery of online/virtual counseling.

THE ROLE OF TECHNOLOGY AND SOCIAL MEDIA

The pandemic has brought about significant disruptions to various aspects of our lives, including the way we work and seek assistance. In Turkey, like in many other countries, the pandemic has underscored the importance of technology and social media in providing employee assistance.

Technology and social media have facilitated easy access to EAPs in Türkiye during the pandemic. Virtual platforms and mobile apps have made it possible for employees to receive immediate support and counseling remotely. The availability of online resources, webinars, and educational materials through social media platforms has increased awareness and accessibility to assistance. Virtual counseling has provided a safe and convenient space for individuals to seek professional help. Technology and social media have facilitated efficient communication channels between employees and EAP providers. Instant messaging and video conferencing tools have enabled real-time communication, enhancing responsiveness and support. Online platforms have allowed EAP providers to disseminate critical information promptly, such as health guidelines and policy updates.

The pandemic has accelerated the adoption of remote work in Türkiye, and technology has played a crucial role in this transition. Virtual collaboration tools have enabled effective teamwork and communication despite physical distance. Social media platforms have provided a means for employees to stay connected, fostering a sense of belonging and reducing isolation.

The role of technology and social media in the employee assistance field in Türkiye during the pandemic has been transformative. These tools have enabled accessible support, efficient communication, and an expedited remote work adaptation process. Investing in technology infrastructure and digital literacy will be crucial for the continued development and effectiveness of Employee Assistance Programs in Türkiye. Harnessing the potential of technology and social media can contribute significantly to the well-being and resilience of employees during challenging times.

EFFORTS TOWARD DIVERSITY AND INCLUSION WITHIN THE FIELD (COUNSELORS, PROVIDERS, CLIENTS)

In recent years, the global discourse on diversity and inclusion has gained attention. Türkiye, with its multicultural heritage and unique blend of cultures, presents an ideal backdrop for acknowledging the importance of diversity. Recognizing that diverse backgrounds, experiences, and perspectives enriches the counseling process, and EAP stakeholders have gradually begun embracing diversity as a cornerstone for effective assistance programs. As a company working in the EAP field, we collaborate with consultants from diverse ethnic, cultural, and religious backgrounds as part of our diversity and inclusion initiatives. By doing so, our aim is to ensure that our clients feel understood and supported. We try to provide language access to clients by adding consultants who are competent in various languages to our network. This initiative helps overcome language barriers and ensures that clients can fully express their concerns and receive appropriate assistance, regardless of their mother tongue.

In addition to recognizing cultural diversity, we work with counselors who can provide psychological support to the needs of underrepresented groups such as LGBTQ+ individuals, refugees, and people with disabilities. We conduct webinars that emphasize the importance of understanding cultural nuances, religious sensitivities, and social contexts to meet clients' needs effectively.

In Türkiye, many individuals and organizations are still unaware of the importance and benefits of diversity and inclusion. Advocacy efforts are needed to raise awareness, engage stakeholders, and foster a collective commitment toward promoting diversity.

EAP organizations should create a more inclusive and effective counseling environment by recognizing the importance of diversity, increasing representation, promoting cultural competency, and providing tailored support. Though challenges exist, the commitment to diversity and inclusion is crucial for empowering individuals from all backgrounds and ensuring the provision of comprehensive support in Türkiye's EAP field.

ABOUT THE AUTHOR

Banu Mercan Öztürk is a Business Excellence Manager at Remed Assistance-AVİTA in Türkiye. Graduate of the Faculty of Economics and Administrative Sciences, Department of Business Administration.

RESOURCES

Turkish Psychologists Association – A national association that brings together professionals in the field of psychological counseling. Find more information on their website at http://www.psikolog.org.tr/.

SPoD – Founded in 2011 with the dream of a fair, equal, and free world under the rainbow, SPoD provides legal, social, and psychological counseling to LGBTI+ people. Find more information on their website at https://spod.org.tr/homepage/.

Healthy Life Centers (HLC) – Established to protect individuals and communities from health-related risks and promote a healthy lifestyle. HLCs operate as additional service units under the umbrella of the public health center. They provide necessary interventions in individual psycho-social counseling/family counseling to address psychological and socio-economic problems related to an individual's mental and/or physical health issues, marriage or couple relationships, communication with family and children, work, and personal life. Find more information on their website at https://shm.saglik.gov.tr/.

YEDAM – Find advice and support for getting help with alcohol, tobacco, substance use, gambling, and internet addiction. YEDAM provides free services in 81 provinces in Turkey. Find more information on their website at https://www.yedam.org.tr/.

UGANDA

John Mary Ssekate

THE IMPACT OF SERVICES DURING THE PANDEMIC

COVID-19 caused a lot of trauma, loss, grief, anxiety, physical and emotional abuse, domestic violence, stigma and discrimination, teenage pregnancies, and many more.

The National Mental Health Technical Working Group was one of the major platforms that was impactful in providing needed services during COVID-19 in Uganda. With over 33 mental health technical organizations under this group, the Ministry of Health shared learnings and best practices on effective responses to COVID-19, coordinated different mental health stakeholders in Uganda, carried out peer support toward suicide mitigation, and facilitated emergency response. The group also carried out research and supported with tele-counselling, which helped to bridge the gap. They developed guidelines, promoted clinical support to health workers, provided home-based care support, and trained front-liners and health workers to effectively support Ugandans during COVID-19 (National Mental Health Conference Report 25th–27th May 2022).

Prior to the COVID-19 period, students' mental health was already at stake, and COVID-19 aggravated the situation. The lockdown caused schools and tertiary institutions to rapidly adopt and pursue remote learning methods. Teachers, students, and their families experienced several different challenges, including increased stress and anxiety that led to the degradation of mental health, sexual abuse, drug addictions, and child labor, all of which remained common features during COVID-19 in Uganda. The Uganda counselling association under Makerere University linked children to the nearby support centers for counselling, provided age-appropriate information, and discouraged risky behaviors like alcoholism and unsafe sexual practices. They enhanced adaptive coping skills for students during the COVID-19 era and boosted the students' mental health in the post-COVID-19 era, steering much-needed counselling services in schools and tertiary institutions.

The broader assessment undertaken by the United Nations in Uganda with a team of researchers from Makerere University on the impact of COVID-19 on local government service delivery shines more light on this subject matter. The study found out that the COVID-19 pandemic disrupted the social and economic structures of service delivery with significant consequences on lives, livelihoods, and general economic development due to government measures, including a partial lockdown of movement of people and closure of places that involve public gatherings such as schools and public transport. Factories and business facilities with a few services considered essential to the population and the functioning of the economy were allowed to operate within the guidelines stipulated in Standard Operating Procedures (SOPs). These services include: health care, security, basic public administration, banking, food distribution, water, energy, transport, and communication.

The closure of education institutions and the requirement that people stay at home not only reduced the production of goods and services but also curtailed demand and trade, as many agricultural industries and services had a direct and indirect linkage with social institutions. Transport and many informal-sector services shut down, leading to massive unemployment. According to this report, the most affected services were basic social services such as health, education, and agricultural extension services that support livelihoods through production and related services, support to the poor and most vulnerable with emergency or regular health care support, and garbage collection. This affected the provision of basic services that were dependent on local resources and work overload for the few staff who were allowed to work and were able to reach the office, according to this study.

VACCINATION SERVICES

Uganda experienced high patient numbers, inadequate oxygen supply, insufficient bed capacity and a high cost of care in the private facilities. The retention of dead bodies by private hospitals increased anxiety in the general public, negatively affecting health care delivery.

The Government of Uganda prioritized COVID-19 vaccination as a strategic intervention for control of the pandemic and for safe and sustainable reopening of the economy. According to Uganda Bureau of Statistics, 22 million people in 2021 above 18 years of age were eligible and targeted for vaccination. 4.8 million were the vulnerable populations including health workers, teachers, security personnel, the elderly of 50 years and above, and those below 50 years with co-morbidities, plus 330,000 students in tertiary institutions aged 18 years and above were included in the priority category to facilitate re-opening of these institutions, according to 4th November 2021 Ministry of Health report to Uganda parliament.

Uganda received 864,000 doses of AstraZeneca vaccines through the COVAX facility and a donation of 100,000 doses of the same vaccine from the Government of India. On 10 March 2021, Government of Uganda launched COVID-19 vaccination with eligible persons only required to report to the vaccination site with national identity cards or any other identification documents like driving permits, work permits, passports or a Refugee Identity Card. According to the Minister of Health Dr. Ruth Aceng's statement to parliament. Uganda also procured 18 million doses of the Sinopharm vaccine from China through the COVAX facility, and it arrived between October and December 2021. Nine million doses of the Johnson and Johnson vaccine were procured through the African Union between September 2021 and September 2022, and 18 million doses of vaccines were obtained through donations from the COVAX facility and other country-to-country donations.

The latest update by the Uganda Mister of Health on 13th October 2023 revealed that the vaccine uptake in the country stood at 59% of the population aged 18 and above, while among children aged 12 to 17, only 6% had received two jabs. This coverage is below our target of 28.5 million eligible Ugandans (22 million adults and 6.5 million children) who are up to date with their vaccination against COVID-19.

However, despite successes in vaccination, COVID-19 vaccination has stagnated in the past 18 months with Ministry of Health recording successive expiry of vaccines with 7,567,200 vaccine doses for COVID-19 set to expire by February 2024 if not administered to Ugandans that have not yet received either their first jab or second jab. The country has recorded 3,632 deaths since the global pandemic broke out in early 2020, but there have been 1,748 cases of COVID-19 between January and September 2023. This brings the total number of cumulative cases in the country since the outbreak of the pandemic to 3,262,447, with COVID-19 cases still being recorded in the country with the Districts of Kampala, Wakiso, Masaka, Kisoro, Gulu, Mbarara and Luwero having the highest numbers since January 2023.

FOOD AND CASH TRANSFER TO THE MOST VULNERABLE

With coordination from the Office of the Prime Minister through the Ministry of Gender Labour and Social Development, Uganda gave out over USh 54.7 billion to 501,107 households from all cities and municipalities around the country. Each one of the persons received USh 100,000 on the mobile money account. The top beneficiaries included bus or taxi drivers, conductors, baggage carriers, wheelbarrow pushers, touts, traffic guides, barmen, barmaids, waiters and bouncers, gym and restaurant workers, boda-boda riders, special hire drivers and Uber drivers, salons, massage parlor workers, teachers, and others.

The Office of the Prime Minister (OPM) relief department also distributed food to over 1.4 million people in urban areas who could not afford to buy food during the lockdown. The distribution of food was conducted at a local council level and saw 10 kgs of maize flour, and three packets of beans and packets of salt to each recipient. Lactating mothers and the sick in urban areas got 2 kgs each of powdered milk and sugar, respectively. This response was complemented by religious organizations through their union, the Inter-Religious Council of Uganda, which supported the government with 22,000,000 shillings in addition to supporting 30,337 households, 1,451,618 persons, and 2,518 institutions with posho, beans, milk and other basic necessities of life, according to the Inter-Religious Council report on food distribution. This complementary effort by IRC was launched on 6th May 2020.

Furthermore, UNICEF stood as one of the strong pillars in providing essential services to the different groups of valuable populations and strengthening systems in collaboration with different government ministries and departments amid changing COVID-19 restrictions and guidelines in Uganda. According to the Country Office COVID-19 situation report no. 2 of May 2020, UNICEF supported district health teams to strengthen coordination, develop COVID-19 district response plans, and functionalize monitoring and reporting on the continuity of essential health services. As a result of these efforts, 32 UNICEF-supported districts got functional district task forces for COVID-19 with response plans and actively implemented mitigation measures to ensure service continuity. 1,393,799 children and women were supported to access essential health care services, including immunization and prenatal services, while 353,833 women and children (176,209 male, 177,624 female) were reached with essential health care services.

Cumulatively by May 2020, 499,929 (248,965 male, 250,964 female) primary caregivers of children were reached with infant and young child feeding (IYCF) counselling through facilities and community platforms. 159,671 people (78,239 male, 81,432 female) were reached with critical water, sanitation and hygiene (WASH) supplies and services. 212 children, parents and primary caregivers were reached with community-based mental health psychosocial support (MHPSS) in May 2020. 61,625 children (30,689 boys, 30,936 girls) were reached with home-based/distance learning to ensure continuity of learning, according to this report.

Through Malaria Consortium and Intra-Health, UNICEF supported the coordination, monitoring and service delivery activities for malaria in 27 most-affected districts in the Karamoja, Lango, Acholi and Teso sub-regions. Out of the 22,815 village health teams (VHTs) in 27 SURMA programme-supported districts, 5,066 VHTs in Karamoja were oriented on IPC to ensure a safe continuation of the integrated management of malaria, pneumonia and diarrhea at the community level with technical support from UNICEF partners.

THE EFFECTS OF ONLINE/VIRTUAL COUNSELING

The Uganda Ministry of Health and her partners like Strong Mind Uganda, the medical concierge group (TMCG), Infectious Diseases Institute (IDI), Baylor Uganda, Uganda Counselling Association, Uganda Psychological Association and the National Association of Social Workers of Uganda virtually supported Ugandans in critical areas like client-seeking counselling support in HIV/AIDS, tuberculosis, maternal newborn and child health, and sexual and reproductive health during COVID-19.

With funding from USAID-HIV/AIDS initiatives at workplaces, activity like USAID regional health integration to enhance services (RHITES), and other health projects—including remote tele-consultations via voice, chat and video platforms; SMS reminders on facility appointments; and mobile SMS health information dissemination and awareness for behavioral change—made a great impact by serving the affected families. People and families remotely consulted health care providers, which reduced the chances of health facility congestion in the face of the easy spread of COVID-19. Tele-counselling providers during the COVID-19 pandemic included private entities like Rocket Health, Twogere Health, Seven Doctors, GoGP+ Nakasero hospital, Case Hospital and research institutions like Infectious Diseases Institute and Baylor Uganda, among others.

The Ministry of Health capitalized on this opportunity by leveraging online platforms to share information regarding COVID-19, including routine infographics. This helped to reach a large critical mass while maintaining social distancing. The adoption of tele-consultation by private traditional health care providers was evidence of the effectiveness of tele-consultation in managing outpatient medical complaints if diagnostic and therapeutic protocols are followed. Therefore, improving this modality of provider-patient interaction, telemedicine helped improve the hospital admissions and referrals to specialist services, diagnostic tests and chronic disease home management.

The Uganda Ministry of Health (MoH) developed tele-therapy guidelines together with the Uganda Counseling Association and other partners from the national mental health working group. The guidelines were made available to the psychosocial support teams that were supporting the COVID-19 response. Because counselling was recognized as one of the frontline services, individual practitioners were able to open up their counselling firms and support in-service provision physically as well as online, especially where the service users could not access the physical premises.

Uganda Counseling Association worked with The Ministry of Education and Sports in response to set up a call center as a measure to handle the psychosocial needs of teachers and students returning to school post-COVID-19. UCA nominated eight counselors to provide the service for a period of six months. Over 120 teachers were able to access the service, and organizations were able to have group counselling sessions for their employees as well as individual sessions.

Psycho-education was majorly done online via Zoom and other conferencing options. Opening up access to information and awareness creation was a success, and the more they appreciated the information, the more COVID-19 patients were able to break the stigma and access individual help.

THE ROLE OF TECHNOLOGY AND SOCIAL MEDIA

Use of technology and social media platforms remained pivotal in enabling the remote delivery of clinical and nonclinical health services in Uganda. Technology innovations like Zoom meetings and Google Meet worked as a catalyst for online health worker training and engagements and as a facilitation tool for medical education, organizing administrative meetings and long-distance patient care.

Technology and social media were harnessed by major health stakeholders like the medical concierge group, Regional Psychosocial Support Initiative (REPSSI), Strong Minds Uganda, the Infectious Diseases Institute, and Baylor Uganda to offer telehealth services in areas such as HIV/AIDS; tuberculosis; maternal, newborn, and child health; and sexual and reproductive health services during this global health catastrophe and challenge of time. Telemedicine applications linked activities from teleconsultations with care providers (including tele-psychiatry and tele-pharmacy services) to effectively disseminate health information and appointment reminders via mobile phones and maintain access to care during the early months of the COVID-19 pandemic in Uganda.

Technology also facilitated the delivery of critical services such as family planning. In the pandemic context, the Uganda Ministry of Health and partners used traditional platforms such as newspapers, radio, television, and billboards, along with a designated website for COVID-19 updates, plus social media platforms like X (Twitter) accounts, Facebook pages, and other social media platforms like WhatsApp to disseminate information to the general public and increase community awareness of key measures ordinary people could take to prevent COVID-19 infection. Health professionals also used social media platforms to share the location of local testing facilities and their availability and later included information about vaccines and vaccine delivery according to the Uganda Ministry of Health (MOH) and Technical Inter-Sectoral Committee COVID-19 Report of December 1, 2020.

The National Association of Social Workers of Uganda (NASWU), together with the Ministry of Gender, Labour and Social Development, and Child's i Foundation, used technology to re-orient services to meet the needs of existing clients and the millions of people whose lives had suddenly been thrown into confusion by the virus. NASWU leveraged technology to remotely engage frontline social workers and different stakeholders through coordinating different social work agencies and academia to share experiences and best practices to promote resilience among children, families and communities in Uganda.

This coordinated intervention of online experience-sharing was a great reason why frontline social workers and health professionals realized that working together as agencies resulted in a high impact, especially in responding to situations of adversity. Webinar meeting discussions and engagements focused on three social protection thematic areas of social work response to COVID-19 in Uganda, addressing online sexual exploitation and gender-based violence during and after COVID-19 in Uganda and prioritizing protection of street children and children under alternative care during and after COVID-19. Key social work agencies and academic institutions were coordinated by NASWU to share their experience and achievements along the webinar themes to empower all frontline health professionals.

YOUTH, TECHNOLOGY AND SOCIAL MEDIA DURING COVID-19

Youth-led innovations promoted resilience during COVID-19 in Uganda. One of the remarkable innovations was a three-month (July 17 to September 21, 2020) national youth-led advocacy intervention using technology to promote positive coping mechanisms for mental health and resilience of children, families and communities amid new and changing restrictions around social interactions and gatherings. This was a viable strategy to continue supporting children and families remotely.

Coordinated by the National Association of Social Workers of Uganda (NASWU) with support from Coordinating Comprehensive Care for Children (4Children), the intervention targeted 100 social work students and recent graduates from 20 social work teaching universities representing five regions of Uganda to promote mental health and resilience amid the COVID-19 pandemic through the innovative use of social media channels to provide important outlets and positively influence their networks of friends and family to promote resilience and unite families amid the evolving situation of COVID-19.

Virtual guidance and support were provided by NASWU for the posting and sharing of accurate and positive information to assist families and communities in coping with the effects of COVID-19, demonstrating the role of professional social workers in situations of adversity. Based on the social work principle of self-determination, the intervention demonstrated the creativity of youth and the power of technology to reach networks and to pass accurate information to the general public. Output in this youth-led advocacy was based on the number of online discussions along major social media platforms, number of online shares, promotion of positive coping mechanisms and creation of an enabling environment for the resilience of children, families and communities.

The following table is a summary of four weeks of online engagement based on selected topics using different social media platforms.

Week	Theme	Facebook		WhatsApp		Instagram		X (Twitter)	
		likes	shares	likes	shares	likes	shares	likes	shares
Week 1 27–31 July	Resilience amid COVID-19 pandemic	15,046	224	143	40	236	21	217	15
Week 2 3–9 August	Protection of children against violence amid COVID-19 pandemic	20,211	325	174	48	292	22	280	25
Week 3 10–15 August	Safety measures in preventing the spread of COVID-19	20,370	351	185	26	365	19	302	21
Week 4 17–21 August	Increasing community vigilance and measures to curb COVID-19	10,887	98	48	6	168	4	272	14
Total output		66,514	998	550	120	1,061	66	1,071	75

Source: (NASWU annual report 2020)

We learned that younger professionals have greater potential when supported to spark positive online exchanges and promote the resilience of families and communities in situations of adversity. We observed that Facebook and Instagram are the most common usable social media platforms by younger people in Uganda and can be explored as a major strategy for further interventions in situations of health emergencies. The creativity of younger people while connecting with fellow youth in different parts of the country to support families in their communities demonstrated the indispensable role of technology and social media in the fight against COVID-19 and its effects in Uganda.

EFFORTS TOWARD DIVERSITY AND INCLUSION WITHIN THE FIELD (COUNSELORS, PROVIDERS, CLIENTS)

Research by Makerere University, Uganda Ministry of Health, and the National Association of Social Workers of Uganda et al. on Refugee Lived Experiences, Compliance and Thinking (REFLECT) in COVID-19 was done in three hosting districts of Kampala, Adjumani and Kyegegwa. Thirteen settlements of refugees gave great insight in regard to diversity and inclusion of refugees in Uganda, which accounts for more than 1.4 million urban and those living in numerous refugee settlements.

The study found great divergence in the knowledge of COVID-19 prevention and compliance, with many members of the refugee communities maintaining their routines and lifestyles, including the risky ones like cultural celebrations, crossing from one settlement to another with close contact and high potential for disease spread, violation of the recommended COVID-19 prevention measures such as social distancing and appropriate use of masks, suggesting low levels of adoption of a new behavior, much more than just a gap in prevention knowledge among refugees.

The UNHCR and the Office of the Prime Minister co-led the inclusive response in refugee settlements in Uganda, coordinating humanitarian assistance, protection and reporting. For example, between March and August 2020, Uganda had confirmed 1,560 COVID-19 cases, including 60 refugees, with 13 deaths, including two refugees. In promoting an inclusive response to COVID-19, Refugee Welfare Officers, Village Health Team (VHT) volunteers and para-social workers and counselors were involved in the fight against COVID-19. The volunteers were trained in risk communication and community engagement for an effective response. UNHCR and its partners worked together with the Uganda Ministry of Health to manage 19 quarantine facilities in refugee-hosting districts, train health workers, strengthen surveillance and infection prevention and control, and trace contacts of positive COVID-19 cases in refugee communities

Efforts toward inclusion and diversity were boosted through financial support from the European Civil Protection and Humanitarian Aid Operation (ECHO) with Euro 6.5 million toward the response, which supported refugees and host communities in continuing to protect their own communities. This enabled UNHCR to construct more than 12 quarantine and isolation facilities at the existing transit and reception centers, buy COVID-19 testing kits and supplies for infection prevention and control, and respond to outbreak alerts with the installation of tippy taps (hand-washing devices) in over 800 homes in the camps, according to the UNHCR press release of June 17, 2021.

However, despite efforts toward inclusion and diversity among refugees, the disparity along socioeconomic spheres among refugee populations in Uganda was imminent. Three rounds of phone surveys by UNHCR, World Bank and Uganda Bureau of Statistics on the socioeconomic impacts of the COVID-19 crisis on refugees conducted between February and March 2020 revealed that the consequences of the pandemic increased despair. Further, a separate UNHCR analysis revealed that the total number of attempted and completed suicides among refugees in 2020 increased by 129% compared to 2019, which had reported 347 suicide incidents. Data on suicides from the first quarter of 2021 was equally worrying, with 76 recorded incidents compared to 68 in the same period of 2020. Most cases concerned young women affected by gender-based violence, as recorded incidents of gender-based violence almost doubled compared to the first quarter of 2020, reaching 1,394. Lack of income and food insecurity within refugee households significantly contributed to these incidents.

The Ministry of Health, working with civil society organizations and the National Union of Disabled Persons of Uganda, supported persons with mental illness and epilepsy who entirely depend on drugs to live healthily to access their medication while minding their safety during this pandemic, ensured persons with disabilities who were infected had equal access to quality health care services without discrimination, provided information about COVID-19 mitigation tips, and offered public guidelines with all presidential addresses having sign language interpreters to better engage people living with disabilities. There was a well-coordinated plan by the District Task Teams on how to handle persons with disabilities by engaging disabled peoples organizations at national and district levels, which was a strong resource to use by the government in the fight against the pandemic. Persons with disabilities were given first priority among those who benefited from the food supplies.

With 5,931 children born every day in Uganda, according to the Uganda Bureau of Statistics, expectant mothers formed a unique category of the population to protect during the COVID-19 response. According to the President of Uganda's address on April 19, 2020, all pregnant women were no longer required to seek the Resident District Commissioners (RDC) permission for health care services like how it was with other categories of the population during quarantine. Village health teams, para social workers and local council leadership supported by identifying expectant mothers and supporting them with access to health services. This was also the same for people living with HIV/AIDS who were supported by social workers, counselors and community COVID-19 response teams through delivering essential medicine for the 2 million patients to prevent relapse and drug resistance. Women working in public markets in the informal sector were allowed to continue working without closure of their businesses but by sleeping at their workplace. The government, through the Office of Prime Minister and Ministry of Health, provided mosquito nets and food support to women in markets.

Inclusiveness and diversity were also shown among the COVID-19 response teams both at national and community levels. The teams included members from health professionals, security teams, cultural leaders, religious leaders, local government response teams, civil society organizations and professional bodies like the National Association of Social Workers of Uganda (NASWU) and the Uganda Counselling Association. This helped to inclusively cascade the information to all categories of people, creating confidence in the public and effectively mobilizing and promoting resilience of individuals, families and communities.

ABOUT THE AUTHOR

John Mary Ssekate is a professional social worker with a Bachelor's Degree in Social Work (Hons) of Kampala International University and a Master of Project Planning with a major in Social Projects. He holds additional professional training in Case Management for Children and Adolescents Exposed to Violence, Sexual Reproductive Health and Rights-SRHR, Health and Migration, from Makerere University, Children's Human Rights, Institute of Inspiring Children Future, University of Strathclyde, Glasgow, Scotland. John Mary has worked as a university lecturer at Kampala International University and Africa Renewal University (2013–2017) and as the National Capacity Building Officer for the National Association of Social Workers of Uganda (NASWU), 2017–2019.

John Mary has worked as the National Coordinator for the National Association of Social Workers of Uganda (NASWU) since 2020. In addition, he has served as an Independent Social Worker for Children and Families Across Borders (CFAB) since 2019. He is a member of the National Child Protection Working Group in the Ministry of Gender, Labour and Social Development and a member of Ministry of Health Mental Health and Psychosocial Support Working Group and a member of International Employee Assistance Program Committee.

RESOURCES

Healing Talk Counseling Services,
P.O. Box 16231
KAMPALA – Uganda
info@healingtalkcounseling.com

National Association of Social Workers of Uganda (NASWU)
naswu2014@gmail.com

Uganda Counselling Association
counsellingassn@gmail.com

Regional Psychosocial Initiative –REPSSI
michael.byamukama@repssi.org

REFERENCES

https://parliamentwatch.ug/news-amp-updates/7-5m-vaccine-doses-to-expire-as-country-still-records-COVID-19-cases/

Uganda Ministry of Health. COVID-19 Response Hub: Coordination structure. Accessed December 1, 2022. https://covid19.gou.go.ug/coordination.html

Uganda Ministry of Health (MOH) and Technical Inter-Sectoral Committee COVID-19. National Community Engagement Strategy for COVID-19 Response. Kampala: MOH; 2020. Accessed December 1, 2022. https://static1.squarespace.com/static/5e7b914b3b5f9a42199b3337/t/5fde38047185ee572d414bd2/1608398854507/NATIONAL+COMMUNITY+ENGAGEMENT+STARTEGY+FOR+COVID-19+Book.pd

Nyoni T, Okumu M. COVID-19-compliant strategies for supporting treatment adherence among people living with HIV in sub-Saharan Africa. AIDS Behav. 2020 Apr 24.

Kanu Ikechukwu A. COVID-19 and the economy: an African perspective. J Afr Stud Sustain Dev. 2020 Apr 20.

UKRAINE

Natalia Nalyvaiko

THE IMPACT OF SERVICES DURING THE PANDEMIC

The pandemic (COVID-19) affected business in terms of changing the practice from work in the office to online consulting. Psychological services were at the greatest demand, including webinars devoted to life during the crisis and work-life balance. The main queries were dealing with anxiety, family conflicts caused by the necessity to share the same premises with many relatives for a long time, fear of getting sick, and fear of being financially disabled because of the possible closure of the employer's company.

WAR

Although the pandemic's influence on the business was the biggest challenge for the company, a greater challenge to its personnel and the clients has become the war: the full-scale Russian invasion on February 24, 2022.

In the best traditions of psychotherapy, IN-Person Corporate, together with the whole Ukrainian community of mental health professionals, started to provide help and psychological support from the very first days of the war in unimaginably difficult conditions. Psychologists worked in bomb shelters, hospitals, in the centers for internally displaced people, in the psychosocial centers, and on the railway stations, providing first psychological aid and other kinds of crisis support. They also contributed through all kinds of online platforms as well as face-to-face consultations, where it was possible.

Due to the special need for crisis intervention and first aid psychological help, all the company's consultants received training in crisis psychological support. The first requests received at the beginning of the war were related to assisting in organizing survival needs after people fled from the places of active fights. The number of legal inquiries has increased significantly. They were related to the issues of accommodation at the places of migration, and the rights and obligations of the mobilized. The main form of support in the first phases of the war was group work via support groups and webinars related to the rules of use during the war, working with children, and basic survival tips.

Since the companies evacuated their offices abroad or to the western part of Ukraine, as well as due to the need to observe security, all services were provided only online. An important feature and peculiarity of this war is that Ukrainian mental health professionals are also in a state of acute stress or fatigue, meaning that they are in a shared reality with their patients. Many of them experienced traumatic events such as occupation, shelling, air raids, and separation from family, some of them are mothers or spouses of combatants fighting on the front line, some are even widows or mothers who lost their sons in the war. Therefore, the state of specialists is, in many respects, similar to the state of clients who turn to them.

In order to cope with these conditions and support each other and regulate their own conditions, there was a "help for helpers" approach implemented in the company, represented by self-support groups, intervention groups and wellness supervisions. These groups proved to be extremely helpful.

Similar groups of support were maintained for the companies' employees on their request on the sites of temporal migration online and offline, as well as webinars, group and individual consultations.

Later in the course of the war, we noticed a growing need for psychological support, in particular for EAP programs. The number of consultations in the office has increased. The main symptoms at that time were guilt, anxiety, depression, loneliness, loss, family separation, financial shortage, and cognitive symptoms.

IN-Person Corporate is currently holding webinars on the topics of living in an ongoing war, sustainability, life after war, and working with veterans. The company's specialists are in continuous training in trauma therapy, conducting webinars and offline seminars with families of veteran employees and with veterans and refugees who have returned to home and work, plus others at the request of the company. The main queries are family breakdown, separated families, anxiety states, returning home, identity issues, and bereavement. They also request legal support regarding the rights and obligations of combatants, their families, and arrangements after return.

There are requests for a webinar on building financial portfolios, and other money management questions have started to pour in, which is a sign that the population is stabilizing and the ability to plan is returning. Throughout the war, the hotline worked without interruption and without delays, responding to 100% of requests. During blackouts, generators were installed to keep things running 24/7/365.

Due to female consultants who fled abroad on the beginning of the war, the network of consultants spread all over the world, which made it possible to provide EAP services anywhere in the world.

THE EFFECT OF ONLINE/VIRTUAL COUNSELLING

The effect of online/virtual counselling was positive. The influence of online/virtual, although it changed the conditions of the setting, did not have a significant impact on the process of psychological counseling itself. On the contrary, it made it more accessible. It enabled more people to use the services. They weren't necessarily bound to the territory and could receive help from any location with the desirable consultant. It activated the usage of the services by the family members. However, most people prefer consultations in the office and try to use it.

THE ROLE OF TECHNOLOGY AND SOCIAL MEDIA

Technology and social media are essential because they allow for greater visibility of the services, quality and involvement of more people, of course.

EFFORTS TOWARD DIVERSITY AND INCLUSION WITHIN THE FIELD (COUNSELLORS, PROVIDERS, CLIENTS)

The company tries to adhere to the values of diversity and inclusion. Diversity, equity, and inclusion are interconnected to its culture. Gender diversity is represented by the counsellors of different genders who work for the company, although, unfortunately due to the mobilization, currently there are more women than men. The company cooperates with the professionals of different ages, from very young specialists to the mature ones near the age of retirement, implementing the idea of age diversity, as well as religious and cultural diversity with our colleagues and clients.

ABOUT THE AUTHOR

Natalia Nalyvaiko, MBA, MPsy, is a psychotherapist, clinician, practitioner, training analyst, and a certified Supervisor of European Confederation of Psychodynamic Psychotherapy (ECPP; Vienna, Austria); Private Practice. She is the founder of IN-Person Corporate. Natalia is a member of numerous national and international professional associations, e.g., European Association of

Psychotherapy (Vienna, Austria) and similar. As a psychologist-practitioner, Natalia has a rich practice as a psychotherapist and a supervisor. She also actively participates in scientific activity connected to theoretical and practical issues of psychotherapy as a speaker at international professional events. Her personal involvement in international business and current active engagement with the psychological societies allows her to be in contact with a wide network of psychotherapists of different modalities.

Natalia founded IN-Person Corporate in 2014, and it was the first Ukrainian company engaged in the field of EAP. The same year, the company became the partner of ICAS International in Ukraine, and in a couple of years, its preferred Partner in Ukraine. IN-Person Corporate is the first in Ukraine proposing a full EAP, which includes psychological support service for employees of organizations as well as other divisions such as legal and financial consultations. It works in order to help people cope with unexpected experiences and pave new paths in their lives.

IN-Person Corporate:

- is an extensive network of psychologists/psychotherapists throughout Ukraine, in all regional centers;
- is a network of specialists: psychologists, psychotherapists;
- has specialists who are members of national and international professional centers;
- conducts constant practice, improves their qualifications, and works with clients face-to-face, online, by phone;
- has extensive work experience in crisis psychology and psychotrauma;
- offers a high level of legal and financial advisers;
- maintains confidentiality, impartiality, and anonymity in accordance with the laws and ethical standards of the profession.

International and local clients of IN-Person Corporate have an opportunity to benefit from unlimited access to its free special hotline that works 365/7/24 and receive psychological, legal or financial advice on issues of concern through any channel: online, telephone, video communication, chat, and face-to-face (personal consultation in the office) in their native language.

Phone number: +380503112300
E-mail: Natalia.nalyvaiko@gmail.com
Location: Kyiv, Ukraine

UNITED ARAB EMIRATES (UAE): UMM AL-QUWAIN, ABU DHABI, DUBAI, SHARJAH, AJMAN, RAS AL-KHAIMAH, AND FUJAIRAH

Hazel Kurian

BACKGROUND

It must be noted that while the term MENA or the Middle East and North Africa—referring to a number of countries in the region—is often used for ease of reference, it belies the complexities of this large area with its many religions, indigenous populations, ethnic groups, and cultures.

The UAE is a perfect example of the breadth and depth of this, with its seven emirates, each with its own ruler. The UAE is the forerunner of countries with a larger immigrant population compared to the local population, edging out Qatar, Kuwait, and Bahrain in the region. Over the last 30 years, the United Arab Emirates (UAE) has had the highest immigration by country, with 88% of its population being defined as immigrants in 2020 (Ross, 2022).

This poses unique opportunities and challenges when it comes to the nature of employment in the country.

EAPs provide a range of support services to employees and their family members, from dealing with work-life stressors to legal and financial consultations. Most, if not all, Fortune 500 companies have established Employee Assistance Programmes (EAPs) embedded into their organisational culture, as do many midsize companies (Jain & Jain, 2020). The basic premise of an EAP is that a healthier and happier workforce is a more productive one. The coronavirus disease 2019 (COVID-19) led to an increased focus on the effectiveness of EAPs (Veldsman & van Aarde, 2021).

The following distinctions can be made between EAPs and traditional mental health programmes (Sonnenstuhl & Trice, 2018):

- **Work Focus:** The main reason most companies strive to implement an EAP is to provide independent, external support structures for employees, with the longer-term intention of taking care of their employees, and to allow for employees to be productive in the work context.
- **Manager Training and Involvement:** Managers are often in a prime position to be EAP champions, given that their position enables them to notice and identify well-being challenges and needs. A robust EAP needs to contain a component of manager training and support to ensure that these key players respond effectively and timeously to issues related to employee well-being.
- **Linkages and Referrals:** EAPs can further assist service users by providing guidance and referrals to external resources that are available in their immediate environment and in the broader community.
- **Anonymity and Confidentiality:** All ethical and professional EAPs need to be built upon a tripartite foundation of trust between employer, employee, and EAP that ensures the confidential handling of all cases. Despite the employer carrying the cost on behalf of the employee, this does not entitle the employer to access private and confidential information related to the nature of the EAP intervention.
- **Short-term Focus:** Historically, EAPs provide short-term support and are not designed for long-term intervention.

THE IMPACT OF SERVICES DURING THE PANDEMIC

The global pandemic of COVID-19 in 2020 catapulted the world into a state of rapid digital transformation and created a hyper-focus on employee well-being. While many industries came to a grinding halt in the face of the pandemic and the numerous lockdowns that ensued, the well-being industry, in particular those focusing on mental health and employee support, seemingly went into overdrive. The book of business for ICAS MENA grew that year, and the utilisation of services *tripled* from 2019 to 2020, with the bulk of service users hailing from the UAE, with the Kingdom of Saudi Arabia and Qatar trailing behind.

In their 2021 study, Veldsman & van Aarde found that the utilisation of EAPs increased because of COVID-19; however, the reasons for accessing these programmes remained largely consistent before and during COVID-19. This finding mirrors ICAS MENA's analysis of utilisation and engagement, as evidenced by Table 1, where the top five presenting issues from the years 2019 to 2022 largely remained the same, with Stress and Mental Health/Psychiatric issues being consistent trends throughout.

2019	Stress
	Mental Health/Psychiatric
	Health & Lifestyle
	Legal Issues
	Relationship Issues
	Child & Family Care
2020	Information & Resources
	Stress
	Health & Lifestyle
	Mental Health/Psychiatric
	HR Issues
	Legal Issues
2021	Stress
	Relationship Issues
	Mental Health/Illness
	Information
	Organisational Issues
	Health & Lifestyle
2022	Stress
	Mental Health/Illness
	Relationship Issues
	Organisational Issues
	Information
	Personal Development

Table 1. Top 5 presenting issues from 2019–2022

THE EFFECTS OF ONLINE/VIRTUAL COUNSELLING

Online/virtual counselling falls under the umbrella of telemental health or teletherapy, which refers to the use of electronically-based communication such as videoconferencing, telephone calls, and mobile apps to provide access to mental health services, typically across distances (Pickens et al., 2020).

Communication and video conferencing tools became the mainstay as COVID-19 prevailed longer than the common citizen hoped or believed it would. As families, friends and work teams were separated due to societal social distancing, tools such as Zoom, Microsoft Teams, Skype, etc., video conferencing platforms made school online learning and remote working possible (Brue, 2023), and therapy followed suit. The use of online or virtual counselling increased rapidly with the start of the pandemic, echoing the trend (Gangamma et al., 2022; van Kessel et al., 2022).

The unprecedently *shared* experience of the pandemic in recent history imparted the importance of taking care of our mental health. Employees and managers, parents and children, leaders and constituents, therapists and clients, etc., almost all experienced the start of the pandemic at similar paces.

Some of the benefits of online/virtual counselling include, but are not limited to:

- **Ease of Access:** Online counselling allows for service users to connect with a licensed therapist or counsellor using any device that has an internet connection, such as a computer, tablet, or smartphone (Cherry, 2022).
- **Can Be as Effective as In-person Counselling:** Studies, such as the ones conducted by Lerardi et al. (2022) and Pescatello et al. (2021), have shown that service users accessing in-person or virtual counselling showed similar levels of psychological distress and that the online counselling intervention was almost as effective as in-person counselling interventions, especially for frameworks such as Cognitive Behavioural Therapy (CBT) treating issues such as moderate depression, panic disorder, social anxiety disorder and generalised anxiety disorder (Andrews, 2018).
- **An Alternative for Remote Areas:** Online counselling via EAPs offers access to professional mental health providers by service users who may live in remote areas where there may be a paucity of such professionals or a literal lack of geographical access, such as client sites that include offshore workers based on rigs or situated in remote rural areas in the MENA region. Having to drive long distances and take significant time out of a busy schedule to seek in-person counselling can be a problem and pose a real obstacle for people in need of help (Cherry, 2022).

- **Accessibility for People with Physical Limitations:** Online therapy provides accessibility to individuals who are disabled or housebound, and mobility can be a big issue when it comes to accessing mental health care (Cherry, 2022; Rutherford, 2016).

Other benefits include the offer of greater privacy by promoting independence where it is possible to access alone. It promotes client well-being, autonomy and empowerment (Rutherford, 2016).

More research is needed both on client populations with a range of different presenting issues and diagnoses and on clients' experiences of different modalities of online therapy in a COVID-19 context. More research is also needed on the therapeutic alliance in online therapy in a COVID-19 context and how this influences clients' experiences. It is important for practitioners to consider clients' individual differences, such as the availability of technology and the impact of clients' different environments, during online therapy sessions. Socioeconomic differences regarding the availability of technology and space can impact clients' experiences of online therapy, suggesting a need for steps to be taken to provide more equitable outcomes (Kessel et al., 2022).

Studies suggest that while some groups of clients are more likely to continue to receive benefits of teletherapy, vulnerable groups such as those in lower socioeconomic conditions may be less likely to be served by it (Gangamma et al., 2022). The many benefits of online/virtual counselling demonstrate the need to continue to research this mode of service, as well as the need for continued training of mental health professionals and investment by communities and organisations to provide even better platforms of communication.

EFFORTS TOWARD DIVERSITY AND INCLUSION WITHIN THE FIELD (COUNSELLORS, PROVIDERS, CLIENTS)

Employers that can demonstrate that they have an EAP that utilises culturally competent and culture-based care practices show their employees that they are invested in employee well-being. ICAS offers culturally responsive care to all service users seeking support through the EAP. This approach ensures that mental health care is more accessible and effective for marginalised communities, such as historically underrepresented groups: Black, Indigenous, and people of colour (BIPOC); people with hearing, visual and physical challenges; and others. For both employees' well-being and employers' bottom lines, it is beneficial for employers to provide EAPs that are more culturally competent, which means they refer employees to the most culturally appropriate providers. To do this, EAP counsellors and case workers must take into consideration a range of characteristics about the employee, such as age, gender, race, religion and sexual orientation (Owens, 2006).

EAPs often face scrutiny related to the efficacy of their interventions due to low engagement, low utilisation and poor awareness among employees, so it's important to expand EAP roles to move beyond only the provision of well-being services to employees to include strategic crisis response and prevention (Frey, 2020) and the ability to be powered by a diverse network of providers, delivering inclusive and personalized support and content so everyone feels like they belong (Sokoler, 2023).

EAPs offer an extra layer of employee support, given that most are independent and external entities to the companies that use them. For many companies, well-positioned EAPs that hold strong relationships with workplace leaders can be part of the solution to addressing diversity, equity, inclusion and belonging goals (Frey, 2020).

With its unique population makeup, the UAE is home to 200 nationalities (UNESCO). Investment and awareness around DEIB initiatives are still relatively new concepts when compared to its global partners, but as the UAE government identifies cultural diversity as a source of strength and enrichment, this will likely continue to grow and expand within community and businesses.

Being an EAP provider in the UAE has offered great opportunities to support individuals who would otherwise never have been able to access professional services such as counselling and consultations with lawyers, financial experts, coaches, dietitians, etc. Individuals in vulnerable groups and who are often overlooked by society and companies are able to be supported with access to services that are free of charge for them, which continues to be one of the feathers in our hat. Being able to promote well-being awareness and work with some of the best, most innovative and industry-leading corporate clients, both local and international, is also a wonderful professional accomplishment. While the challenges exist, these are part-and-parcel of EAP work, and more research and evaluation are needed in order to address these. EAP work can continue to benefit organisations and society as a whole, and the work must continue to upskill counsellors, build awareness with clients, and implement consistent evaluation measures (Masi, 1997) that will allow us to do so.

*There is a scarcity in research linked to EAP work within the United Arab Emirates, which may be linked to the fact that there are very few Employee Assistance Professionals Association (EAPA) registered EAPs working in the country, with even fewer having a local presence (ICAS being one of the only organisations practicing at a local level).

ABOUT THE AUTHOR

Hazel Kurian, Associate Director of Clinical Operations and Diversity, ICAS Middle East & North Africa (MENA), is a psychologist with 15 years of extensive clinical and EAP experience. She is an Associate Director of Clinical Operations and Diversity at ICAS MENA, with experience in clinical supervision, training and psychotherapy. She is a strong advocate for well-being in the workplace and the promotion of positive change. Her areas of clinical interest include working with people from marginalized groups and social advocacy. ICAS is a global EAP provider and a leader in the market, supporting 18 countries within the MENA region.

RESOURCES

Paul Firth
Country Manager – ICAS MENA
Paul.firth@icasworld.com

Hazel Kurian
Head of Clinical Operations and Diversity – ICAS MENA
Hazel.kurian@icasworld.com

REFERENCES

Ross, J. (2022, April 18). *"Mapped": Immigration by Country, as a Percentage of the Population.* Visual Capitalist. https://www.visualcapitalist.com/cp/mapped-immigration-by-country-as-a-percentage-of-the-population/

Veldsman, Dieter, & van Aarde, Ninette. (2021). *The impact of COVID-19 on an employee assistance programme in a multinational insurance organisation: Considerations for the future.* SA Journal of Industrial Psychology, 47(1), 1-10. https://dx.doi.org/10.4102/sajip.v47i0.1863

Jain, R. & Jain, S. (2020). *The Science and Practice of Wellness: Interventions for Happiness, Enthusiasm, Resilience, and Optimism (HERO.)* W. W. Norton & Company

Sonnenstuhl, W.J., & Trice, H.M. (2018). *Strategies for employee assistance programs: The crucial balance.* New York, NY: Cornell University Press. [Google Scholar]

Veldsman D, van Aarde N. *The impact of COVID-19 on an employee assistance programme in a multinational insurance organisation: Considerations for the future.* SA Journal of Industrial Psychology. 2021 Sep 27;47:1863. doi: 10.4102/sajip.v47i0.1863. PMCID: PMC8517698.

Brue, M. (2023, March 3). *Zoom Gears Up For Post-Pandemic Growth As competition Heats Up.* Forbes. https://www.forbes.com/sites/moorinsights/2023/03/03/zoom-gears-up-for-post-pandemic-growth-as-competition-heats-up/?sh=59753df07ff6

Gangamma R, Walia B, Luke M, Lucena C. *Continuation of Teletherapy After the COVID-19 Pandemic: Survey Study of Licensed Mental Health Professionals.* JMIR Form Res 2022; 6(6):e32419 doi: 10.2196/32419

van Kessel, K., de Pont, S., Gasteiger, C., & Goedeke, S. (2022). *Clients' experiences of online therapy in the early stages of a COVID-19 world: A scoping review.* Counselling and Psychotherapy Research, 00, 1–12. https://doi.org/10.1002/capr.12610

Pickens J, Morris N, Johnson D. The Digital Divide: Couple and Family Therapy Programs' Integration of Teletherapy Training and Education. J Marital Fam Ther. 2020 Apr;46(2):186–200. doi: 10.1111/jmft.12417.

Cherry, K (2022, May 16). *The Pros and Cons of Online Therapy. https://www.verywellmind.com/advantages-and-disadvantages-of-online-therapy-2795225*

Ierardi, E., Bottini, M. & Riva Crugnola, C. *Effectiveness of an online versus face-to-face psychodynamic counselling intervention for university students before and during the COVID-19 period.* BMC Psychol 10, 35 (2022). https://doi.org/10.1186/s40359-022-00742-7

Pescatello MS, Pedersen TR, Baldwin SA. *Treatment engagement and effectiveness of an internet-delivered cognitive behavioral therapy program at a university counseling center.* Psychother Res. 2021;31(5):656-667. doi:10.1080/10503307.2020.1822559

G. Andrews, A. Basu, P. Cuijpers, M.G. Craske, P. McEvoy, C.L. English, J.M. Newby. *Computer therapy for the anxiety and depression disorders is effective, acceptable and practical health care: An updated meta-analysis.* Journal of Anxiety Disorders, Volume 55, 2018, Pages 70-78, ISSN 0887-6185, https://doi.org/10.1016/j.janxdis.2018.01.001. https://www.sciencedirect.com/science/article/pii/S0887618517304474

Rutherford, H (2016, October 27). *The benefits of online therapy if you have a disability.* https://disabilityhorizons.com/2016/10/benefits-online-therapy-disability/

Owens, D. (2006, October 1). *EAPs for a Diverse World.* HR Magazine: Society for Human Resources Management. https://www.shrm.org/hr-today/news/hr-magazine/pages/1006agenda_div.aspx

Frey, J. J. (2020, October 14). *How Employee Assistance Programs Can Help Your Whole Company Address Racism at Work.* https://hbr.org/2020/10/how-employee-assistance-programs-can-help-your-whole-company-address-racism-at-work

Dale, M. (1997). *Evaluating Employee Assistance Programs.* Research on Social Work Practice, 7(3), 378-390. OMB Digital Archive

UNESCO. *Awareness and Promotion of Cultural Diversity Values.* https://es.unesco.org/creativity/policy-monitoring-platform/awareness-promotion-cultural#:~:text=The%20UAE%20is%20home%20to,source%20of%20strength%20and%20enrichment.

THE UNITED KINGDOM

Eugene Farrell

I am Eugene Farrell, twice Chair and currently Immediate Past Chair of UK EAPA, with awarded Emeritus Membership. In 2022, I returned to the EAPA International board after a 10-year gap. I have over 25 years' experience in mental health and EAP work in the UK, Europe and across the world. I work for a major health insurance business in the UK as a mental health consultancy lead. I am writing for England as part of the UK where EAPs have been in existence since the mid-1980s. According to research by UK EAPA, the UK EAP market is valued at £118 m annual turnover, covering 24.45 m employees. EAPs delivered 1.375 m counselling sessions to users in 2022.[50] Data on the market size for England only is not available; it would, however, be a considerable proportion of the total.

In England, EAPs are all delivered by external EAP providers, some of which are specialist EAP organisations, and others are part of health insurance businesses or specialist counselling businesses. EAPs are staffed by qualified counsellors, where qualifications are granted by one of several accrediting professional bodies. Some EAPs have State Registered Psychologists on staff who may provide clinical escalation, clinical supervision and policy-setting. The staff within EAP providers may provide intake and assessment as well as scheduled telephone and online counselling. After assessment, service users are passed to a contracted network of counsellors who

---

50 UK EAPA Holding it together. UK mental Wellbeing and the role of Employee Assistance Programmes 2023.

supply face-to-face counselling, in the room and remotely. The typical EAP models provided in England are five to seven sessions of brief intervention, person-centred counselling.

THE IMPACT ON SERVICES (MENTAL HEALTH, SUBSTANCE ABUSE AND EAPS) DURING THE PANDEMIC

The COVID-19 pandemic started a change in focus on mental health within England, and this has continued since then. Throughout the pandemic, the Office for National Statistics published data on well-being measures that included happiness, depression, life satisfaction and worthwhileness. The data showed that self-reported anxiety increased significantly at the start of the pandemic and peaked in the second wave, falling after that. The level of anxiety has been consistently higher in females compared to males and still is so.

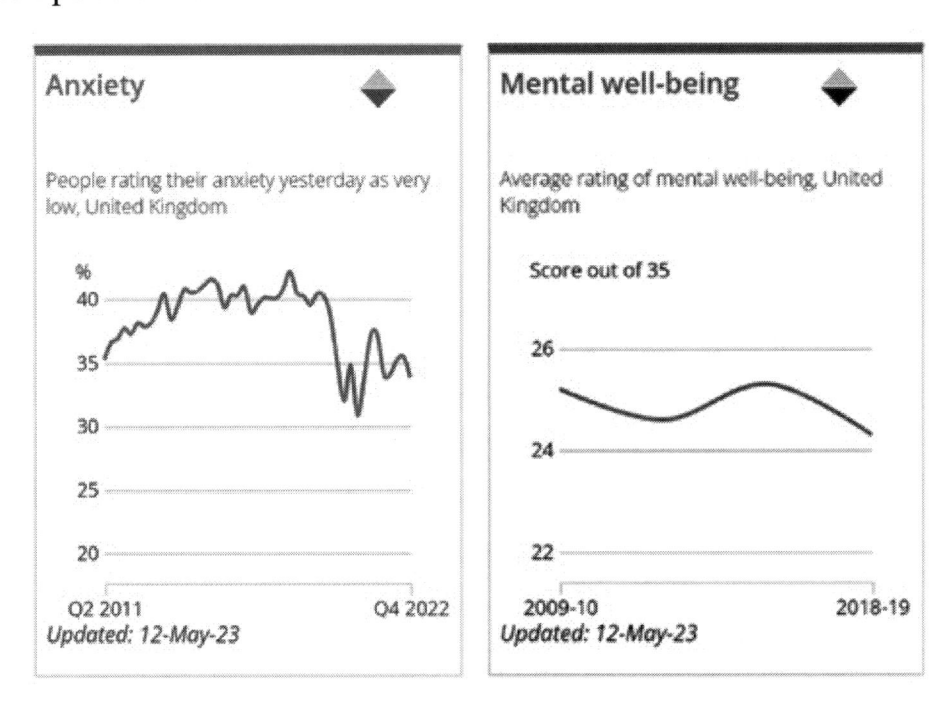

UK Office for National Statistics – Measures of National Well-being Dashboard: Quality of Life in the UK, May 2023

Tracking the anxiety data across the pandemic period to the current date, the level of anxiety felt by people is still above the level pre-COVID-19. This is an interesting phenomenon, and it is debatable that this has become the "new normal" and will never return to the pre-COVID-19 level. It may well be reflective of the ongoing concerns and changes both in England and across the world. Data published by the mental health charity Mind showed that two-thirds (65%) of adults and more than two-thirds (68%) of young people with mental health problems say their mental health has gotten worse since the first national lockdown, with nearly half (46%) of adults and over a half (51%) of young people saying their mental health got much worse since the first national lockdown.[51]

Throughout the pandemic, the UK media highlighted how the population's mental health was being adversely affected by the pandemic, and this increased attention on mental health as a health and social issue. The increased media mentions shone a spotlight on mental health and may well have been a cause of increased discourse around mental health by the population. We continue to see this increased attention to mental health.

Whilst many organisations closed operations during the pandemic with employees staying at home, EAP providers in England remained open and available for calls. With travel prevented, EAP providers very quickly adapted to provide services using staff working from home.

EAP providers in England rely upon a network of accredited counsellors to provide face-to-face counselling services to service users. The pandemic meant that face-to-face counselling services were not allowed to be delivered and the EAP market quickly adapted to remote services using telephone, online chat and video counselling.

EAPA UK conducted a survey of affiliate counsellors in August 2020. Before the pandemic, some 93% of counsellors primarily delivered counselling in the treatment room. During the pandemic, a range of modes were used to deliver counselling: telephone 92%, video 86%, email 6% and text and chat 4%. This adaptation was outside of the training received by counsellors, with 54% saying they had been trained in telephone counselling, 52% in video counselling and 10% in text and chat.[52] There has not been a follow-up study.

Subsequently, the British Association for Counselling and Psychotherapy published an updated competence framework for online and phone therapy to assist in setting standards and minimum competence levels for this type of work. Stating, "The original framework (telephone and e-counselling competence framework) was first published in February 2016. Since then, this area of counselling has changed markedly as technology has evolved and new media have been developed. The COVID-19 pandemic and the requirement for many of our members to move to online or phone counselling reinforced the need for the framework and curriculum to be updated."[53]

For many counsellors providing in-person, in-the-room services, they have either not returned to in-the-room work or now provide a mix of in-person and virtual counselling therapy. Consequently, demand from service users has now become a mix of in-person and virtual

---

51 MIND Corona Virus: The consequences for mental health – July 2021.
52 EAPA UK Survey of counsellors experience during the COVID-19 pandemic – August 2020.
53 BACP Online and phone therapy (OPT) competence framework, user guide and training curriculum.

support, with EAP providers looking to meet the user preference for digital interaction as well as in-person traditional therapy. It seems that EAPs have not yet become fully digital, most likely because service users continue to demand traditional telephone and face-to-face services as well as digital options.

EFFECTS OF ONLINE/VIRTUAL COUNSELLING

Since the pandemic, England has seen the emergence of a plethora of digital-only providers of mental health support as the market for services has increased through customer demand and a shift in market conditions. Some service providers use market materials that are, in many ways, anti-EAP in their approach, claiming that EAPs are not meeting customers' needs and some going as far as to say that EAPs let customers down. No evidence of the claims is provided, and this can be viewed as a tactical measure to claim a difference in proposition and service from traditional EAPs to gain new customers and market share.

EAP providers have made some service changes that introduce more technology, and this mostly includes app access to informational services or online counselling support or E-CBT programs. This is by no means universal yet, and most likely, the investment demanded is challenged by the sectors' profitability. However, there have been strategic partnerships with established app providers to widen both the service offer and the product appeal.

THE ROLE OF TECHNOLOGY AND SOCIAL MEDIA

Social media has played a big role and has since increased in prominence in mental health awareness and campaigning. Providers are using social media to promote their services through regular posting of campaign messages, national and international mental health awareness days and thought leadership. All the EAP providers have presence in social media these days. UK EAPA itself increased its social media presence over the last few years with weekly posting of articles and commentary, looking to further promote the role of EAP within England and the UK. The major mental health charities in England have been very active on social media over a number of platforms. These have been important contributors to the wider and continued discussion on England's mental health, government lobbying and campaigning.

EFFORTS TOWARD DIVERSITY AND INCLUSION WITHIN THE FIELD (COUNSELLORS, PROVIDERS, CLIENTS)

Following George Floyd's death in 2020, there has been an increase in organisational awareness of diversity and inclusion. Pressure from client organisations has meant that EAP providers have needed to consider how to respond to questions about diversity and the requests from services users to receive counselling from a counsellor having similar life experiences or being "like them." This has not been easy because provider networks have traditionally not recorded counsellors' cultural expertise, heritage or ethnicity. Today, more effort is put into meeting the specific cultural, gender or ethnicity requests of services users.

In addition, the professional bodies in counselling and psychology have responded with both statements around diversity and inclusion and policy. The BACP published its Diversity and Inclusion Strategy in 2020 and updated its Good Practice Guidelines on Equality, Diversity and Inclusion in 2020. The British Psychological Society has taken a different direction and included diversity as a major feature of the strategic framework, published in June 2021.

ABOUT THE AUTHOR

Eugene Farrell, GMBPsS, BSc, DCRt, is the Mental Health Consultancy Lead for AXA Health in the United Kingdom.

RESOURCES

UK EAPA: https://www.eapa.org.uk/

British Association for Counselling: https://www.bacp.co.uk/

National Counselling and Psychotherapy Society: https://nationalcounsellingsociety.org/help/contact

British Psychological Society: https://www.bps.org.uk/

THE UNITED STATES

Jodi J. Frey

I was asked to address trends affecting EAPs in the US in the following three areas: 1) effects of online/virtual counseling on EAP, 2) role of technology and social media in EAP, and 3) efforts toward diversity, equity and inclusion (DE&I) in the EA field, with trends and future predictions. I conclude with references to organizations and research sources that support some of my observations and provide additional detail and context for anyone searching for a more empirical perspective.

COVID-19 AND BEYOND: IMPACT ON EAP SERVICES IN THE US

During the COVID-19 pandemic, the EA field was constantly adapting to changing needs and demands from US employers and employees. With regular workplace shutdowns during the early stages of the pandemic, causing disruption to many workplaces, EAPs had to quickly pivot to provide 100% remote services. While many EAPs were already offering various counseling modalities, including online options, only a few embraced a completely virtual approach, and many needed to identify new methods and platforms to provide secure and confidential services. This shift to 100% online involved a need to quickly train counselors on best practices for virtual counseling, updating security and digital counseling platforms and working with employers to promote EA services in a new way.

The availability of online and virtual assessments, counseling, and support services has significantly expanded the range of options available to employees. In numerous instances, the adoption of online and virtual platforms for mental health services has enhanced the accessibility of such resources. Prior to the pandemic, employees who had children or other dependents at home faced challenges in accessing EA services. However, the introduction of virtual modalities has now made it more feasible for them to seek and utilize these services. Furthermore, virtual EA services have been particularly beneficial for employees with mobility and transportation challenges.

Despite not all employees being able to work remotely during COVID-19, the majority of EA services were provided virtually. However, industries like health care, construction, and emergency services lacked the option to work from home, leading to additional challenges in delivering services within a hybrid work environment. This posed difficulties for a workforce regularly exposed to safety risks and potentially traumatic events. In response, EAPs partnered with workplace leaders to provide crisis intervention services for individuals, in addition to training for managers and education for employees on topics such as grief/loss, isolation and loneliness, stress management, mindfulness, and trauma.

Additionally, for industries such as those listed and others where online services were not possible to deliver or would not have been used, EAPs were flexible with hours offered to try and provide services to employees during off-work hours. Some EAPs were able to provide on-site support during the pandemic, when needed, ensuring that they and employees received services in a way that was safe and that minimized as much of the risk of COVID-19 transmission as possible. While some services for emergencies were offered in person, the vast majority of EAPs relied on virtual support programming for individual assessment and counseling and group sessions and training. They also provided additional education about crisis calls and text lines, some managed by the EAP and others provided by the broader community, that could be used to provide support 24 hours per day.

As the US acknowledged the mental health strain experienced by children during the pandemic, working parents and employers increasingly relied on their EAPs to offer enhanced support for parents. The need for employee-parent support services persists to this day, particularly given the concerning rise in suicide deaths among younger adults and adolescents. Suicide overall has been an area that has grown in recognition by workplace leaders. During the pandemic, the US saw a slight overall decrease in suicide deaths. This decrease was not consistent across all demographics and the most recent Centers for Disease Control and Prevention (CDC, 2023) statistics show that suicide death rates are again increasing. EAPs have been expanding suicide-screening services and reviewing policies and procedures for managing suicide risk, given the increased demand for crisis services.

In addition to concerns about increased suicide risk, the workplace has seen increases in employee substance use relapses and new substance use problems during the pandemic (NIDA,

2022). Historically, EAPs have been a cornerstone of prevention and support services for employees struggling with substance misuse or needing recovery support, and the need for more proactive and supportive services in the workplace to support recovery are critical post-pandemic. Additionally, the need for EAPs to provide training for managers on recognizing and responding to signs of impairment is once again increasing in the workplace.

A focus on helping employees to feel included and valued at work increased during the pandemic as employers' attention to DE&I initiatives also increased. EAPs played a pivotal role in partnering with business leaders to provide support and guidance in their endeavors to foster inclusivity and establish anti-racist workplaces. While trying to support workplace clients, EAPs also had to do their own internal work with their companies, something I wrote about during the pandemic in a *Harvard Business Review* article (Frey, 2020). The lack of diversity in workplace leadership, but also within the EA field, has always been problematic, but with the recent increased focus on DE&I, coupled with new modalities for accessing care and employees demanding more diverse counselors, EAPs are needing to take a continued hard look at workforce development issues and how to encourage people with diverse racial and ethnic backgrounds to enter and stay in the field.

Beyond an increased demand for employee choice and diverse counseling specializations, employees are also looking for more holistic mental health services that are also culturally responsive. Recognizing that certain employee groups face unique barriers and challenges to accessing care EAPs continue to be pushed to examine their more traditional services and work to improve the cultural responsiveness of services while breaking down barriers to engagement. Employers have encouraged EAPs to adopt a proactive approach toward well-being, prioritizing early engagement and establishing connections with employees before crises arise and shifting the focus to include more attention to sub-clinical concerns and prevention.

The demand for more preventative and proactive approaches to holistic care connects directly to technological changes observed during COVID-19. As a result of COVID-19, the field focused more on the emergence of artificial intelligence (AI) and its influence on the landscape of US EAPs. AI is being used to help EAPs initially screen employees for risk and schedule employees to see a counselor, which is intended to reduce wait times and offer more employee choice. Additionally, EAPs are using technology to develop new online screenings for topics such as suicide, trauma, and anxiety. The screening can be conducted by a chatbot (AI-powered technology) and other types of virtual assistants that ask screening questions about mental health, but are programmed and trained to respond in a more conversational manner, similar to a live person. The responses from employees to the technology assistants can be analyzed using a variety of different types of AI analyses to look for patterns in language, tone, behaviors, and voice that might suggest a possible mental health concern or problem.

Use of such technology can help to provide a foundational assessment from which a live counselor can then pick up and continue with the employee. These AI-supported screenings help to provide an immediate response to employees and cut down on time needed for screening with a live counselor. Employee responses to AI-supported screening can also help the EAP identify what type of counselor would be a good fit for the employee, or any specialized services that a counselor needs to offer. This technology can also be used at follow-up and before additional counseling sessions to track responses and changes over time. These screening interventions are often built into mobile applications that include mental health tracking and real-time support for employee clients.

The use of these online support programs helps to track and monitor employees' mental health and provide data to counselors, allowing them to respond with tailored, real-time personalized feedback and support. Having increased access to data has already helped EAPs evaluate their clinical services even more. Some of the evaluation and research has been published in the *Journal of Workplace Behavioral Health,* many of which are available freely through the EA Archive.

We have also seen a surge in the creation of online support groups and peer support programs. These virtual communities are designed to provide a safe space for employees and other adults to connect with others who share their experiences and who can provide support in times of crisis and recovery. While peer support programs, with their focus on lived experience, are not new, they are having a resurgence in the workplace as employers look for novel ways to provide support in a timely manner and work to reduce stigma while building up psychological safety.

In addition to AI, EAPs became more aware of the potential uses for social media during the pandemic. EAPs have historically minimized their use of social media to promote services, in part, to protect confidentiality. Not using social media in the past has had drawbacks for the field as EA professionals and organizations are not viewed as the leaders or "influencers" on social media platforms and therefore have not been shaping workplace mental health conversations. However, their presence is increasing and will continue to increase beyond COVID-19.

THE FUTURE OF EAPS IN THE US

Although I cannot predict the future with certainty, there are several trends regarding the future of EA in the United States that I can confidently anticipate. Employers will continue to request more mental health services, both through traditional EAPs and newer models of service provision. Given the continued decrease in mental health stigma in the workplace, it is expected that even more employees (and their covered family members) will request access for service. This will increase EAP utilization but also place continued pressures on a broken mental health care system. The existing state of the mental health care system in the US poses an ongoing challenge for EAPs as they strive to address issues such as lengthy wait times, quality of service, and customized matches to professionals who can provide specialized and culturally responsive care.

As the demand for mental health support continues to rise, there remains a concerning increase in the stigma associated with those seeking help for substance use issues within the workplace. While new and existing cases of substance use disorders during the pandemic increased, services to provide support and recovery did not adequately match this increased demand. Recently in several states, there have been notable changes regarding the legalization of marijuana, and workplaces continue to face challenges stemming from the opioid epidemic, with the emergence of new and complex substances. These ongoing issues place strains on existing support systems, including EAPs. One bright spot is the increased attention and support for Recovery Friendly Workplaces expanding throughout the US (RWF New Hampshire, 2023) and work by the US Department of Labor on Recovery Ready Workplaces (DOL, 2023). These programs continue to grow and include EAPs as an important partner.

EAPs have traditionally played a role in risk management related to mental health and substance use. However, the extent of their involvement in this area has significantly increased, and this trend is expected to continue in the future. Risk management focuses not only on clinical outcomes but also linking clinical care to workplace outcomes such as absenteeism and presenteeism. As employers become more informed about research methods and outcomes, they will continue to put pressure on all workplace programs, including EAPs, to quantify their impact on productivity and safety and to demonstrate effectiveness and return-on-investment.

The explosion of technology within the EA field will continue to push the boundaries of service delivery and meeting employees' preferences, while there will be a continued focus on evaluating ethics and the effectiveness of different modalities and technology options. Most EAPs have adopted some level of technology into their services (i.e., assessment, scheduling, apps, and digital cognitive behavioral therapy or CBT). Some of the newer companies to enter the EA scene during the pandemic have already blended live and technology-based counseling to provide additional support using digital CBT. This integration of live and AI-based services can allow for greater access to real-time EAP client data and feedback to help tailor personalized interventions. The use of technology might also have a positive impact on the broader mental health and substance use fields, which are facing a shortage of counselors. How AI and technology will be harnessed and used in the EA field has yet to be determined. With increased demand for customized and holistic care that can be delivered quickly and effectively, there is pressure on the field to adopt more AI practices into their existing services. Research is only starting on how AI can best be used to support overall behavioral health and well-being.

The continued push toward more upstream approaches to prevent workplace mental health issues and other crises opens opportunities for EAPs to continue to play an important role in organizational culture change. Educating and supporting leaders and managers with coaching and consultation services that include a focus on mental health will be key. EAPs must also fully embrace other aspects of well-being such as health promotion, safety, and risk management. The future for EAP is bright, but how the field will continue to evolve to meet complex challenges in a post-pandemic work world remains to be seen.

Acknowledgment: Dr. Frey wants to acknowledge editing contributions to this chapter by Amanda Mosby, MA, and Sahrah Marcellin, BS, both from the University of Maryland, Baltimore.

ABOUT THE AUTHOR

Jodi J. Frey, PhD, LCSW-C, CEAP

For 25 years, I have had the honor of serving in various capacities within the Employee Assistance (EA) and broader workplace behavioral health fields. My career commenced as a Licensed Certified Clinical Social Worker (LCSW-C), where I transitioned into the realm of EA as a Certified Employee Assistance Professional (CEAP). I obtained a PhD, with my dissertation focusing on EA and workplace crisis intervention. Since 2004, my career has predominantly revolved around academia, culminating in my current position as a tenured Full Professor and the Associate Dean for Research at the University of Maryland School of Social Work (UMSSW). My scholarship focuses on adult behavioral health and well-being, with a specific emphasis on exploring the interplay between work and well-being. I have focused a significant portion of my professional career on suicide prevention, substance use, and mental health research.

I co-founded the International Digital Employee Assistance Archive (EA Archive) in 2013 to provide free access to historical and current EA-focused materials. Within this collection, one can find contributions from esteemed authors such as Dr. Dale Masi, Dr. Marc Attridge, Dr. Patricia Herlihy (EA Archive Co-Founder), and Dr. David Sharar, among hundreds of others. I have also served as Co-Editor-in-Chief for the *Journal of Workplace Behavioral Health* for the past 14 years. For over a decade, I have served as Co-Chair of the National Workplace Suicide Prevention and Postvention Committee. I am also active in the Employee Assistance Professionals Association (EAPA), one of the leading professional organizations for the EA field. The breadth of these diverse experiences serves as a foundation for shaping and informing my perspectives throughout this chapter.

REFERENCES

Centers for Disease Control and Prevention (CDC). (2023, May 11). Suicide Data and Statistics. National Center for Injury Prevention and Control. Accessed online July 9, 2023: https://www.cdc.gov/suicide/suicide-data-statistics.html#print

Frey, J. J. (2020, October 14). How employee assistance programs can help your while company address racism at work. Harvard Business Review, Available online from the EA Archive: https://archive.hshsl.umaryland.edu/handle/10713/14035

National Institute on Drug Abuse (NIDA). (2022, February). COVID-19 and Substance Use. Accessed online July 9, 2023: https://nida.nih.gov/research-topics/comorbidity/covid-19-substance-use

Office of Governor Chris Sununu. (2023). Recovery Friendly Workplace, New Hampshire. Accessed online July 9, 2023: https://www.recoveryfriendlyworkplace.com/

U.S. Department of Labor (DOL). (2023). Recovery-ready workplace. Accessed online July 9, 2023: https://www.dol.gov/agencies/eta/RRW-hub/Recovery-ready-workplace

Printed in Poland
by Amazon Fulfillment
Poland Sp. z o.o., Wrocław
17 May 2024

4a5b4ef3-c78b-4ff5-9778-7e0ebde2a8caR01